The Edinburgh Companion to
Sir Walter Scott

Edinburgh Companions to Scottish Literature

Series Editors: Ian Brown and Thomas Owen Clancy

Titles in the series include:

Visit the Edinburgh Companions to Scottish Literature website at
www.euppublishing.com/series/ecsl

The Edinburgh Companion to Sir Walter Scott

Edited by Fiona Robertson

EDINBURGH
University Press

© in this edition Edinburgh University Press, 2012
© in the individual contributions is retained by the authors

Edinburgh University Press Ltd
22 George Square, Edinburgh EH8 9LF

www.euppublishing.com

Typeset in 10.5/12.5 Adobe Goudy
by Servis Filmsetting Ltd, Stockport, Cheshire, and
printed and bound in Great Britain by
CPI Group (UK) Ltd, Croydon, CR0 4YY

A CIP record for this book is available from the British Library

ISBN 978 0 7486 4130 7 (hardback)
ISBN 978 0 7486 4129 1 (paperback)
ISBN 978 0 7486 7019 2 (webready PDF)
ISBN 978 0 7486 7020 8 (epub)
ISBN 978 0 7486 7021 5 (Amazon ebook)

The right of the contributors
to be identified as authors of this work
has been asserted in accordance with
the Copyright, Designs and Patents Act 1988.

Contents

Series Editors' Preface

The fourth tranche of the *Companions* series marks in its own way the underlying themes of the series as a whole: Scottish literature is multivalent, multilingual and vibrant. Each volume also reflects the series ethos: to challenge, set new perspectives and work towards defining differences of canon in Scottish literature. Such definition of difference must always be sensitive and each volume in the 2012 tranche shows not only the confidence of up-to-date, leading-edge scholarship, but the flexibility of nuanced thought that has developed in Scottish literary studies in recent years. A tranche which balances a volume on women's writing with volumes on two major male writers subverts, even on the most superficial reading, any version of an older tradition which depended on a canon based on 'great' writers, mostly, if not exclusively, male. In approaching Scott and Hogg contributors have demonstrated fresh thinking and recontextualised their work, opening them to new insights and enjoyment, while the authors in the volume on *Women's Writing* reinterpret and reorganise the very structures of thought through which we experience the writing explored.

Scott, often in the past taken to represent a stuffy old-fashioned male-dominated literary canon, is revisited, reassessed and brought to our minds anew. One is reminded of the remark of the great European scholar Martin Esslin to one of the series editors that Scott was the greatest artist in any art form of the nineteenth century. Such a statement may embody the generalising attitudes of an older generation, but Esslin's argument was based not just on Scott's range and innovations, but on the importance of his influence on his successors, not just in literature but in other arts. Hogg, meantime, has often previously suffered by comparison with Scott, misunderstood and misread in ways the *Hogg* volume makes clear as it demystifies past perceptions and opens new vistas on his work's scope. The *Scottish Women's Writing* volume completes a trio of innovative *Companions* in its range of disparate viewpoints. Avoiding easy categories or theories, these demonstrate with rigour and vigour that, though in some genres, like drama, women's writing has had a difficult time historically, it has, not least in the Gaelic tradition, always played a crucial role. The volume rightly and lucidly interrogates any system of classification that obscures this insight. The 2012 tranche as a whole continues the *Companions* series project of reviewing and renewing the way we read and enjoy the rich diversity of Scottish literature.

Ian Brown
Thomas Owen Clancy

Brief Biography of Sir Walter Scott

Walter Scott was born on 15 August 1771 in College Wynd, in the Old Town of Edinburgh. His father, also Walter, was the eldest son of a tenant farmer in the Borders, and had become a Writer to the Signet; his mother, Anne, was the eldest daughter of Dr John Rutherford, one of the foremost Edinburgh scientists of his day. Scott was the tenth child born to them, and the third of the five boys and one girl who survived infancy. Poliomyelitis, contracted when he was about eighteen months old, permanently lamed him; and to restore his health he spent six of the first eight years of his life living as an only child with his paternal grandparents at Sandyknowe Farm near Smailholm Tower in Berwickshire. His aunt Janet taught him to read, and in 1775–6 took him to Bath, where he first visited the theatre; in 1783 he stayed with her in Kelso, where he met James and John Ballantyne, who would later publish many of his works.

He attended Edinburgh High School from 1779 to 1783, then Edinburgh University from 1783 to 1786, after which he was indentured to his father for five years. Returning to the university, he qualified as an advocate in 1792: he was appointed Sheriff-Depute of Selkirkshire in 1799 and in 1806 a Clerk to the Court of Session. In 1795 he proposed to Williamina Belsches, but she chose instead a rich banker's son, and in December 1797 he married Charlotte Carpenter (or Charpentier: 1770–1826) in Carlisle. They lived in the still-expanding New Town of Edinburgh and in a rented summer cottage in Lasswade, buying 39 Castle Street, Edinburgh, in 1801. Their four children – Sophia (1799–1837), Walter (1801–47), Anne (1803–33), and Charles (1805–41) – were brought up in Edinburgh and at Ashestiel, the house near Galashiels which Scott leased from 1804. In 1811 he bought a farm on the banks of the Tweed, which became the basis of the estate surrounding Abbotsford, the house which was one of his greatest projects (completed 1825). His first novel, *Waverley*, was published anonymously in 1814 and, until his financial ruin in 1826 forced him to acknowledge authorship, the identity of the 'Author of *Waverley*' was, officially, a mystery until 1827. He accepted a baronetcy in 1818 (gazetted 1820). Scott had bouts of serious illness in the late 1810s and sporadically throughout the 1820s, suffered strokes from 1830, and died at Abbotsford on 21 September 1832. He is buried, next to Charlotte, at Dryburgh Abbey. The grave of Sophia's husband John Gibson Lockhart (1794–1854), whose *Memoirs* of Scott were published in 1837–8, lies at his feet.

List of Abbreviations

The following abbreviations are used throughout for all references to Scott's works:

Journal   *The Journal of Sir Walter Scott*, ed. W. E. K. Anderson (Oxford: Oxford University Press, 1972)

Letters   *The Letters of Sir Walter Scott*, ed. H. J. C. Grierson et al., 12 vols (London: Constable, 1932–7)

Minstrelsy   *Minstrelsy of the Scottish Border*, ed. T. F. Henderson, 4 vols (Edinburgh: William Blackwood, 1902)

MPW   *The Miscellaneous Prose Works of Sir Walter Scott, Bart.*, ed. J. G. Lockhart, 28 vols (Edinburgh: Robert Cadell, 1834–6)

PW   *The Poetical Works of Sir Walter Scott, Bart.*, ed. J. G. Lockhart, 12 vols (Edinburgh: Robert Cadell, 1833–4)

WN   *The Edinburgh Edition of the Waverley Novels*, gen. ed. David Hewitt, 30 vols (Edinburgh: Edinburgh University Press, 1993–2012)

Introduction

Fiona Robertson

'A hundred lines of *Marmion*', Muriel Spark's Miss Gaunt sets as punishment for Rose Stanley, 'famous for sex' but unsure how to spell 'possession', in *The Prime of Miss Jean Brodie* (1961).[1] Specifying *Marmion* (1808) seems to punish Scott, too, though Spark's first moment of literary recognition was the First Prize she won, aged 14, for a poem commemorating the centenary of Scott's death; and she was writing afresh about Scott in 1994, when she was 76.[2] For Spark, as for many Scottish writers and readers, Scott was the literary edifice she inhabited, knowingly, sometimes wryly, and just a little possessively. Whenever Spark wrote about Edinburgh, where she and Scott were born one mile and 147 years apart, her cityscape had a way of reflecting not identifiable scenes or passages in Scott's poems and novels but a structure of thought shaped by Scott. In 'What Images Return' she describes the Castle Rock:

> To have a great primitive black crag rising up in the middle of populated streets of commerce, stately squares and winding closes, is like the statement of an unmitigated fact preceded by 'nevertheless'.[3]

Scott's writing interweaves, and shows to be mutually defining, fact and fantasy, landscape and populace, the primitive and the commercial, the apparently 'unmitigated' and the always possible. As in Spark's description, each of these can be seen as preceding and determining the other. In Miss Gaunt's unimagining punishment for Rose, too, there are ironies left unstated. *Marmion* approaches a national historical event – the 1513 Battle of Flodden Field – through a tale of private deception and betrayal, at the emblematic centre of which a nun is entombed alive for breaking her vow of chastity. Miss Gaunt metes out *Marmion* as if it were void of implication. Spark does not.

Scotland's greatest writer was also its most prolific and diverse, influencing poets, novelists, artists, composers, architects, designers, dramatists, and legislators worldwide. Scott published in his lifetime nine volume-length narrative poems, twenty-seven novels, five plays, translations of Bürger and Goethe, collections of Scottish ballads, a nine-volume biography of Napoleon, studies of witchcraft, demonology, and 'Border antiquities', histories of Scotland and France written for children, essays on contemporary and historical affairs, numerous shorter works of fiction and verse, and an array of literary scholarship and commentary including editions of medieval romance and of the works of Dryden and Swift, studies of literature in old Scandinavian and Germanic languages, reviews, literary compilations, memoirs, and introductions to the works of other novelists and to his own collected novels (the 'Magnum Opus', 1829–33).[4] His private writings include a voluminous correspondence and the posthumously-published *Journal*.[5] Adapted and dramatised versions of his poems and novels proliferated during and after his lifetime, and in political and wider cultural terms his influence was especially marked in what is now called 'the invention of tradition' and in the conception, and realisation, of nationhood and national independence.[6] In 1936 Edwin Muir called Scott 'by far the greatest creative force in Scottish literature as well as one of the greatest in English'.[7] There is, of course, an implicit difference between 'creative force' and 'writer'. For many years Scott was more widely recognised for his cultural impact than for his literary finesse – though the publication over the last two decades of the *Edinburgh Edition of the Waverley Novels*, which has radically changed perceptions of his approach to composition and revision, has done much to transform this view. One of the purposes of this *Companion* is to re-focus attention on the qualities of Scott's thought and style, highlighting their complexities and sensitivities.

In the 'Memoirs' he began at Ashestiel in 1808, Scott describes a boyhood spellbound by story – by ballads, folklore, fairytale, and books of all kinds. He called his early reading 'totally unregulated and undirected' and, although his 'Memoirs' reports the gradual imposition of discipline, first through his studies at Edinburgh University and then by his training in law, his intellectual excitement is clearest when he describes the Literary Society, which he co-founded in 1789, and the Speculative Society, to which he was elected in 1790. In these groups he debated with other talented and 'disputatious' young men topics in literature, philosophy, and science.[8] Scott read omnivorously throughout his life. His library at Abbotsford is the most important single collection of books and manuscripts gathered by any British literary figure. Catalogued in 1838, the Abbotsford collections are currently the focus of specialist new cataloguing and research, and testify to the range and eclecticism of Scott's reading.[9]

Equally important, intellectually and imaginatively, were personal friendships, correspondence, and literary and intellectual circles, especially the literary circles of Edinburgh. Scott grew up in a city dominated by some of the great names of the Scottish Enlightenment – Adam Ferguson (whose son was his lifelong friend), Dugald Stewart, William Robertson (like Ferguson, professors at Edinburgh: Scott attended their lectures), and the new men of science, including the chemist Joseph Black and the geologist James Hutton. Later he maintained close literary friendships (with James Hogg, Joanna Baillie, Maria Edgeworth, William Wordsworth, Robert Southey, Lord Byron, Washington Irving, Charles Robert Maturin, Susan Ferrier) and exchanged visits, ideas, and letters with fellow scholars and antiquarians, scientists, politicians, dramatists, and actors. The conversations he had in his letters capture something of an extremely sociable and socially engaged disposition. With books, too, he was in a permanent state of conversation. He played a prominent part in the wider world of letters and the theatre, and was the prime mover behind the *Quarterly Review*, the periodical established in 1809 as a rival to Francis Jeffrey's *Edinburgh Review*, and which became one of the dominant cultural forces of its time. Although he declined editing the *Quarterly*, he wrote extensively for it, producing essays on translations, biographies, histories, and contemporary literature ranging from Austen's *Emma* and Byron's *Childe Harold's Pilgrimage* to Robert Cromek's *Reliques of Robert Burns*. The political partisanship typified by this venture generated criticism. William Hazlitt divided his account in *The Spirit of the Age* (1825) between an appreciation of Scott's 'new edition of human nature' in the Waverley Novels and an attack on his political prejudices.[10] The belief that Scott pandered to established power has persisted, though this *Companion*, in considering the variety and experimentation of his work, demonstrates the many ways in which it resists easy categorisation formally, thematically, and politically.

Hazlitt's essay on Scott also suggests the doubleness and internal contradiction conjured up by Muriel Spark's 'nevertheless'. Hazlitt's Scott exists by division: looking to the past, never to the future; maintaining a reactionary politics in 'real life' while filling his 'romance' with an egalitarian cast of characters; founding his 'loyalty' to Britain's Hanoverian monarchy and to Unionism 'on *would-be* treason'.[11] Most of all, Hazlitt depicts Scott's fictions as the intellectual and emotional currency of the age. Characters and scenes 'come thronging back upon our imaginations'.[12] Since Scott's death they have done so, pervasively, and in ways which are not only broadly cultural (Waverley Station, the Scott Monument, or, remembered in this volume, the Ivanhoe restaurant in Chicago) but also intensely literary. Scott's influence on other national literatures was profound, and remains most obvious in historical works, from the explosion of historical fiction in the United States in the 1820s–40s to Tolstoy's *War and Peace* (1863–9) and the novels of Ingemann, Hugo, Dumas and Manzoni.[13] To follow through the example plucked from Spark, however, 'a hundred lines' of *Marmion* made this poem one of the imaginative touchstones of the Brontës – in their turn, deeply important to Spark, who edited and extensively discussed their writings.

In chapter 33 of *Jane Eyre* (1847), Jane closes herself off from a snowstorm by reading *Marmion*, from which St John Rivers interrupts her, coming through 'the blocked-up vale' to join up the scattered fragments of her history, setting her feelings and actions in motion but also under new constraint.[14] Canto 2 of *Marmion* describes the bricking-up alive of a nun, Constance de Beverley, in the vaults of Lindisfarne. The memory, and threat, of sexual/religious transgression haunt *Villette* (1853), with its spectral nun and buried letters. In chapter 8 of Anne Brontë's *The Tenant of Wildfell Hall* (1848), 'an elegant and portable edition' of *Marmion* occasions a charged exchange between Gilbert Markham and Helen Huntingdon about gifts, obligation, and financial control.[15] Scott's tale of sexual double standards and forged documents becomes the highly suggestive intertext of their personal and textual relationship. In the 1996 BBC dramatisation, Gilbert gives Helen a copy of Wordsworth's poems instead.[16] The substitution makes Gilbert's gift less recondite, for most viewers. But Anne Brontë, like Spark, specified *Marmion* not because it was natural, but because it was dangerous, and because it suggested not truth, but falsity.

This *Companion* sets out to be more than a collection of essays on the many different topics and approaches into which Scott's writings can be divided. It is designed to give a narrative of a writing life, by combining a broadly chronological with a thematic scheme. All the chapters emerge from new research by their authors, and can stand independently as investigations of complex questions and texts. They are, individually, feats of selection and compression. The chapters can also be read sequentially, as a whole, tracing at particular stages in Scott's writing life concerns which affect his work more generally, but which are concentrated in the years and works in question. A sequential reading will bring back into play far more of Scott than is available anywhere else, except in Scott's works themselves.

Ina Ferris's opening chapter examines the literary world Scott entered and the ways in which he changed it. From antiquarian and editorial beginnings a global publishing phenomenon emerged, Scott's success being not only unprecedented but also, as Ferris shows, symptomatic of conditions in the wider literary field of the Romantic period. This chapter emphasises different kinds of 'crossing' – between genres of writing, literary and historical conventions, oral and print cultures – as a special, and charged, condition of writing in the early nineteenth century. The status of the novel as a literary genre was under pressure; while traditionally regional works, such as ballads and folklore, increasingly crossed cultural and national borders throughout Europe. What Ferris concludes by calling 'Scott's antiquarian-commercial model of authorship' is essential to an understanding of his work as a whole. Scott's early work as compiler, editor, imitator, and analyst is the subject of Kenneth McNeil's chapter on *Minstrelsy of the Scottish Border* (1802–3), Scott's first major publication. The uses of orality, the problems of forgery (represented by ongoing debates in Scott's time about the authenticity of James Macpherson's Ossian), and the role of the poet as 'minstrel', make the *Minstrelsy* an important work in its own right, as well as one that anticipates the relationship between localisation and internationalism in Scott's later writings and their reception. The figure of the minstrel reappears in Alison Lumsden's and Ainsley McIntosh's chapter on Scott's long narrative poems, a captivatingly successful series which began with *The Lay of the Last Minstrel* (1805) and included some of the most popular long poems of the Romantic period, notably *Marmion* and *The Lady of the Lake* (1810). Although Scott's poetry has largely been overlooked in present-day discussions of Romanticism, its characteristic concerns – history, nationhood, and social responsibility – accompanied stylistic innovations which, as this chapter argues in its analysis of *The Lay of the Last Minstrel*, developed the aesthetic of Romanticism while exploring its limitations. Taken together, Chapters 2 and 3 testify to the re-emerging importance of Scott's poetry and to the pleasures of reading Scott in all his genres not by the metre, but for the metre – that is, for his inflections, turns, and nuances of style.

Scott's move to prose fiction with the publication of *Waverley* in 1814 prompts Caroline McCracken-Flesher's analysis of his 'Jacobitical plots'. *Waverley* was the first of Scott's accounts of the several attempts in the eighteenth century to reclaim the British throne for the Stuart line: subsequent treatments include *Rob Roy* (1818), *Redgauntlet* (1824), 'The Highland Widow' (1827), and *Tales of a Grandfather* (1828–31). *Waverley* also extended Scott's characteristic figure of the 'wavering' hero, caught between loyalties and ideologies. The problem of choice, as this chapter argues, structured Scott's representations of the historical past – intriguingly, since no modern choice could change the outcomes of past conflicts. Focusing on the early to middle years of Scott's novel-writing, Catherine Jones next suggests the ways in which Scott could, nevertheless, re-plot history. In examining Scott's relationship to the theory and practice of writing Scottish history, Jones reveals the new emphases and patterns exemplified by novels such as *The Heart of Mid-Lothian* (1818) and *The Bride of Lammermoor* (1819). Scott redefined the intellectual frameworks of historical writing, combining popular memory and the tradition of philosophical history in ways that redirected understandings of the past.

The immediacy of Scott's present day is brought home in Samuel Baker's chapter on the significance of war in his fictions. It is fitting that the chapter which marks the halfway point in this volume should be a reflection on war, the most pressing and most dangerous condition of Scott's lifetime but also the fictional topic which opens up what Baker calls Scott's 'worlds' – a series of conflicts which by the end of his career would encompass ancient Rome, the Crusades, and the sweep of British imperialism. Moving from *Waverley* to

Woodstock (1826), this chapter focuses on *Guy Mannering* (1815), *The Tale of Old Mortality* (1816), *The Heart of Mid-Lothian*, *Ivanhoe* (1820), and the two *Tales of the Crusaders* (*The Talisman* and *The Betrothed*, 1825). Baker's emphasis on conflict leads into a new reading of the importance of the topic, which, as George Marshall's chapter demonstrates, drives many of Scott's fictions – religious dispute. Scott's representations of faith have often been seen as incidental, a necessary part of describing certain periods of history. In showing how individuals define their beliefs in times of crisis, however, Scott draws on deep reserves of linguistic and rhetorical empathy. Marshall places Scott's depictions of religious dispute in the context of the principles of 'moderation' governing the Scottish church in his day, while highlighting the linguistic excesses and excitements which mark religious expression in *The Tale of Old Mortality*, *The Bride of Lammermoor*, *The Monastery* and its sequel *The Abbot* (both 1820).

As Scott shows in all the most concentrated exchanges of his writing, style matters. In a chapter linking the passions of Scott's writing to his role in developing the aesthetic preferences of the Romantic period, Fiona Robertson moves the volume's narrative to some of the most intensive years of Scott's writing life, the early 1820s. Although Scott had not yet acknowledged authorship of the Waverley Novels, the curiously mixed pressure, thrill, and ennui of being that Author were stamped all over his work. In *Kenilworth* (1821), *The Pirate* (1822), *Quentin Durward* (1823) and *Saint Ronan's Well* (1824), Scott emerges as one of the great interlocutors of Romantic literature. Robertson identifies the keynotes of Scott's aesthetics as 'latitude, freedom, originality, and excitement'. Maintaining the focus on the middle years of Scott's career, Tara Ghoshal Wallace gathers the Stuart monarchs of *Peveril of the Peak* (1822), *The Abbot*, *The Fortunes of Nigel* (1822) and *Woodstock* into a study of performativity in power: the body politic. Far from making readers complicit in 'tushery', the novels in which Scott gives his monarchs most freedom to speak are also those which linger over their inadequacies. In writing these fictions, Scott was responding to crises of monarchy in his own time – royal executions in revolutionary France, the madness of George III replaced by the flummery of George IV in Britain, and the parliamentary 'trial' of the latter's wife, Caroline of Brunswick – but doing so in a way which conspicuously ironised the Stuart sympathies deduced by many early readers of *Waverley*. Driving the fictions of these years ever more insistently is the apparently very different but actually closely related topic of Alexander Dick's chapter on Scott and political economy: the insecurities of value. As Dick shows in a discussion which takes in the debate on the Corn Laws, the population problem, the bullion controversy, and a range of early economic theorists including David Ricardo and Thomas Malthus, political economy was a developing and far from stable discipline in Scott's time. The significance of economic thought emerges from *The Antiquary*, *Woodstock*, and 'The Highland Widow', but is even more explicit in *The Letters of Malachi Malagrowther*, 'On Planting Wastelands' and *Tales of a Grandfather*.

Dick's focus on economics at this stage in Scott's career is timely, for in January 1826 financial disaster struck. Scott found himself personally liable for debts totalling some £126,000 (in the region of £5,500,000 today) incurred by the collapse of the printing firm in which he was a partner, James Ballantyne & Co., in the wake of the collapse of his publishers, Archibald Constable & Co., and Constable's London agents, Hurst Robinson & Co. These events initiated the final phase of Scott's writing life. Meditating on Theodor Adorno's reflections on a 'late style' in Beethoven, Ian Duncan considers Scott's last novels, adding to discussions of *Woodstock*, *The Fair Maid of Perth* (1828), and *Anne of Geierstein* (1829), extended analysis of 'The Two Drovers' (1827) and the two last *Tales of My Landlord* (the long-neglected *Count Robert of Paris* and *Castle Dangerous*, 1831).[17] In a telling phrase, Duncan notes the ways in which these later works 'return with a vengeance' to the topics and tropes of Scott's earlier fictions. How could we have overlooked for so long *Count Robert of Paris*, which, in Duncan's words, has a cast of characters including 'Greeks, Turks, Normans, Varangians, Africans, Scythians, a bluestocking princess, a ferocious warrior-countess, a seditious philosopher nicknamed "the Elephant", a real elephant, a tiger, a mechanical lion, and an eight-foot-tall captive orang-utan'? Emanations of this expansive eccentricity come, as Nicola Watson shows in her concluding chapter, to characterise Scott's afterlives in literary and material culture. From Sheridan Knowles's theatrical spectacular, *The Vision of the Bard* (a death-masque of 1832) to present-day Scottish tourism, Scott has entered public and domestic spaces in a variety of parlour games, fancy-dress entertainments, *tableaux vivants*, street-, mansion-, institute- and city-names. Watson specifies the iconicity of *Ivanhoe*, probably the work that most clearly reveals the 'cultural saturation' Scott achieved; but, as in every chapter of this *Companion*, the particular case stands for many others.

Several chapters bring Scott into present-day cultural and political debates. Kenneth McNeil's chapter ends with reflections on minstrelsy of the US/Mexican border and on modern Chicano studies, a reminder of how wide ranging and evocative, but also how particular and focused, ideas of borderlands continue to be. Alison Lumsden and Ainsley McIntosh conclude that Scott's poetry is especially relevant to twenty-first-century readers, its concerns and methods serving as precursors for 'our own, more troubled, condition of postmodernity'. Caroline McCracken-Flesher finds in the peculiar conditions of choice exemplified in Scott's 'Jacobitical' plots the template of all post-Scott approaches to the world: how not to choose. George Marshall's reappraisal of Scott's portrayals of religious fervour demonstrates that although Scott's depictions of seventeenth-century Scottish Covenanters and sixteenth-century Roman Catholics are convincingly particular, reflecting an apparently effortless command of historical materials, they also step out of their historical frame, speaking to present-day concerns about religious intolerance and the endemic politicisation of faith. Nicola Watson ends with a snapshot of afterlives ongoing and still to come – Scott's new textual life in the *Edinburgh Edition of the Waverley Novels*; the redevelopment of Abbotsford; the contrasts which stimulate tourism. In addition, the debate on Scottish independence has reactivated terms that have come to seem natural, politically, emotionally, and economically.

Fabled in his own lifetime as 'the Wizard of the North' and as the long-anonymous 'Author of *Waverley*', Scott played a unique role in the dissemination of an idea of Scottish culture and history. From his early work as a collector and editor of traditional balladry to the widespread popularity and fame of his poetry and novels, and to his influential writings on history, economics, folklore, and literature, he refashioned the culture of his day and continues to shape our own. This *Companion*, the first collection of its kind devoted to Scott, brings together new thinking across the range of his work, drawing on and adding to the research and scholarship which have revitalised it for a modern readership.

CHAPTER ONE

Scott's Authorship and Book Culture

Ina Ferris

Reviewing an anonymous collection of ballads entitled *Minstrelsy of the Scottish Border* in 1803, the *Monthly Review* observed that its Dedication was signed by one Walter Scott. 'We have been informed that this gentleman belongs to the Faculty of Advocates at Edinburgh and is Deputy Sheriff of the county of Selkirk', the reviewer reports, evidently regarding the volumes produced by this provincial gentleman as what we would now call a vanity publication. Thus he stresses that the editor has encased negligible local content ('rude lays of his marauding ancestors') in a pretentious production featuring 'a handsome frontispiece, fine cream-coloured paper, the beautiful and recent type of a border press, and a learned and polished introduction consisting of 110 pages, five numbers of appendix, and a laudable munificence of notes and commentaries'.[1] For this reviewer, both time and paper would have been more effectively distributed had the 'motley materials' been sorted out and issued as separate modest publications, and the review concludes by advising 'Mr S' to 'employ his pen on more important and useful subjects'.[2]

Thirty years later the obscure 'Mr S' had metamorphosed into the celebrated 'Sir Walter Scott', having parlayed his early antiquarian and editorial beginnings into the extraordinary literary career that made him a global author and publishing phenomenon. 'His novels, his poems, have been translated into every civilised language; his heroes and heroines have become household words all over the world', declared *Fraser's Magazine* on news of Scott's death in 1832. Nor had the impact of his books been limited to literary genres. *Fraser's* notes a spillover into a broad range of artistic media, as well as into areas outside the sphere of strictly cultural production: 'The painter, the sculptor, the engraver, the musician, have sought inspiration from his pages. The names of his works, or the personages introduced into them, are impressed on the man-of-war or the quadrille, the race-horse or the steam-boat.'[3]

Obituaries conventionally allow for a certain hyperbole, but *Fraser's Magazine* does not greatly exaggerate: Scott's success was unprecedented. It was also symptomatic, a manifestation of the innovative dynamic of generic reciprocity and interchange that produced the broad movement known as European Romanticism in the early decades of the nineteenth century. With the emergence of new forms (and sites) of national sentiment in the wake of the French Revolution and its aftermath, literary culture across Europe was increasingly understood as an emanation of local or national place. This led to a new sense of literary history as national history and to a revived interest in overlooked writers and genres of the past, as well as to generic experiments such as Wordsworth's and Coleridge's 'lyrical ballad'. At the same time, the publishing boom of these decades combined with increased efficiencies in distribution, on the one hand, and the rapidity of translation, on the other, to mean that literary works entered one another's national space ever more quickly. Scott's own career is inextricable from the vibrant literary and publishing milieu of post-Enlightenment Edinburgh, wherein the modern idea of national culture was influentially shaped.[4] But Edinburgh was also part of lines of cross-cultural transmission through which European writers and scholars articulated notions of the national past and its relation to the national present. The ballad collecting slighted by the *Monthly Review*, for instance, appeared all over Europe as a reflex of the fascination with local traditions in the late eighteenth century, and it set in motion networks of literary migration among nations. In particular it activated a German-Scottish axis of cultural interchange in which Scott participated and which underlines the fact that contemporary interest in local cultures was not simply a transnational phenomenon, popping up in different places at around the same time, but importantly an international publishing phenomenon at once rooted in and promoting interlaced circuits of influence among cultures.[5]

Scott's own earliest publication was a translation of two ballads by Gottfried Bürger in 1796, a publication reflecting the fact that his interest in ballads had been in part inspired by Johann Gottfried Herder's ground-breaking collections of *Volkslieder* (1778–9). Herder's translations of European folk songs had itself been stimulated by Thomas Percy's influential *Reliques of Ancient English Poetry* (1765). Scott's *Minstrelsy* furthered cross-pollination between Scottish and German cultures: it lies behind the edition of legends and folk songs by Clemens Brentano and Achim von Arnim, *Des Knaben Wunderhorn* (1805–8), a fertile source of adaptations, re-mediations, and further collections for the rest of the century. The important point is that these kinds of linkages, zig-zagging across geographical space and historical time, identify literary cultures less in terms of an aesthetic matrix of representation and imaginative creation than in relation to broad circuits of publication and transmission in which the spheres of letters, learning and commerce overlap. The role of the 'Author of *Waverley*' thrust Scott on to the international stage, but that role was forged out of a rich complex of literary-historical practices as editor, collector, imitator, and periodical essayist in a range of intermediary genres. Scott's print-saturated model of literary culture (itself part of an intensified turn to print in the period) placed him at the intersection of antiquarian interests and commercial practice. Through the form of public authorship this produced Scott reinvented historical romance as the modern historical novel, and in so doing altered the status of fiction for the nineteenth century.

1

In the years around 1800, history became a public concern, a shift in emphasis that profoundly affected the literary field (a term used here in Pierre Bourdieu's sense, to mean more than strictly literary culture).[6] As cultural historians have noted, history became public in a quite literal sense in these years, when historical materials were being rapidly transferred from restricted private venues to more public ones, especially on the Continent.[7] Although this process had been going on for some time, it was accelerated in the wake of the French Revolution and Napoleonic conquest, as massive numbers of texts were released from monastic and aristocratic spaces into the public sphere, becoming available to a larger public in unprecedented numbers and for the first time. The transfer from private to public took place not just in a concrete-material sense with the founding of museums, archives, and libraries but also (more important for an understanding of Scott's career) in an intellectual sense, as historical knowledge was more widely disseminated through, on the one hand, the printing of archival materials and, on the other, the assimilation of the historical past into popular genres such as novels, plays and paintings. In Scotland, as throughout Great Britain, the transfer of private collections to public spaces was neither forced nor on the same scale as on the Continent – it took place gradually and in piecemeal fashion – but in both Europe and Britain antiquarianism both accompanied and promoted such transfer. By the end of the eighteenth century antiquarian practice, traditionally élite, began to shift down the social scale to be embraced by numbers of the 'middling' classes; at the same time, booksellers became interested in publishing antiquarian works suited to more general readers (such as topographical tours or engravings of antiquities).[8] While many such publications responded to imperatives of fashion and taste (expensive volumes of picturesque engravings, for example), the proliferation of antiquarian-related genres testifies to a growing interest on the part of a wider public in access to, and participation in, the national past. By the early nineteenth century this interest had created a space of generic crossing, even as historiography itself was moving closer to imaginative and biographical genres, as it reconfigured its own territory to include the unofficial realm of social and private life.[9]

Alert to the public appetite for the past, Scott made this space his own, and became by far the best-seller of the age.[10] From the start his contemporaries understood both his innovation and his success as intimately linked to his ability to infuse the antiquarian interest in life in the past with imaginative power. Reviewing *Marmion*, the *Scots Magazine* commented: 'Antiquarian pursuits had before been confined chiefly to mere men of research, plodding and laborious, but incapable of communicating any charm to the study. The *poetry* of antiquities, if we may use the expression, was a subject hitherto untouched.'[11] Scott himself placed antiquarianism at the heart of his authorship. While he consistently sought to distance himself from the obsessions and pedantry of 'the severer antiquary', it was through antiquarian figures that he articulated his reflections on and definitions of historical fiction. The character among his own creations with whom he most closely identified was Jonathan Oldbuck of Monkbarns, the eponymous hero of his third novel, *The Antiquary* (1816), and to this same Oldbuck can be traced the set of antiquaries who people the fictional frames in the later Waverley Novels, starting with Oldbuck's friend Dryasdust. Oldbuck himself often features in these frames; suggestively, he surfaces for the last time in a text left unfinished at Scott's death, *Reliquiae Trotcosienses*, where he figures as the deceased owner of a mansion (doubling Scott's own Abbotsford) to which the book serves as a guide.[12]

Much of *Reliquiae Trotcosienses* details the books in Scott's actual library at Abbotsford, underlining the way that his antiquarianism assumed a predominantly bookish cast. Scott certainly collected antiquarian objects with zeal, filling Abbotsford with remnants and relics of all sorts (armour, weapons, bits of buildings, clothes), but his primary commitment was to textual rather than material remains. From the outset he was intent on printing and circulating what could be found in the archive. He published a collection of private memoirs in *Secret History of the Court of James the First* in 1811, for instance, and he put together a 13–volume edition of *Somers' Tracts* between 1809 and 1815, working on both collections in the years that he was writing *Waverley*. He himself also wrote essays on Scottish antiquities, and founded the pioneering Bannatyne Club to publish works illustrative of the history, topography, and literature of Scotland. 'Old and odd books', he told his readers in 1827 when formally discarding his incognito in the Introduction to *Chronicles of the Canongate*, were an enduring 'quarry' for his historical novels (*WN* 20:5). Nor was such bookishness confined to writers like Scott or to fellow antiquaries and learned persons: the success of the Waverley Novels and the historical poems owes a great deal to the intense bookishness of the literate classes as a whole in the early decades of the nineteenth century. These decades experienced a publishing and reading boom, driven in part by the reprint market that opened up following the end of perpetual copyright in 1774, and they saw the emergence of new forms of periodical publication and bookselling, along with the flourishing of bibliophilic writings of all sorts and the emergence of phenomena like the book 'bubble' known as bibliomania, a fashion for collecting rare early modern printed books to which Scott's fictions often allude.[13]

This bookishness reflects the fact that for the first time printed matter became part of everyday life for large sectors of the British population, at once familiar but not taken for granted, as it would be later in the century. Books assumed a widespread and palpable presence, and the specialised idiom of book production (such as 'octavo', 'black letter', 'tall copies') moved into public discourse, showing up in casual remarks and sayings, from informal letters to periodical reviews to poems. Most striking is the way that long-standing metaphors of the book, typically derived from the 'idea' of the book or long since stripped of any material resonance, became more concrete. In the opening chapter of *Waverley*, Scott's narrator clears a space among sentimental and fashionable novelistic genres for his own venture, and he concludes by declaring that although his novel is set 'sixty years since', it is grounded in the universality of 'passions common to men in all stages of society'. To make this point, he states that he proposes to 'read a chapter to the public' from the 'great book of Nature', but as he elaborates this venerable trope 'Nature' turns strangely bookish: 'the great book of Nature, the same through a thousand editions, whether of black letter or wire-wove and hot-pressed' (WN 1:6). The novel that follows is itself thickly bookish, crammed with the book allusions and prominent book-objects that have prompted Peter Garside to characterise *Waverley* as a book 'created amongst, out of, and in reaction to other books'.[14] It is true that the novel as a genre was self-consciously bookish from its inception – we need only think of *Don Quixote* – and *Waverley* takes its place in this novelistic line. But the ubiquity and concreteness of its attention to books points to an intensified and wider book-consciousness in the early nineteenth century, when even the authors of anonymous romances could assume their readers would be familiar with the language of typography and paper-making, and fully alert to its semiotic cultural import.

The Antiquary emerges from exactly this broadening of the public stake in print culture and national history. Much of the novel is taken up with conspicuous scenes of debate over questions of national origin among unremarkable characters in a quiet corner of Scotland – debates that draw on recent or ongoing public controversies of the day. Not incidentally, such debates were often sparked by rival antiquarian publications, as in the debate over the origin of the Picts that was still being agitated at the time the novel appeared. Set in the mid-1790s, the novel inhabits a time very close to the present of its first readers. In a certain sense *The Antiquary* may be said not to be a historical novel at all, and Scott sets it up in the Advertisement as the culmination of a trilogy illustrating 'the manners of Scotland', which (starting with *Waverley*) moved ever closer to the present day (*WN* 3:3). Lacking the historical sweep and play of historical forces usually found in the Waverley Novels, despite its setting in the turbulent 1790s, *The Antiquary* is best understood as a reflection on the form of authorship Scott had initiated when he entered the novelistic field, striking the keynotes he would sound when he came to define his historical romance more explicitly in later works.

The antiquary Oldbuck himself is a familiar generic type, the ridiculous figure long caricatured in European literature: obsessed with detail, chaotic in thought, fanciful, self-deluded. But he also exhibits the scepticism that identifies antiquarian inquiry as the historical outgrowth of an enlightened modern rationality suspicious of arguments from authority and tradition. Odlbuck's own particular target is the aristocratic notion of hereditary right and the Tory form of antiquarianism attached to it. Repeatedly, he clashes with the dim and impecunious Sir Arthur Wardour over the latter's allegiance to the dubious 'sacred list' of one hundred and four Scottish kings; more seriously, he challenges his upholding of the Celts as privileged national origin, a hypothesis canvassed by George Chalmers, whom Sir Arthur cites and who was still living at the time of the novel's publication (*WN* 3:38, 48). Oldbuck clashes as well with another defender of descent and heredity, his nephew, Hector MacIntyre, a bellicose Highlander who prides himself on a paternal 'pedigree of fifteen unblemished descents' and remains a staunch proponent of the authenticity of the Ossian poems (*WN* 3:151, 243). In his scepticism about arguments of national origin, Oldbuck exemplifies the way that the antiquarian focus on the past through its broken bits and illegible traces inevitably foregrounded the discontinuities of historical time and hence put it at odds with a conservative sense of national-historical time as continuity and inheritance.[15] But Oldbuck's antiquarianism has a double valence, and its relationship to the question of origins is complicated, for in one sense he too is fully governed by the idea of origin. Oldbuck is obsessed with matters of derivation, although in his case it is the derivation of words – all kinds of words, but especially the names of places.[16] In his etymological riffs he seeks to motivate the linguistic sign, and hence ultimately to stabilise the relationship both between word/world and between present/past. Thus he argues that the name 'Kaim of Kinprunes' has a Latin origin, keen to support his theory that the spot so named was the site of an ancient Roman camp; and he discourses at great length on how the word *shathmont*, referring to a certain measure, must derive from *salmon-length* (*WN* 3:28, 66).

In such moments Oldbuck appears at his most fanciful and absurd, the target of the novelist's mockery. At the same time, however, he exhibits a wry self-understanding, aware that he is only speculating (even when most swept away), and his attraction to words exceeds the pragmatic logic of establishing origins or authenticity. He takes great pleasure, for example, in reading out loud, 'with a rapturous voice', the elaborate titles of the broadside ballads he collects (WN 3:25). That this pleasure is linked to a printed text is not incidental: Oldbuck's antiquarianism (like that of his author) is deeply invested in print. A collector of old and rare books, he has published small antiquarian pieces in the *Gentleman's Magazine* and the *Antiquarian Repository*, and he remains eager to participate in what he terms 'author-craft' (WN 3:106). From the printing press too he derives his alternative story of origins, taking pride in tracing his own ancestry to a German printer exiled for printing the Augsburg Confession, 'the foundation at once and the bulwark of the Reformation' (WN 3:85). Venerating this ancestor as 'labouring personally at the press for the diffusion of Christian and political knowledge', Oldbuck (in contrast to Sir Arthur and Hector) bases his story of origins not on lineal descent but on a public act of 'diffusion'. His too is a romance, one that privileges the European Reformation as the emancipation of modern knowledge and the modern subject. Importantly, however, this is not a strictly national romance (although it may be appropriated by nations). Rooted neither in place nor in a pure line, it foregrounds an activity and an act of migration, yielding a model of national identity (and of authorship) based less on conservation and consolidation than on production and 'diffusion'.

Over a decade after *The Antiquary*, Scott revisited the debate over ancient Scotland he had incorporated into his early novel, writing a long review of Joseph Ritson's posthumous publication, *Annals of the Caledonians, Picts, and Scots*, for the *Quarterly Review*. Scott dismisses the 'dream of antiquity' in which, he says, the Scottish people long indulged, and he takes pleasure in noting that this dream was dispelled by the Catholic Scottish antiquary Thomas Innes. But the key point for an understanding of his own authorship is the way he counters the emphasis on pure descent advanced by both sides in the debate over the ancient Scots. Conceding that such a thing as 'national character' may exist, he contends that it does so in the manner of 'family resemblance' in that both nations and families 'are perpetually subjected to the most extraordinary changes'.[17] Even as Scott sought to promote a sense of national culture through his romances, he detached the idea of national culture from notions of authentic lines of descent or innate national character. Instead, his fictions reflect the argument he makes in the review of Ritson that if one wants simply to reproduce the same narrow set of characteristics, then one stays within the tribe; but 'if we seek patterns of general excellence, we shall be more likely to find such amongst nations whose original race has been repeatedly crossed'.[18] The import of such a position for the project of constructing a new British identity out of the diverse components making up the kingdom in the years following Waterloo is not hard to discern, but it also yields a combinatory model of authorship, downplaying both originality and singularity. This combinatory model established Scott's historical novel as paradigmatic for the nineteenth century, and helped to alter the status of the novel itself.

2

The novel entered the nineteenth century as an undeniably low genre but one in flux. Relegated to the sub-literary margins of the literary sphere, it continued to be dismissed in the reviews as a commercial genre of popular entertainment directed mainly at new inexperienced readers, from the provincial apprentice to the proverbial 'milliner's miss' routinely invoked in the press. Such readers were widely perceived to be entering the reading public in 'multitudes', threatening a dilution of the very notion of the 'reading public' as they 'devoured' rather than read texts. Their taste was represented as restricted to 'the common novel' churned out by low-status publishing houses like the Minerva Press, which supplied circulating libraries with endless, rapidly produced volumes of generic fiction such as Gothic novels, novels of sentiment, and adventure tales. But at the same time the 'common novel' was being countered by more serious and enterprising forms of fiction, particularly from the British peripheries; while the reviews themselves were also coming to recognise that they could no longer ignore a genre and readership that loomed ever larger on the cultural landscape. Novels began to receive more coverage; ideas about fiction were debated; the history of the English novel began to be sketched out.[19] The 'proper novel' of manners was greeted as a responsible counter to the debased 'common novel', and new novelistic genres like the national tale garnered attention for their innovative representation of cultural difference. Indeed, Maria Edgeworth, co-founder of the national tale along with the more flamboyant Sydney Owenson (later Lady Morgan), became the most reviewed and respected novelist before Scott (who cites her as a model in the Postscript to *Waverley*).[20] Even so, Edgeworth's fiction, however worthy, was seen as limited in scope and imagination, inevitably confined by gender. Contemporary fiction was perceived across the critical spectrum as a female realm, a genre aimed at female readers and dominated by women writers (no matter the actual make-up of authorship and readership). In large part this was owing to the prominence of female novelists in the early years of the century. As the *Antijacobin Review* noted, 'among the novellists [sic] of the present day, the female writers have borne away the palm';[21] but this had not always been the case, and the reviews set about constructing an eighteenth-century male canon by which to measure the novel's current decline. The critical stage was thus set for the entry of a 'manly' writer like Scott, whose historical novel infused masculine energy into a feminised field, and decisively repositioned the novel in the hierarchy of genres.

Not that the anonymous *Waverley* was the instant success it is sometimes credited with being. The novel certainly received immediate and widespread attention upon its publication in 1814, prompted in no small part by rumours that the best-selling poet, Walter Scott, was its author; it was also typically reviewed as a cut above the type of 'common novel' manufactured by the book trade. But it was not heralded as a new form of fiction nor was its author accorded any special powers. Just over five years later, however, Francis Jeffrey proclaimed in the influential *Edinburgh Review* that the 'Author of *Waverley*' had 'founded a new school of invention; and established and endowed it with nearly thirty volumes of the most animated and original composition that have enriched English literature for a century'.[22] In this brief period and almost single-handedly, thanks largely to his extraordinary productivity, Scott had given the novel literary respectability; moreover, he had done so through one of its most widely scorned and dubious modes, the historical romance. In the very year of the publication of *Waverley*, for example, the *British Critic* declared that it had 'insuperable objections' to the species of romance denominated 'an historical romance': 'We consider the words 'historical' and 'romance' as at hostility with each other, and utterly unreconcilable [. . .] we must enter our protest against blending and confounding together historical truth and romantic fiction, each of which ought to be rigidly restrained within its own peculiar province.'[23]

The derogation of historical romance reflects uneasiness over the popularisation of history, but it points as well to what Richard Maxwell calls the intractable 'dilemma' of historical fiction as a genre: how to maintain the integrity of history and yet retain the rhetorical impact of fiction.[24] Scott himself directly entered this debate in the 'Dedicatory Epistle' to *Ivanhoe* (1820), using the occasion of his first foray outside familiar Scottish space, as well as into a remote historical period, to reflect on the propriety and protocols of historical romance. Addressed to Oldbuck's friend the Reverend Dr Dryasdust, the 'Dedicatory Epistle' is written by a fellow antiquary, Laurence Templeton, supposed editor of the manuscript that is the ostensible source of *Ivanhoe*. Templeton anticipates dismissal of his work as an idle tale by 'the more grave antiquary', and he mounts a pre-emptive defence (*WN* 8:5). Along the way, he confronts the standard (and enduring) charge that historical fiction 'pollut[es] the well of history with modern inventions', and hence inculcates in naïve and young readers false ideas about the period in which the novel is set (*WN* 8:8). Admitting the force of this charge to a point – Templeton cheerfully declares he may well have 'confused the manners of two or three centuries' (*WN* 8:12) – he argues that the fictional project of communication to 'the modern reader' trumps obligation to the historical record. Templeton pursues this argument on several fronts and spells out limits to the 'fair licence' permitted a novelist, but he consistently maintains a set to the audience and foregrounds authorship as an act of mediation, a 'translation' of the past for the present (WN 8:9). Such mediation requires Templeton to operate outside categories of transparency or authenticity, and he takes as the emblem of his authorship a 'minstrel coronet' composed 'partly out of the pearls of pure antiquity, partly from the Bristol stones and paste, with which I have endeavoured to imitate them' (WN 8:12).

The interfusion of original pearls and paste imitations in the 'minstrel's coronet' exemplifies the combinatory method of generic mixing David Duff has dubbed 'smooth-mixing' (synthesis) in contrast to 'rough-mixing' (juxta-position).[25] Mixing of both sorts was endemic in the period; indeed, generic hybridisation is the signature of Romantic literary innovation. But in Scott's historical romance not only the genre was composite; so too was the author. In this 'species of composition' writing takes the form of re-composition, re-cycling and collaboration, and the author himself emerges as a distinctly 'rough-mixed' construct. The annotations and introduction to the 'Magnum Opus' edition at the end of Scott's career make this most visible, as Scott identifies the diverse texts and other sources that went into the making of his narratives. If the 'Magnum' built on and consolidated the authority of Sir Walter Scott, however, it did so on the basis of what Fiona Robertson terms the 'inbuilt plurality' evident in the role of the 'Author of Waverley'.[26] From the start, Scott's novelistic authorship operated under signs of multiplicity and proliferation. As early as the Preface to the third edition of Waverley in October 1814, he joked that the unknown author might be a poet, critic, lawyer, clergyman or perhaps (echoing Mrs Malaprop in Sheridan's The Rivals) 'three gentlemen at once'.[27] The fictional frames Scott began attach-ing to his novels with the first series of Tales of My Landlord a few years later reinforced this scattering or fragmentation of the single author, featuring a set of multiple (often foolish) authorial figures like Jedediah Cleishbotham, Captain Clutterbuck, and Dr Dryasdust. The significant point, however, is that these are editor-figures rather than originators, transmitters of the stories of others. Translating the implication of these sportive frames into a referential discourse of retrospection and scholarship, the annotations to the 'Magnum' make explicit the degree to which Scott's narratives were gener-ated out of and even rendered in the words of others. 'We find in his novels not one author', Robert Mayer aptly comments, 'but a whole grab-bag of authors' from various professions, historical eras, and different genres.[28]

The Waverley Novels thus immerse the author in an intergeneric network of reading/writing/transmission, drawing attention to the generic reciproc-ity and adjacency that characterised the early nineteenth-century literary field. Scott's novels drew particular authority from their distinct alignment with historical genres and archival documents, an alignment reinforced by the extensive historical notes he added to them. But such annotations also blurred the line between the author as novelist and the author as antiquarian historian, allowing for a reversal of the trajectory of authorisation with the popular romances underwriting historical documents. Thus Archibald Constable published a collection of historical pamphlets about Captain John Porteous, featured in *The Heart of Mid-Lothian* (1818), not only at the same time as he published Scott's novel but in exactly the same format. Indeed, *Criminal Trials, Illustrative of the Tale Entitled 'The Heart of Midlothian', Published From the Original Record*, appears authorised by the novel rather than the other way around. Nor were Scott's sources always textual or historical; many were local, personal or oral. *The Heart of Mid-Lothian* itself is a famous example, its central figure and plot having been suggested to Scott in a letter from Mrs Goldie, whose tale of the obscure Helen Walker captured his interest and informed the creation of Jeanie Deans in the novel.

In contrast to historical authorities, the 'correspondents' and other informal sources placed the novels within a contemporary sphere of circulation and attached them to current readers, locating the fiction rather differently. Scott's historical novel was always Janus-faced: one face turned to the past and the archive, the other to the present and the literary market. The turn to the commercial world of publishing and readers was decisive in cementing the demystification of authorship already activated by the notion of the editor-author, and from such demystification arose much of Scott's popularity with the reading public. If his material was often obscure and scholarly, the figure of the author developed in the novels was homely, familiar, and often funny; this was an author who inhabited the same mundane world as his readers. Scott took these readers seriously even as he tweaked their propensities and appetites, as he tweaks the circulating-library reader, Miss Martha Buskbody, whom he abruptly introduces in the coda of *The Tale of Old Mortality* (1816). As a stereotypical female romance reader, Miss Buskbody demands certain predictable satisfactions from her novels, and she badgers Peter Pattieson, the authorial figure in this text, to deliver them. Pattieson finds delivering such satisfactions tiresome, as Scott did himself, but Buskbody's brisk and unenchanted view of novel-writing as a 'trade' requiring certain skills (much like her own as a lace-maker) resonates with the notion of authorship he advanced throughout his career.

Like his friend William Wordsworth, Scott understood the modern writer to be 'a man speaking to men'; unlike Wordsworth, he also understood him to be fully within modern commercial society. Where Wordsworth distinguished himself and his poetry from the realm of popular genres – the 'frantic novels, sickly and stupid German Tragedies, and deluges of idle and extravagant stories in verse' famously dismissed in the Preface to the second edition of *Lyrical Ballads*[29] – Scott happily engaged in producing texts as numerous and popular as possible.

His prodigious output and rapidity of publication, as novel after novel (not to mention works in other genres appearing under his name) poured from the press, led to a growing chorus of complaint in the reviews about over-production and crass mercenary motives. On this front too Scott directly entered the debate. The 'Introductory Epistle' to *The Fortunes of Nigel* (1822) meets these charges in a spirited exchange between the Eidolon of the Author and another of Scott's antiquarian personae, Captain Clutterbuck. Importantly, the exchange itself takes place in a commercial venue: the back of the bookshop of Scott's publisher, Archibald Constable. Responding to Clutterbuck's insinuation that 'an unworthy motive may be assigned for this rapid succession of publication', the authorial Eidolon admits the profit motive may join with others in accounting for his rate of production. However, he argues, his publications support not just himself but (among others) the paper-manufacturing and the printing trades, so that the local economy is in fact greatly obliged to him for having established 'an exten-sive manufacture' (WN 13:13). When universal suffrage arrives, he quips, he intends to stand for Parliament on behalf of 'all the unwashed artificers connected with literature' (WN 13:14). The tone is light; the point serious. Rather than repudiating the literary market, Scott inserts authorship fully within it, contesting Adam Smith's designation of authors as 'unproduc-tive labourers' by arguing that an author's 'bales of books' are as much a part of 'the public stock' as the goods of any other 'manufacturer' (WN 13:14). Taking up the demeaning vocabulary of 'manufacture' thrown at him, Scott absorbs it into an argument for circulation and publication. For his part, declares the authorial Eidolon, he refuses 'to disclaim the ordinary motives, on account of which the whole world around me is toiling unremittingly' (WN 13:15).

Scott's antiquarian-commercial model of authorship depends on notions at once of inexhaustibility and of impermanence. On the one hand, the anti-quary's archive is an immense reservoir of materials. 'The stores of history are accessible to every one', declares the authorial Eidolon in the preface to *Peveril of the Peak* (1822), defending himself from charges of adulterating historical knowledge, 'and are no more exhausted or impoverished by the hints thus borrowed from them, than the fountain is drained by the water which we subtract for domestic purposes' (WN 14:9). Fountains may be so drained, of course, but for Scott water symbolises a public good, a good whose availability is not diminished by individual usage: the archive cannot be used up. On the other hand, in immersing his authorship in the com-mercial current of present time, Scott writes it under signs of transience and ephemerality. Subject to fashion and taste, his novels appear in his fictional frames as mere creatures of an hour: the novels can be (and will be) used up. These two motifs conjoin to generate a flexible notion of circulation at once grounded and open. Re-inflecting historical romance through the notion of circulation, Scott's bookish authorship in the Waverley Novels not only reshaped the literary culture of his time but significantly extended its reach.

CHAPTER TWO

Ballads and Borders

Kenneth McNeil

In one of the most important scenes in *The Antiquary*, Jonathan Oldbuck and his party come upon Elspeth Meiklebackit 'chaunting forth' what he recognises as a scrap of a historical ballad. Instantly enraptured, Oldbuck begins to write it down as a 'genuine and undoubted fragment of minstrelsy' (*WN* 3:310). One refrain of the ballad describes Lowland men-at-arms deriding the prowess of the Highland Host, and Oldbuck cannot resist taunting his young Highland friend, Hector MacIntyre. Hector's reaction is to dismiss the ballad as doggerel and to reopen his long-standing quarrel with Oldbuck about the authenticity and superior quality of the Ossianic songs of Selma, as transmitted by James Macpherson a generation earlier. However, Oldbuck is adamant that they have discovered a fragment of a historical ballad that Joseph Ritson and Thomas Percy, two of the most revered authorities of the time, would have both admired and declared as genuine.

In this scene, Scott stages key elements of a literary antiquarian discourse in the late eighteenth century, which he had helped shape, and which was in turn to have a major influence in the shaping of his career. Scott himself had relied on Percy and Ritson, citing their work to undergird the authority of his own antiquarian collection of ballads, *Minstrelsy of the Scottish Border*, published in three volumes in 1802–3. The *Minstrelsy* was Scott's first significant foray into the literary world. What began as a modest proposal to collect and edit a small volume of a handful of Borders 'riding' (or raiding) ballads grew into a finished collection of no fewer than seventy-seven ballads, forty-three of which had never appeared in print before – surrounded by a vast scholarly apparatus of footnotes, headnotes, prefatory material, and appendices. Scott eventually organised his material into three categories: 'historical ballads' (the riding ballads), 'romantic ballads', and 'modern imitations of ancient ballads' (comprising twenty-one imitations by Scott and others). Much of this collection grew out of a lifelong exposure to, and fascination with, ballad material. Scott describes hearing border ballads and tales as a child at Sandyknowe, the home of his grandparents, where Scott's grandmother would recount the raiding exploits of ancient Border families, including his own. These were tight-knit, fiercely independent, patriarchal clans living in isolated, desolate moss and hill country; many deemed outlaws or renegades by the crown authorities on either side of the border. As an adult, Scott set about collecting these border ballads, while also depending on the efforts of a cadre of friends and collaborators, including James Hogg and John Leyden. *Minstrelsy of the Scottish Border* launched Scott's literary career; the first edition of two volumes sold well enough for Scott to issue the third volume a year later, in May 1803. The publication also inaugurated Scott's relationship with the printer James Ballantyne, which would lead to Scott's greatest literary glories and his eventual financial downfall.[1] Although for many years readers of the *Minstrelsy* were content to appraise its value solely in relation to the novels that came after, more recent scholars have come to recognise it as a key work of British Romanticism, part of the great 'ballad revival' of the late eighteenth and early nineteenth centuries, which shaped new understandings of literature and history in Britain, in Europe, and around the world.[2]

When Scott wrote *The Antiquary* he was, like Oldbuck, already in middle age and busily accumulating artefacts of Scottish history while at the same time building up the museum-house at Abbotsford in which he would display them. But by this time Scott, unlike Oldbuck, was not primarily an antiquarian, but a novelist. It might be more accurate to say that Oldbuck's character allowed Scott to poke fun at his early antiquarian preoccupations and the career he might have had, had his ambition not moved him into a literary realm offering freer creative rein. As such, a winking irony and gentle scepticism attend much of the antiquarian discussion in *The Antiquary*. Oldbuck's insistence, for example, that no less a figure than Ritson would have found Elspeth Meiklebackit's ballad genuine alludes to a preoccupation of much antiquarian writing of the era, which alternatively defended and attacked claims of ballad authenticity – this while some of the most famous examples of 'ancient' ballad material turned out to be imitations of contemporary manufacture. The irony, however, is that Ritson most certainly would not have found the ballad genuine since, as Caroline Jackson-Houlston has shown, Scott himself made it up.[3] By 1816 Scott could smile at the obsessive pedantic debates that not only preoccupied the minds of antiquarians a generation before but were the cause of serious anxiety for the young Scott himself, who had his own antiquarian contributions to make. In doing so, a literary past, of which Scott himself played a part, is plotted in *The Antiquary*. Ballad collecting and editing becomes an earlier, and outdated, mode of cultural expression enfolded within a more modern one, the historical novel, which can describe and historicise the cultural forms that preceded it.

While Scott exposed the excesses of antiquarian discourse in his fiction, he clearly valued the ballad form as an expression of a more traditional and localised world view, an alternative mode of recalling the past, a folk memory, in contrast to the historical/antiquarian mode embodied by Oldbuck. Collecting and preserving this localised view of the past informed Scott's task as editor of the *Minstrelsy*. However, as T. F. Henderson shows in his edition, the complete locality Scott seems keen to assign to the ballads in the collection is of little account since place names and personages are not identified in most of the originals (*Minstrelsy* 3:3). In both novel and ballad collection, Scott tampered with his source material, adding particular local details to a certain interpretation of the past, and, as examined later in this chapter, a certain family history – his own.

Scott's *Minstrelsy*, then, instances simultaneously an invention of tradition, an imaginative recounting of the historical and regional parameters that defined the author's own community; and an (in)authentic (auto)ethnography in that it forges, in both senses of the word, a historical and genealogical continuity that is set against the disruptive forces of modernisation. Scott's first contribution to the literary marketplace reveals the ironic complexity at work in grappling with material that seeks to define a people and their ties to a particular place and to a particular past, while making visible the ways in which a culture of modernity both licenses the search for this material and is critiqued by it. Scott was always interested in what happens at the borders, enunciating categories associated with the formation of national culture while at the same time putting them into play. As a recent study of Scottish Romanticism puts it, Scott 'installs the "Border" chronotope of a dynamic liminality' for a modern national/imperial identity.[4] What has not been remarked on, however, is how Scott's *Minstrelsy* – a work that compiles a long history of repeated border crossings – both announces and inaugurates this border chronotope. As the first note of Scott's profound contribution to Romantic culture in Scotland, Britain and beyond, the *Minstrelsy* is not so much an authentic expression of a homogenous collective, the immanent culture of a national community (imagined or otherwise), but a vehicle for staging a contemporary exploration of the boundaries between key sets of oppositions associated with modern notions of national identity: the present and the past, the authentic and the imitative, orality and literacy, the local and the national/imperial.

The Uses of Orality

Antiquarianism and ballad collecting both reflected and promulgated a shift in thinking about orality and oral sources of literary expression in the late eighteenth century. Samuel Johnson had famously doubted the authenticity of Macpherson's Ossian because there was, as Macpherson would later admit, no textual source material, no ancient manuscript. However, Macpherson's work proved to be a landmark in the move toward renewed interest in, and validation of, oral sources in the latter part of the century.[5] Johnson's out-of-hand dismissal of Ossian nevertheless reveals the antiquarian historicisation of language art: orality is the sign of an earlier form of culture superseded by a more advanced form under the sign of writing. Recent scholars have pointed out that this historicisation of orality and the ballad form has a history itself. Penny Fielding, for example, has traced the genealogy of the categorisation of orality in Scotland. The oral, Fielding writes, is always writing's other, and through this opposition literate Scots of the eighteenth century articulated a host of cultural assumptions and norms.[6]

For Scots of the period, the most urgent social evaluation for which the currency of orality was put to use concerned their national identity. On the one hand orality, expressed as a problem of 'scotticisms' that had to be purged from the polite speech of educated Scots, was the sign of a national lack, a linguistic reminder of the nation's struggle to achieve economic and social parity with the nation's more advanced neighbour to the south.[7] Imperfections of Scottish speech indicated the imperfections of the nation, and both required improvement in order to fulfil the social and economic benefits offered by union with England. On the other hand, as assertions of national backwardness gave way to a Scottish cultural nationalism later in the century, orality became associated with the recovery of the nation's vanished origins. Orality, as that which precedes literacy, became the authenticating imprimatur of antiquarian material deemed uniquely Scottish. Through the validation and historicisation of orality, the ballad form was no longer deemed expressive merely of the doggerel of the lower classes, but instead became the repository of the nation's heritage, the undiluted expression of the people. The 'vulgar' became the 'volk', and the ballad form concomitantly offered a singular, if ephemeral, glimpse into the life of the nation.

Scottish writers of the late eighteenth and early nineteenth centuries, like Robert Burns and James Hogg, continued to move within increasingly divergent literary cultures. On the one hand they exploited the new-found interest in untutored ploughmen and shepherds to sell their written work to a reading public; while, on the other, they partook of a balladeering culture in which originality and authorship are secondary to the quality of recitation and the poet's ability to replicate the collective folk memory of the listeners. Burns's poems, for example, both drew on oral sources and fed back into them. Late eighteenth and early Scottish popular culture reveals the rich complexity of oral/textual interaction and imbrication, but the dominant assumption in Scottish literary culture was increasingly insistent on separating these worlds, hardening the distinction between them.

Embalming the Dead

Paradoxically then, the oral achieved iconic status as national expression only when, and because, it was deemed to be no longer living. Eighteenth-century literary culture's investment in the ballad form is bound up with the anxiety that it was dead or nearly dead, rendering the investigation of the oral archaeological or historical. As the wellspring of the nation's cultural identity, the oral world was found in fragments, fossilised under layers of literary sediment, or in living transmutations that were pale shadows of the original. The tension between the dead (but pristine) past and the living (but corrupted) present gave rise to the antiquarian editor-function. In a kind of contravention of the Whig historiography of culture and society that Scott as novelist has been said to promulgate, Scott as compiler-editor of the *Minstrelsy* adopted the conventional antiquarian stance that the passage of time meant degradation and distortion, not refinement. The emendations of various latecomers to the source material – often identified in antiquarian writing as careless monk transcribers, sloppy itinerant troubadours, or, in the more recent past, old spinsters with faulty memories – required the editor to rescue his source material, to restore it to its original state while at the same time preserving it by rendering speech into text.[8] In doing so, antiquarians reinforced orality's static deadness. As Janet Sorenson argues, orality is always 'preliterate', always anterior to the present as conventional antiquarian discourse 'anachronised' both oral material and the 'common' people who drew upon it.[9]

As documenting the provenance of source material became increasingly necessary to establish claims of authenticity, of ancientness, antiquarian writers relied increasingly on extensive framing apparatuses. Headnotes and footnotes served to contextualise and legitimise each source within the collection, while lengthy dissertations and essays preceding or appending the entire collection served to contextualise and legitimise the claims of the writer within the antiquarian scholarship that preceded him. By Scott's time, the increasing acceptance of living reciters of ballads as sources necessitated an additional kind of framing material: lengthy notes detailed the circumstances that surrounded the transcription – name and occupation of the 'informant', background upon which to establish the informant's authority to present the material, and the time and date of transcription. The structure of the *Minstrelsy of the Scottish Border* – its lengthy introductory essay, headnotes and footnotes (many taking up more space than the ballads to which they are attached), and multiple appendices – reveals a keen desire on the part of its author to secure legitimacy in the conventional antiquarian discourse of his time. The struggle to secure bona fides, of both the writer and his source material, perhaps underlies the emergence of antiquarian ballad editing as a key vehicle for the establishment of the formal science of 'culture', manifested in inquiry that would diverge later in the nineteenth century into separate fields – historiography, anthropology, folklore, linguistics, ethnography, aesthetics, and literary criticism. In this way, antiquarian discourse was instrumental in shaping the forms and assumptions by which we now investigate 'culture', while also establishing literary expression as a key marker of cultural distinctiveness.

The *Minstrelsy*'s three-part taxonomy – historical ballads, romantic ballads, and modern imitations of the first two categories – signals for the most part Scott's investment in presenting his ballad material as an authentic vestige of a Scottish cultural past. It also injects an alternative impulse apparently at odds with its antiquarianism. Particularly in the last category, the apparently unassuming 'modern imitations', the *Minstrelsy* diverges from its alignment with emerging fields of cultural study. Indeed, with the addition of this third category, Scott's taxonomy seems to undermine the authenticating function of the ballad collection in the first place, drawing attention to the uncertainty that had long surrounded the genre rather than bolstering Scott's own claims as to the authenticity of his material. In the history of antiquarian publication, as Scott well knew, it had not always been possible to distinguish the imitation from the genuine article. The ballad revival was haunted from the start by accusations and counter-accusations of forgery. As long as the value of the ballad was wholly bound up with its relative antiquity, the modern imitation could have no value. They could not signify as the literature of the nation, but instead were fakes and lies, the work of a charlatan.

Scott's own solution to this dilemma was to reorient the terms of the debate, reshaping the categories upon which ballads or oral material must be judged. In an 1805 review of the *Report of the Committee of the Highland Society of Scotland, Appointed to Inquire into the Nature and Authenticity of the Poems of Ossian*, Scott affirms the judgement of the committee. Ossian is indeed a fake. Yet at the same time, Scott invests its forger with the laudatory status of national spokesman, Scotland's bard:

> [W]e are compelled to renounce the pleasing idea, 'that Fingal lived, and that Ossian sung,' [but] our national vanity may yet be flattered by the fact, that a remote, and almost a barbarous corner of Scotland, produced, in the 18th century, a bard capable not only of making an enthusiastic impression on every mind susceptible of poetical beauty, but of giving a new tone to poetry throughout all Europe.[10]

The nation's literary legacy must be judged not on its antiquity but on its aesthetic merits. In Scott's formulation, it is not Ossian who gets the praise, who casts glory on the nation, but his modern-day imitator. Here, Scott articulates a stance that is only partially developed in the *Minstrelsy of the Scottish Border*, published just a few years before, which, though it aligns literary expression with national identity, undermines the assumption that such expression needs to be the long-buried work of a long-dead poet.

The tension in the *Minstrelsy* between the categories of 'ancient' and 'ancient-like' reveals not so much a contradiction but a complex notion of the role Scott had assumed for himself as a latter-day ballad editor and of his relation to his source material. As subsequent folklorists have shown, Scott not only inserted his own imitations of ancient border ballads, but also actively reworked some of his original source material. If he did not manufacture 'ancient' ballads wholesale, as others had done, he certainly rewrote them: changing phrases, adding whole stanzas, and (as discussed later) inserting the names of specific historical figures and locales where his source material was non-specific or ambiguous. Scott's inclusion of contemporary imitations of ancient material signals, in Maureen McLane's words, the work's 'retro-neo chronotope' as it both seeks to preserve the past but also, through emendation and imitation, revitalise forms assumed to be anachronistic, belonging to the past.[11] In doing so, it is possible to see Scott already chafing at the restrictions imposed on him as 'ballad editor' and moving toward a potentially more authoritative position.

In the 1830 edition of the *Minstrelsy* Scott rehearses the antiquarian debate on the significance of the historical minstrel figure, a debate that was bound up with larger debates of the ballad revival as to the integrity of oral ballad tradition and material deemed 'ancient'. In contrast to antiquarians like Ritson, who, Scott writes, had dismissed the minstrel as a figure of small merit, a mere musician who sang other people's verses; and Percy, who had granted the minstrel a prominent place in medieval courtly society as a singer of verses he himself composed, Scott argues that the both antiquarians saw only one side of the gold and silver (minstrel) shield. Yet it is also clear, as the title of his own ballad collection suggests, that Scott seeks to reclaim the minstrel idea, arguing that in any society '[a]ll professors of the fine arts [. . .] hold their professional respectability by the severe tenure of exhibiting excellence in their department' (*Minstrelsy* 1:34). Ritson's picture of the 'poor and wondering glee-man purchasing his bread by singing his ballads at the ale-house to drunken revellers', is for Scott an example of the minstrel profession's substrata and not indicative of the potential laudatory greatness to which the talented minstrel could aspire. Scott's assertion, and his generalising use of the term 'poet' to describe literary figures ancient and contemporary, is significant because in a summary of a debate grounded in historiographical claims and counter-claims, Scott inserts an ahistorical condition, 'exhibiting excellence', which exerts its pressure on all 'professors of the fine arts' throughout time. In this way, historical distinctions between bard/minstrel/poet are less significant than the fact that 'literary great men' have always been fêted and rewarded by their societies for their talents.

Scott's pronouncement on the minstrel debate reveals some of the earlier anxieties of authority that had preoccupied him in his early career, and the extent to which, by 1830, he felt he had mastered the subject. It also suggests the extent to which Scott had also pushed questions of authorial status, authenticity, preservation, and literary merit beyond the scope of antiquarianism. After the publication of the *Minstrelsy*, he wasted no time securing his own position as poet, and in 1805 published the first work he claimed as wholly his own, *The Lay of the Last Minstrel*, a poem originally intended for the third part of the *Minstrelsy*. More than an imitation of an ancient Scottish Border ballad, however, the *Lay* foregrounds the tale-teller himself, mediating the past and present and the role of the modern poet in both re-animating and legitimising the figure of the minstrel. Scott mimics the style of the minstrel, in an act of historical ventriloquism, while at the same time self-consciously legitimising his own status as modern-day heir to the minstrel tradition.[12] In the *Lay*, thematically aligned with the *Minstrelsy*, Scott makes the transition from the role of antiquarian editor, a forger of an invented national tradition, to the role that would make him both famous and enormously rich – the national author, whose own work narrates the mediation between the various components, past and present, of a fragmented national community. The nation's literary voice is found not in the archives, in the dusty remnants of its bards and minstrels, but in the synthesis of material both archival and imaginative: the foundation of the historical novel.

Local Knowledge

A cataloguing of the emendations Scott made to his source material reveals a telling component of Scott's larger agenda for his ballad collection. Scott is always keen to locate narrative settings in the Scottish Borders, even when his source material makes no reference to specific place names or indicates an alternative setting altogether. Thus, Scott assigns a 'complete [Borders] locality' to 'The Douglas Tragedy' through his reference to historical personages, even though no such reference appears in the original. Scott also identifies the setting of 'Annan Water' as located near where the title river empties into the Solway Firth, even though his source is Allan Ramsay's *Tea-Table Miscellany*, where the ballad is entitled 'Allan Water', which is in Perthshire (*Minstrelsy* 3:348). This localisation is part of a larger ordering of space that features in much of Scott's work. The local, whether the Borders, the Highlands, or rural Lowlands, becomes a site of both spatial and temporal difference, of disjuncture between a literate cosmopolitan culture self-aware of its own alienated contemporaneity and a naïve primitive culture holding on to the residue of traditions and folkways that are always in danger of becoming 'lost'. As he does in much of his later work, Scott imbues his borderlands with their own unique spatial and cultural integrity. While doing so, however, he also abstracts them, removing them from their local context in so far as the habits and manners of Borders society illustrate the universal condition of 'primitive society'. In this, the Minstrelsy reveals Scott's debt to the theories and methodology of Scottish Enlightenment philosophy that sought to identify the peculiar collection of attributes that marks a people, a 'culture', while ordering all differentiated cultures along an axis of stadial development toward increasing complexity and sophistication. Scott displays the profound influence on his thinking of Scottish Enlightenment figures – especially Adam Smith, John Millar, and Adam Ferguson – when he argues that any interest in the literary expression of ancient Borders society must be premised on its fascinating and instructive exemplarity. Scott articulates this most fully in his 'Introductory Remarks on Popular Poetry', which he appended to the 1830 edition of the Minstrelsy:

> Yet the investigation of the early poetry of every nation, even the rudest, carries with it an object of curiosity and interest. [. . . I]ts resemblance to, or dissimilarity from, the popular rhymes of other nations in the same stage, must needs illustrate the ancient history of states; their slower or swifter progress towards civilisation (Minstrelsy 1:6)

At the same time, in the headnote to 'Archie of Ca'field' he argues for this ballad's merit in containing 'minute particulars, highly characteristic of Border manners, which it is the object of this publication to illustrate' (Minstrelsy 2:146). Scottish Enlightenment categories of the local and the universal reinforce and feed on one another in the Minstrelsy of the Scottish Border, as the local ('particulars characteristic of Border manners') serves as illustration for the universal ('the progress toward civilization of primitive nations'), which, reciprocally, endorses the local.

The inherent tension between a particular local culture and universal laws of culture in Scott's work, and the complex overlapping of spatial and temporal orderings of difference that such a tension produces, have been identified as Scott's integral contribution to the ways in which Britons of the period made sense of the vast array of discrete cultural encounters within an emerging imperial world-system. In Scott's (imperial) modernity, cultural difference is acknowledged and even celebrated, while the 'primitive' is safely anachronised, made an object for self-satisfyingly detached but sentimental reflection on the part of a contemporary reader.[13] In this line of argument, Scott's work is aligned with the consolidation of national and imperial cultures. His novels, while giving utterance to the violence and inevitable loss that attends the historical clash of cultures, nevertheless describe new and compensatory identities in the overarching narrative of peace and progress. No wonder then, that Scott became the author of choice for British imperial reading publics, many of whom could trace their lineage to Scotland and the Celtic peripheries, around the globe.[14]

Balladeering as Autoethnography

The worldwide popularity and influence of Scott's *Minstrelsy* and of ballad collecting in general demonstrates the exportability of Scott's imperial registry of cultural identity. For example, the tropes and methods of Anglo-Scottish ballad collecting were adopted wholesale in the United States among collectors who concerned themselves with 'Negro Minstrelsy' or 'Indian' song traditions – forms which continue to register as signs of cultural appropriation in American culture.[15] Yet in no other work does Scott himself more readily align his own identity with the culture he describes. Scott dedicated the *Minstrelsy* to Henry, third Duke of Buccleuch, who was not only Scott's patron but was also the chief of the Scott clan, and throughout the *Minstrelsy* there is frequent mention in the ballads of Scott's Borders ancestors. Exaggerating their roles in the history recounted in the *Minstrelsy*, Scott maps his own genealogy (and his name) on to the history and geography of the Borders. Scott's narrative stance in relation to historical personages and to the historical ballads themselves is positively reverent and in contrast to the later sceptical or ironic stance he adopts in his novels.

Scott's unique relation to the archival material may have granted him the creative licence to shape his ballad material, as Scott was not only the editor but also, in folklorist terms, his own 'informant'. The emphatic identification between author and subject culture in the *Minstrelsy* suggests that the work can be considered no less an ethnographic account of the self, an 'autoethnography', defined in contemporary anthropological study as a transcultural mediation in which a native subject undertakes to represent himself in ways that engage with the terms of the dominant metropolitan culture.[16] Scott's insistent localisation of both his archival material and his family heritage within the border space framed in the *Minstrelsy* suggests that the work is closer in keeping with an autoethnography than any of his later treatments of discrete cultures. (He was, for example, always careful to proclaim himself an outsider in relation to the Highlands.) Scott's authorial stance in regard to the Borders reveals an earnestness, an attachment, a partisanship, that is neither wholly touristic nor wholly indigenous but something else in-between, both inside and outside. The irony in all this is, of course, that the border space in which Scott locates himself most insistently is itself defined by an intrinsic geographical and cultural ambivalence, an 'in-betweenness'.

Debatable Lands

Frontier spaces are often synonymous with the 'contact zone', the transcultural space in which the autoethnographic text is produced.[17] As a geographical demarcation between one place and another, one nation and another, one culture and another, 'frontierness' is, of course, the very function of the border space; Scott's historicisation of the region emphasises the permeability and instability of the boundary line and the repeated 'border crossings' that give the space and its people their unique character, which is marked by violent interaction and contestation. In the Borders, Scott sums up, 'the hands of rapine [are] never [. . .] folded in inactivity, nor the sword of violence returned to the scabbard' (*Minstrelsy* 1:108). Violent conflict brands itself on the culture of the Borderers who succumb to a kind of geopolitical, rather than strictly geographical, determinism, which in turn gives rise to the ballad form. Endless conflict creates shifting boundaries, shifting loyalties, and shifting allegiances. Summarising the long-term cultural psychological effects of this history, Scott writes: 'The Borderers had, in fact, little reason to regard the inland Scots as their fellow-subjects, or to respect the power of the Crown.' Instead they were, even in times of peace, 'a kind of outcasts, against whom the united powers of England and Scotland were often employed' (*Minstrelsy* 1:115). Conflictedness, the insistent theme of all Borders history, produces a strange paradoxical collectivity: a shared sense of not belonging to either nation. The outsider status of the Borderers comes to define them, as a consciousness of exclusion becomes the tie that binds them together. In other words, Scott's historical recounting of cultural, political, and spatial discontinuity and marginalisation manifested in the ballads of the *Minstrelsy* provides the basis for a powerful sense of continuity, of communal tradition.

Scott acknowledges that Borders culture seems perhaps attractively freewheeling to those who are accustomed to the monotony of polished society; yet Borders nostalgia is, at best, only a partial compensation. The Borderer's world has faded or is fading away, in what Scott describes in the relentless processes of cultural assimilation. Through means both evolutionary and revolutionary, 'Border marauders were, in the course of years, either reclaimed or exterminated; though nearly a century elapsed ere their manners were altogether assimilated to those of their countrymen' (*Minstrelsy* 1:110).[18] Scott ultimately resolves the conflict and disunity of the borderlands, consigning their attractive heterogeneity to the past and replacing it with a homogeneity of an undifferentiated present.

Return to the Border

That the Borderer belongs to the past suggests that Scott's intent is to shunt his independent primitives into the narrow confines of a melancholic modernity. The simple, rural, preliterate world of the Borders is forever at the cusp of annihilation, always dying but never quite dead; its demise always deferred in an endless cycle of memory and the desire for return. Yet our contemporary critical moment has seen a revitalisation of the borderland as the figuration of ambiguity and uncertainty, of living in-between, in our postcolonial world. The border has become both the frequent theme of much recent cultural criticism and its primary critical trope. Homi K. Bhabha, for example, famously identifies 'a contingent, borderline experience' within 'the discourse of colonialism [that] opens up *in-between* colonizer and colonized. This border space of cultural and interpretive undecidability is produced in the "present" of the cultural moment'; it represents an 'interstitial future that emerges *in-between* the claims of the past and the needs of the present'.[19] For Bhabha and many subsequent postcolonial critics, the border is a figurative site of critical resistance to rigidity, fixity, boundaries, and limitation, which is reflected in postcolonialism's concern with the global, trans-oceanic reach of European colonialism and on the condition of diasporic and migrant cultures fomented in its aftermath.

The ascendancy of the border in the contemporary disavowal of the Manichaean structure of colonial discourse paradoxically provides the context for one of the most influential and interesting returns to Scott's formulation of the borderlands as the topographical sign for a particular ethnic identity. *'With His Pistol in His Hand': a Border Ballad and Its Hero*, Américo Paredes's 1958 study of the US–Mexican border ballads of the lower Rio Grande – the *corridos* – has come to be considered a seminal account of a cultural studies field now well-established in the United States. Chicano studies, like other American ethnic and multicultural studies, grew out of the 1960s civil rights movement, as Chicano activists drew upon a critique of American racism and Anglocentrism, but uniquely looked to the US–Mexico border for their critical and political point of departure. The success of this effort is reflected in the indispensable contribution that Chicano studies have made to the concept of the border in American cultural studies.[20]

Paredes's Chicano ur-text makes no direct reference to the *Minstrelsy of the Scottish Border*, though he said in an interview that his interest in ballads was inspired by reading Francis Child's version of 'Sir Patrick Spence' (Spens) in graduate school. (Child, for his part, had relied heavily on the collection at Abbotsford to supply him with material for his own exhaustive collection of *The English and Scottish Popular Ballads*.) Paredes's debts to ideas first enunciated in the *Minstrelsy* a century and a half earlier, however, are clear.

Adapting the trope of cultural comparison that Scott himself adapted from
Scottish Enlightenment inquiry, Paredes argues that the ballad tradition that
most closely parallels the *corrido* tradition of the lower Rio Grande – which
recount the exploits of men who belonged to tight-knit, fiercely independent,
patriarchal families living in isolated, desolate scrub and hill country and who
were deemed outlaws or renegades by the federal authorities on either side –
can be found in medieval Scotland, as both traditions arise from a history of
border conflict. Paredes's autoethnography, like Scott's, articulates a kind of
universal border culture, whose cultural integrity is shaped by the constant
of its own geopolitical marginalisation.[21]

Reading the border consciousness of Scott's own *Minstrelsy* in the context
of Paredes's study of the *corridos* and the rise of Chicano studies and its
concomitant identification of a Chicano volk, as it were, is testament to
the widespread proliferation and transmutation of Scott's border vision as it
spread to America, Europe, and around the globe. As a force of cultural and
outright political nationalism, as a vehicle for an invented (folk) tradition,
of autoethnography, of cultural appropriation of minority culture (that is
later recuperated), the border chronotope that Scott installed in Scottish
Romanticism continues to shape worldwide understandings of national/
ethnic identity and cultural difference. Through it we come to comprehend
our own modernity, our own awareness of living in a present time that stands
in relation to something other than itself. Scott gave us modernity's alienation from other worlds, other times, which nevertheless encompass us living
in the here and now.

CHAPTER THREE

The Narrative Poems

Alison Lumsden and Ainsley McIntosh

Walter Scott's poetry has received little critical attention in recent years and there is as yet no modern scholarly edition. Seldom included even in anthologies of Romantic poetry, his poems have been all but written out of critical constructions of Romanticism.[1] This belies their phenomenal popularity at the time of their publication and their influence throughout the nineteenth century (and, through Victorian intermediaries, their continuing presence in twentieth- and twenty-first-century poetry). The de facto critical consensus overlooks Scott's innovative treatment of the relationship of poetry to the past and to both personal and national identity. It also occludes the pivotal role his poetry plays in negotiating theories of creativity and in formulating what we now define as Romanticism.

In the opening decade of the nineteenth century Scott's poetry enjoyed a high, as well as a popular, status. His first major narrative poem, *The Lay of the Last Minstrel* (1805), won both critical acclaim and commercial success: by 1807 there were already over 11,000 copies sold. This encouraged Scott's publishers to make the unprecedented offer of 1000 guineas, in advance, for his second experiment in narrative poetry, *Marmion* (1808).[2] Two years later, 16,000 copies of this poem had been sold. Such was Scott's reputation that by the time *The Lady of the Lake* (1810) was published there were eight editions issued in that year alone and over 20,000 copies sold.[3] This poem consolidated Scott's position and proved his most popular poetic work.

So how did a poet who was once so popular, and whose works coincide with what is generally agreed to be the 'high Romantic' period, come to be omitted from modern constructions of Romanticism? The answer resides in part in the problematic nature of the term 'Romantic' and its shifting status; what constitutes Romantic poetry is notoriously difficult to define. While many writers of this period share a concern with formal experimentation, landscape, memory and subjectivity, not all are now termed 'Romantic'. As Ian Duncan recognises, post-war criticism generated a version of Romanticism that foregrounded the lyric poem with its concentration on precision of form and subjectivity and thus privileged an art which is in excess of 'the collective pressures of society and history'.[4] Scott's poems' thematic concerns with history, nationhood and social responsibility do not lend themselves to this formulation.[5] Scott's narrative poems were also excluded from the canon more generally as they failed to conform to a Modernist aesthetic that values complexity and precision. While the lyric poetry of the Lake School could be accommodated within Modernism's requirements, Scott's poetry, which on the surface (although not upon closer reading) is narrative driven and generated by demands of rhythm and rhyme, could not be rehabilitated in this way. Ironically, the recent critical rehabilitation of Scott's fiction has also served to overshadow the significance of his poetry.

Scott is not the only writer to be ousted from modern formulations of the Romantic canon. Most notably, Robert Southey's poetry also has been eliminated from twentieth-century constructions of what characterised the literature of the early nineteenth century, and perhaps for similar reasons. However, in more recent years critics have sought to re-examine the parameters of the Romantic period to accommodate his thematic engagement with history, politics and nationhood in poems such as *Thalaba the Destroyer* (1801) and *Madoc* (1805).[6] Recognising that his poetry is significant because of its experimentation in form, its tropic innovation and its scepticism, Marilyn Butler posits that Southey was in fact the exemplar poet of the Romantic period.[7] Scott's poetry is similar in its scepticism, innovation and experimentation: he too should be read as offering a significant contribution to a revised Romanticism. In his narrative poems Scott adumbrates a theory of creativity that accords with Romantic sensibilities and simultaneously adopts an ironic scepticism towards its processes that positions him as a poet particularly relevant for the twenty-first century.

In spite of their recently neglected status, both Southey and Scott were central to early nineteenth-century constructions of poetic sensibility and were part of a network of poets now considered intrinsically Romantic. As well as his correspondence with Southey, Scott formed a long-standing correspondence and friendship with both Wordsworth and Byron and was acquainted with Coleridge. Scott's position within the framework of Romanticism is further implied by the origins of his career and the overlap of his own interests with those of, in particular, Wordsworth and Coleridge. Nowhere is this more evident than in what Scott himself described as his 'German-mad' phase when he learnt the language so that he might absorb the work of Schiller and the Schlegel brothers (*Letters* 10:331). As David Hewitt suggests, it was this 'encounter with German Romanticism' which was the 'actual transformative experience' that forged Scott as a writer.[8] Years later he was to describe his excitement concerning this literature which 'liberated [him] from the constrictions of eighteenth-century English poetry',[9] and it is consequently no surprise that Scott's first published poetical works were

translations from Bürger's 'Leonore' and 'Der wilde Jäger', published anonymously in 1796 as *The Chase and William and Helen: Two Ballads from the
German of Gottfried Augustus Bürger.*

Equally important to his development as a writer and to his connection
with a matrix of ideas that formulated his Romanticism, however, was Scott's
activities as a ballad collector and his absorption of a Scottish oral tradition.
The collection of material from a vernacular tradition was already well established by the end of the eighteenth century, exemplified most clearly within
a Scottish context by Alan Ramsay's *The Evergreen* (1724) and David Herd's
Ancient and Modern Scots Songs (1769). Such collections privileged vernacular culture and frequently set it within a national or regional context. More
significantly, however, they also laid the foundations for Romantic poetry,
for they promoted a naïvety which broke the boundaries of the Augustan
style and facilitated the generic experimentation foregrounded in the title
Lyrical Ballads which fused this vernacular tradition with original poetry. As
Kenneth McNeil's chapter has shown, Scott's *Minstrelsy of the Scottish Border*
can be located within this tradition but also offers interesting departures from
it. Defined spatially as arising from the traditions of the 'Lands Debateable',
it offers an interesting intervention on the question of national identity. By
describing itself as 'minstrelsy' it implies an authority to the material contained within it, aligning it generically with a noble poetic tradition and with
the developing concept of the 'bard' or minstrel which by 1802 had accrued
a whole host of connotations concerning national identity and forms of
creativity.[10] Moreover, the notes and paratexts which accompany the edition
also demonstrate Scott offering a negotiation between print and oral cultures
which was to remain significant throughout his career.[11]

As its title suggests, *The Lay of the Last Minstrel* began life as an 'imitation'
of the sort Scott had conceived for the *Minstrelsy*. In his 1830 'Introduction'
to the *Lay* Scott outlines its origins aligning these with his ballad collecting activities, describing it as 'the attempt to return to a more simple and
natural style of poetry [. . .] likely to be welcomed [. . .] when the public had
become tired of heroic hexameters, with all the buckram and binding which
belong to them of later days' (*PW* 6:30). He indicates that his intentions in
writing the poem are similar to those claimed for the *Minstrelsy* (the record-
ing of remarks, legends and superstitions which 'if not now collected, must
soon have been totally forgotten') since the *Lay*, he writes, was generated
by the desire of the young Countess of Dalkeith to make 'herself acquainted
with [Scotland's] traditions and customs' (*PW* 1:238, 6.21). However, in this
'Introduction' Scott also indicates the ways in which the *Lay* departs from
traditional material; it is these departures which are, perhaps, most crucial
to our understanding of the poem. Writing an imitation or 'modern' ballad,
he notes, poses a problem for the poet, since 'the ballad measure itself, which

was once listened to as an enchanting melody, had become hackneyed and sickening'. However, an encounter with John Stoddart was to lead to Scott's introduction to Romantic poetry, forging a renewed familiarity 'with the poetic effusions which have since made the Lakes of Westmoreland, and the authors by whom they been sung, so famous wherever the English tongue is spoken' (*PW* 1:23). While he was already acquainted with Southey's work, Mr Stoddart 'who possessed a strong memory with an excellent taste, was able to repeat to [him] many long specimens of their poetry, which had not yet appeared in print' (*PW* 1:24). Among these specimens was, famously, Coleridge's 'Christabel', a poem which impressed Scott by 'the singularly irregular structure of the stanzas, and the liberty which it allowed the author to adapt the sound to the sense' thus making it ideally suited to 'such an extravaganza as [he] meditated on the subject of Gilpin Horner' (*PW* 1:24). The idea of the minstrel frame, likewise, was prompted by suggestions made by friends (*PW* 1:28).

It is the introduction of this frame which marks the *Lay*'s move away from mere ballad imitation and adds to its complexity. Moreover, it allows Scott not only to imitate the Lake poets but to contribute to a growing aesthetic which may be defined as Romantic. This is evident in the poem's subject matter and its adoption of both overt romance elements (the themes of border warfare and love) and in the supernatural features of the poem that are clearly indebted not only to traditional Scottish lore but to the German Romanticism in which Scott had so immersed himself. The stylistic freedom that Scott so admired in 'Christabel' is also evident in the poem since it takes liberties with genre, mixing traditional ballad forms alongside its overarching romance structure. This was a feature of the poem identified by its early critics who noted the generic complexity of the *Lay* by describing it as 'such a romance as we may suppose would have been written in modern times'.[12] This formal dexterity is also illustrated in the 'minstrel competition' with which the poem ends, and in one of the most memorable passages in the poem, the ride of Deloraine by night to Melrose Abbey in order to recover the magic book of Michael Scott (*PW* 6:65–8). Passages like these show Scott at his poetic best, adapting 'sound to the sense' so that the shifting rhythm and rhyme patterns mimic Deloraine's ride.

The *Lay*'s most overtly Romantic features are contained at the opening and close of each canto, where the minstrel speaks directly to his audience and where there is a repeated elision between that voice, located in the seventeenth century and the voice of the modern poet, writing in 1805. This is evident, for example, in the famous passage that opens Canto 2:

IF thou would'st view fair Melrose aright,
Go visit it by the pale moonlight;

For the gay beams of lightsome day
Gild, but to flout, the ruins grey.
When the broken arches are black in night,
And each shafted oriel glimmers white; (PW 6:73)

Francis Jeffrey remarked that 'the reader will observe how skilfully the
Author calls in the aid of sentimental associations to heighten the effect of
the picture which he presents to the eye' (PW 6:73). Landscape is described
in terms of the sublime, with light and shade employed to add to the effect.
Moreover, as in, for example, *The Prelude* or Byron's *Childe Harold*, it is not
used neutrally, but as an emotional corollary that introduces a contradictory
psychological undercurrent.

This intervention of what might be described as a neo-Romantic voice
into the dominant romance structure of the poem is also evident in its treatment of time. Scott's description of the minstrel frame whereby readers would
be reminded 'of the time, place and circumstances of the recitation' (PW
1:28) encapsulates the fact that it allows for three time frames: the 1805 point
of publication, the sixteenth-century setting for the story told by the minstrel, and the seventeenth-century world inhabited by him. This suggests a
collapsing of the normal historical distinctions between different periods but
there are also points where the relationship between time and poetry is more
explicitly addressed. At the opening of Canto 4, for example, the minstrel
laments the death of his son, suggesting that while the River Tweed rolls on
through history so that 'all is peaceful, all is still', 'the tide of human time [. . .]
Retains each grief, retains each crime' and is 'stain'd with past and present
tears'. Here time is envisaged within a teleological Enlightenment model (the
idea of it as a river in ceaseless flow). However, an alternative Romantic paradigm is also proposed by which 'human time' does not function by a linear
dynamic but via an interaction with imagination so that in 'memory's eye'
the present is stained with both 'past and present tears'.[13] Memory, imagination and, by implication, poetry thus operate to create a complex version of
both past and present. This paradigm is also embedded in the structure of the
poem so that what seems like a simple romance 'imitation' is, in fact, offering
a complex meditation on the role of the present to the past and the relationship of both to poetry. For example, as Deloraine makes his way towards
Melrose he passes sites that resonate with echoes of the past: 'And sternly
shook his plumed head, / As glanced his eye o'er Halidon; / For on his soul
the slaughter red / of that unhallow'd morn arose / When first the Scott and
Carr were foes' (PW 6:67–8). Here his encounter with landscape re-enacts
the ways in which memory operates associatively to create an imaginative
bond between past and present.

This passage also demonstrates another aspect of the poem that cuts across a post-war construction of Romantic aesthetics since it incorporates within it a commentary on the dynamics of Scottish history and the processes by which national identity has been forged. No discussion of Scott's poetry can ignore this aspect of it but for many critics this preoccupation is contentious since it is seen as the site where Scott sidesteps modern concerns and retreats into the conservatism of romance proper. However, a more complex dynamic may operate whereby this social aspect of the poetry may be seen not as a retreat, but as part of a negotiation where Scott both engages with and generates Romantic concerns and simultaneously explores their limitations.

Andrew Lincoln has argued that: 'The pose [of minstrel] distinguishes Scott from the visionary romanticism of Wordsworth [. . .] it anticipates the more sceptical and ironical romanticism of Byron and Keats, for whom the poet's imaginings may always be unmasked as deceiving fantasies'.[14] Again, it is the minstrel frame that facilitates Scott's questioning of the Romanticism which, elsewhere, the poem appears to formulate. For many critics the minstrel's history is one that offers a narrative of rejuvenation and this goes hand in hand with what they see as a trajectory towards the pacification and reconciliation of the Scottish border. This reading of Scott's poetry (which facilitates a pro-Union agenda) persists in spite of the fact that it has been called into question in recent criticism of his fiction.[15] However, just as Scott's use of landscape suggests a darker reading of its romance impulses, so too the *Lay* as a whole is open to far more disruptive readings than this, which, in turn, cut across the optimism and faith in creative processes symptomatic of his first-generation Romantic contemporaries. While the end of the poem sees the minstrel rejuvenated and reintegrated into a social circle via his act of narration, the care Scott has taken to remind his readers at all times of the 'place and circumstances' of the narration also pulls apart this optimistic reading. Such is the pressure of time, and the constant reminders of this via the minstrel frame, that no reader can fail to note that by the time of the 1805 time frame of the text the minstrel, and indeed everyone else in the poem, is long dead.[16] While the past may be recalled and reinvigorated by memory, imagination and poetry such recovery is only temporary. Murray Pittock contends that in his poetry Scott 'thrust his buried men back in the human mind again';[17] but Scott is all too aware that this is, in fact, no more than an 'artifice',[18] and that poetry cannot ultimately defeat death.[19]

In the *Lay of the Last Minstrel* Scott can be seen to be both developing a Romantic aesthetic and exploring its limitations, looking beyond its earlier optimism to the darker visions of the second generation of Romantics and their resonant foreshadowing of the concerns of our own times. This complexity of approach to romance and Romantic impulses is again evident in Scott's second major narrative poem, *Marmion* (1808). Scott weaves the conventional and the experimental together to create a poem that both draws upon romance elements and moves beyond this to offer a Romantic meditation on the events inscribed. However, the change in mode from the imitative to the experimental, and from the medieval to the Romantic is even more marked in this poem than in the *Lay*. Here Scott's innovation is manifested in genre-mixing, in the poem's treatment of time, experimentation with characterisation, and in its revolutionary framing device. The blending of traditional literary conventions with new modes of articulation is demonstrated in the poem's form. In the Introduction to Canto 5, Scott claims that he 'scorns pedantic laws' of verse and throughout the poem he highlights that he is drawing on various literary poetic models (including the poetry of classical antiquity, French medieval lays, Chaucer's metrical romances, Malory's chivalric romance *Le Morte D'Arthur*, the epic poetry of Milton and Spenser, the verse epistles of Dryden, and the Germanic Gothic ballad tradition), while subverting verse form and incorporating non-literary modes traditionally associated with oral culture, such as ballads, songs, folklore, legends and lays. Moreover, he pushes beyond this identification with the bardic and poetic past by inscribing experimental modes of expression, such as literary autobiography. Thus, a new, distinct sense of poetic identity emerges. *Marmion*'s generic heterogeneity proved challenging for Scott's contemporary readership and, as a result of their mixed reaction to it, he was never so innovative in poetry again. However, Scott's subversion of poetic 'rules', and this fusion of form, is potentially what makes the poem so fascinating for scholars of Romanticism today.

Another marker of Romanticism within *Marmion* is Scott's treatment of time. Through the contrasting depiction of the unchanging landscape and the altering architecture of an area, Scott frequently elides historical distance so that temporal perspective can shift between one line of the poem and the next. For example, the perspective of the morning of the Battle of Flodden in September 1513 is abruptly replaced by Scott's present-day view of a 'hawthorn glade', through which the English troops rode that day and which now 'In spring-tide bloom[s] so lavishly' (*PW* 7:334). The martial scene of mass bloodshed is mapped onto a pastoral setting where nature peacefully flourishes and the past coexists with the present. As Tara Ghoshal Wallace has expressed it, the poem thus 'allows consciousness of multiple historical moments', generating an accumulative process of associative emotion and meaning.[20] This layering of time is further suggested in the characterisation of the poem's protagonist. Lord Marmion inhabits both the romance world of the sixteenth century and the Romantic period, simultaneously embodying the values of the collapsing chivalric system and, through his crime of forgery, the commerciality and the individualist sensibilities of the nineteenth century. Moreover, through his depiction of the psychological (and physical) effects of guilt upon Marmion, as well as James V and Constance de Beverley,

Scott explores that most Romantic of subjects: the divided self. Despite the narrative interaction with events leading up to and including the Battle of Flodden, Scott's focus is on a form of conflict that is more localised and internalised than that between or within Scotland and England.[21] Marmion's haughty demeanour and dark qualities further qualify him as a Byronic hero long before the literary birth of Childe Harold or Manfred. In these various ways, Scott's fractured, flawed protagonist prefigures the fragmentation felt and expressed by the second generation of Romantics and foreshadows the protagonists of twentieth-century realist fiction, even as the poem's tropic engagement with existential angst anticipates the literature of the Modernist movement and beyond.

However, nowhere in *Marmion* is an experimental, Romantic voice more evident than in the six verse epistles that introduce each canto. As in the *Lay*, embedded narrative devices provide an 'enactment [. . .] of the stages by which Scott moves into his romance world'.[22] However, in *Marmion*, the form of enactment is also self-consciously and self-reflexively constructed as Scott's voice replaces that of the minstrel as narrator, and the epistles are addressed to his personal friends rather than to a general audience, puncturing any easy location within the medieval world. A significant proportion of contemporary readers reacted negatively to this innovative appropriation of narrative voice. As Richard Heber, a dedicatee of one of these epistles, commented: 'With respect to the introductory addresses prefixed to the Cantoes, they are *all* highly poetical & interesting – but they do not possess the appropriate charm of being links in the story like those of "the lay"'.[23] Similarly, many recent critics have suggested that while they are 'too important to ignore', the epistles 'defy all efforts to integrate them into the body of the poem'.[24] However, the introductory epistles make *Marmion* the most ambitious and the most challenging of all Scott's narrative poems. They give Scott's personal meditations on who he is, and on 'the nature and status of [his] art'.[25] In them he suggests connections between the current of history, the flow of the imaginative process, and the course of his own poetic development. Indeed, *Marmion* represents Scott's attempt to trace the creative process from its source, the imaginative capacity of the poet, and to examine the formative influences that nurture that creative faculty; *Marmion* thereby becomes 'a poem about the workings of the imagination which produced it'.[26]

All six Introductory Epistles encompass ideas that are now identified as key preoccupations of the Romantic poets, but which had not been articulated fully before *Marmion*; when Scott explores the formation of poetic identity and the relationship between poet and poetry he is not employing established Romantic modes of articulation, but developing them, pre-empting Wordsworth's treatment of these concerns in *The Prelude* (unpublished until 1850). Scott engages with these ideas most overtly in the Epistle to Canto

3, which traces the connection between childhood and the growth of poetic power; the poet's communion with nature; the primacy and growth of the imagination; and the relationship between memory and imaginative 'vision'. Scott recalls childhood incidents that he considers key to his poetic development, thereby suggesting that the poet's exploration and recreation of the past must be understood as a psychological activity, as well as an artistic one. Like other Romantic-period poets, he is keenly aware of the emotive power of nature, locating the first stirrings of poetic creativity during his childhood spent in the hilly rural region of Smailholm. This is further fuelled by a love of reading medieval romances, adventure tales of knights and kings, and Shakespeare, and listening to fireside tales. The boy's emotional response to his physical, intellectual, and cultural environment acts as a catalyst for his imagination, which in turn creates connections between landscape, literature, and legend. Shaped by the sense of a special communion with this environment the child's imagination peoples the lonely landscape with legendary heroes, courtly lovers, fairytale creatures, and 'forayers' (Introduction to Canto 3) who have returned from pillaging in the south.

As the physical landscape becomes the point of communality between present and past, reality and fiction, Scott fittingly describes his capacity for creativity through analogies drawn from the world of nature, such as the swell of the wind, the fitful flow of the tide or the freely growing foliage (Introduction to Canto 3). He then likens his 'wild' poetic form to the rude and uneven measure of a bard's 'wild harp', which has the power to evoke emotive memories and feelings that 'Glow in the line, and prompt the lay' (Introduction to Canto 3). This further suggests the emotional and animating capacity of the interaction between memory, imagination and creativity and after the poet has explored this connection he may better understand his own role and his relationship to his work. This articulation of poetic impulse firmly situates Scott within the Romantic tradition and also aligns him with the optimism of the first-generation Romantics, as does his description of the imaginative process in the first introductory epistle. However, the futility of the poet's attempt to ascend to an ideal state simultaneously becomes apparent as the transformative vision fades and the mundane 'reality' of the natural world reasserts itself:

> It will not be—it may not last—
> The vision of enchantment's past:
> Like frost-work in the morning ray,
> The fancied fabric melts away;
> (PW 7:33–34)

Scott's awareness of the transitory nature of the poet's escape from reality further suggests his scepticism about the limitations of the poetic process and foreshadows Keats's treatment of the same experience in stanzas 4 to 6 of 'Ode to a Nightingale' (1819).[27]

This awareness of the limitations of poetic transformation is also fundamental to the poem's narrative. The plot of *Marmion* hinges upon a forgery, and is thus driven by a literary act which claims an authenticity that masks its deceptive and manipulative nature.[28] The plot therefore mirrors the 'lying legend[s]' (*PW* 7:67) upon which romance is based, and suggests the need for a degree of scepticism when engaging with any form of poetic utterance. Ultimately, neither the forged documents nor the performative act of confession by which they are uncovered provide closure. Through the temporary ascendancy and the ultimate failure of either discourse, the poem points to the transfigurative power of art as well as to the limits of it.

Scott's third long narrative poem, *The Lady of the Lake*, was his most commercially successful, and marked his first literary excursion to the Highlands, crucial to subsequent discussions of his romanticisation of Scotland. Much of its popularity arises from its depiction of scenery and Scott's employment of light and shade and sublime description that he had honed in his earlier work and perfects here. However, for many critics this has been seen as resulting in a lack of engagement with history and the politics of the Highlands and a retreat into a kind of romantic fairy land that divorces Scottish identity from contemporaneity.

If we consider *The Lady of the Lake*, like the *Lay* and *Marmion*, in terms of both an engagement with and a sceptical critique of the preoccupations of both romance and Romanticism an interesting dynamic begins to emerge. James Fitz-James enters a terrain which, on first appearances at least, occupies the discourse of traditional romance. The stage is set with spectacular scenery ('The stag at Eve' with which the poem opens) and inhabited by exotic Highlanders who speak a different language (the Gaelic of the boat song), and who have different cultural markers, such as the fiery cross. Moreover, this is a space inhabited by the eponymous 'Lady of the Lake' herself, so beautiful that she captures the heart of the King, tempting him back to the Highlands at the risk of his own life. It is hardly surprising that these elements gave birth to a whole school of Romantic paintings and have led critics such as Andrew Hook to conclude that through Scott 'the aura of romance finally settled upon Scotland'.[29]

A closer examination of the poem itself rather than just the set pieces and images that are so easily extracted from it, however, serves to suggest that Scott is offering a far more complex engagement with the limits of romance, and indeed, Romantic poetry more generally. This is evident if we consider the historical moment against which the poem is set. There is a sense in which *The Lady of the Lake* is Scott's first real engagement with the historical process that was to become so large a part of his fictional career. While

The Lay of the Last Minstrel is set in the past it deals historically with a very local moment of Scottish history. The Battle of Flodden, similarly, forms a backdrop to *Marmion*, but it is not actually the subject matter of the poem, which concerns itself far more with the personal story of Marmion. *The Lady of the Lake*, however, looks forward to dynamics that operate in Scott's fiction; while the love story of Ellen and Malcolm Græme forms a significant part of the poem the impediments to their marriage lie in the 'national' narrative that evokes the relationship of the Douglas family with the crown and the relationship of the Highlands to the rest of Scotland. As Roderick Dhu recognises, James's real purpose in visiting the region is his desire to pacify the Highlands, incorporate them into his modern version of Scotland and to erode the markers of difference which the poem itself seemingly inscribes. Moreover, this trajectory is essentially that which is reinforced in the poem's conclusion with the marriage of Ellen, the forgiveness of her father, and the benevolence of James all seemingly suggesting the movement towards reconciliation and progress that so many readers find in Scott's fiction.

Yet if we revisit the Romantic Highlands suggested in the poem a more fractured version of Scottish identity emerges. James Hogg suggests that *The Lady of the Lake* is a '*lying poem*', drawing attention to the constructed nature of the Highlands presented within it.[30] Hogg is in many ways correct, but while he sees this as a flaw in the poem, it is in fact part of its effect, since this Romantic and constructed version of the Highlands is largely presented as the version of it perceived by James. This is evident in the opening scenes of the poem which are focalised through James as he follows the stag. As such it is James who perceives the scene in overtly Romantic terms, and ones that are foregrounded as artificial: 'So wondrous wild, the whole might seem / The scenery of a fairy dream' (*PW* 8:37). As James's encounter with Roderick Dhu demonstrates, his blindness to the alternative discourse by which the Highlands operates and the real threat it poses to the security of his kingdom is a failure of his own kingship.

This becomes even more apparent when James returns to Stirling, for here the problems of his authority become overt as the pageant that greets him, like his view of the Highlands, is presented as a sham when 'chiefs, who, hostage for their clan' 'deem'd themselves a shameful part / Of pageant, which they cursed in heart' (*PW* 8:240). The success of Douglas in the tournament that takes place there equally calls into question the king's real power. Finally, the close of the poem, when 'Snowdoun's Knight' is transfigured into 'Scotland's King' so that he can pardon Douglas, grant Ellen a boon, and bring about the supposed reconciliation that heralds the close of the poem is framed in romance terms that mirror the descriptions of the scenery at the opening of the poem as a kind of fairy land, thus suggesting that this apparent seat of power may be as much of a delusion as James's construction of the Highlands:

> Within 'twas brilliant all and light,
> A thronging scene of figures bright;
> It glowed on Ellen's dazzled sight,
> As when the setting sun has given
> Ten thousand hues to summer even,
> And, from their tissue, fancy frames
> Aerial knights and fairy dames. (PW 8:292)

In his 1816 review of Duncan Forbes's *Culloden Papers* Scott warns that if the Highlands are cleared by brutal economic policies they will become 'the fairy ground for romance and poetry' (MPW 20:93). While space precludes a lengthy discussion of *The Lady of the Lake*, even a brief reading of it suggests that at the very moment when Scott was laying the foundations for a Romantic view of the Highlands that emerged as a consequence of the poem's success, he was simultaneously reminding his readers, as he would in his later fiction, of the dangers of romance, and its limitations as a valid paradigm for interpreting Scottish experience.

The complex negotiation of romance and Romantic impulses alongside a scepticism towards the very modes that he employs is in fact the hallmark of Scott's narrative poetry. While it is developed in the three great poems discussed here it persists in his later work, such as *Rokeby* (1813). Set in the aftermath of the Civil War the poem both inscribes the romance of the period and explores its overshadowing by discussion of guilt, and personal and collective responsibility. As Marshall Brown points out, the highly experimental *Bridal of Triermain* (1813) also offers 'an interesting combination of the near-contemporary, the vaguely historical, and the magically legendary' which deconstructs the authority of any one poetic mode as sufficient to express experience, suggesting that meaning can only reside in the fragmentary and indeterminate.[31]

Andrew Lincoln's suggestion that Scott is best positioned as a precursor of the second generation of Romantic poets and that in his poetry, as in his later novels, Scott helps both to define the conditions of modernity and offers a retreat from it is helpful, for it recognises that Scott's poetry embeds within it a contemplation of Romantic aesthetics and the limits of such poetics. However, this overlooks the fact that, just as Scott both articulates the key concepts of Romanticism and moves beyond them in his work, so too he both retreats from modernity and moves beyond that moment, suggesting, as a consequence, a more fractured, sceptical and fragmented model of poetry and its complex relationship to the past, nationhood, and society that may offer a precursor for our own, more troubled, condition of postmodernity.

CHAPTER FOUR

Scott's Jacobitical Plots

Caroline McCracken-Flesher

Under which King [. . .]? speak, or die!

Waverley (WN 1:[xvii])

He has robbed me of himself.

Redgauntlet (WN 17:177)

Waverley (1814), Scott's first 'Jacobite' novel, begins with a startling impera-
tive: 'speak, or die'. Of course, the choice, too, risks death. Scott's heroes
must declare for a cause, and perhaps suffer terminal consequences. Such
choices, we might presume, are worth their risks, and the costs are easy to
avoid if we choose aright – as real heroes must. Yet however much Scott's
novels of national identity and Stuart risings are celebrated for helping
countries across Europe assert their cultural difference and choose their own
political path, they repeatedly emphasise the responsibility, the difficulty,
and even the impossibility of choice.[1] In novels full of pressing oppositions,
Scott demonstrates how to choose *not* to make a choice – how to steal oneself
away, and live.

This argument may seem counter-intuitive, for Scott encouraged dualistic
thinking. In July 1813, while writing *Waverley*, he joked to Miss Clephane:
'I am very glad I did not live in 1745 for though as a lawyer I could not
have pleaded Charles's right and as a clergy-man I could not have prayed
for him yet as a soldier I would I am sure against the convictions of my
better reason have fought for him even to the bottom of the gallows' (*Letters*
3:302). Moreover, by publishing *Waverley* Scott was establishing an opposition and making a choice in his own life, leaving behind poetry for fiction.
Predictably, then, the Jacobite novels that follow *Waverley* are all about
choosing – between Stuarts and Hanoverians, romance and history (often
cast as poetry versus prose), and past and present, so aligned.

Thereby, Scott led generations of scholars to read his novels in terms
of making choices between extremes – the opposition between 'head' and
'heart' is much cited.[2] These implied choices communicated an oppositional

47

structure to criticism of his work, too, which often manifests its own Caledonian antisyzygy, suffering the strains of opposed terms that never shall meet. The cautious Francis Jeffrey saw *Waverley* as 'too recent to be romantic, and too far gone by to be familiar'.[3] To this contemporary, *Waverley* manifested the complex reality that is 'nature'. Yet even in his day, Scott was read reductively as a Tory by James Hogg, but as a bourgeois novel manufacturer by Thomas Carlyle.[4] Early in the nineteenth century, Scott was appreciated for his use of Jacobitism to emphasise Scottish difference and imply strength and possibility. He replaced the eighteenth-century image of the degraded highlander – Sawney invading the bog-house that divides savagery and civilisation, plaid kilted up and a leg down each hole – with the striking Fergus Mac-Ivor of *Waverley*.[5] Perhaps more importantly, he offered the tartanised George IV, visiting Edinburgh in 1822. Preening in kilt and pink fleshings, Hanoverian George was convinced of his Stuart ties and cunningly committed to Scottish difference by stage-manager Sir Walter.[6] Nonetheless, by mid-century, although Scott's works set patterns for the 1848 'Year of Revolutions' across Europe, Hugh Miller lamented that such Jacobitism 'formed merely a sort of laughing-gas, that agreeably excited the feelings'.[7] For the twentieth century, the same literary phenomena display either an author who leads in the depiction of historical forces, or one romancing in a cultural vacuum, administering outmoded Jacobite tales to support 'an ideology of noisy inaction' that distracts a British Scotland from the nothing it has become.[8] More recently, Scott has been reprimanded for failing to give full expression to Jacobitism's extent and powers, but also praised for purveying codes that lock him on one side of these ongoing debates about politics and literary genre.[9] And in many cases, Scott the instigator of the national novel is said to have delimited his own nation. This trend runs so deep that even Cairns Craig, who criticises Scotland for scapegoating her authors as too national and thus not doing enough to energise the nation – and observes his own drift in that direction – continues to question Scott's plots. To Craig, repetitions of Jacobite tales, in particular, posit the incipient barbarism of Scotland as dangerous and energising, yet distressingly recursive.[10]

Judith Williamson argues that in the commercial discourse running rampant since the nineteenth century, the idea of 'choice' is paramount: *Coke* or *Pepsi*; the burger with or without the cheese – history or romance; Byron or Scott?[11] The one choice we do not have is *not* to choose. This chapter tracks the dualities that seem to require choice in Scott's major Jacobite utterances – *Waverley*, *Rob Roy* (1818), George IV's Edinburgh visit, *Redgauntlet* (1824), 'The Highland Widow' (1827), and *Tales of a Grandfather* (Third series, 1829) – showing how oppositions become confused, and distinct choices prove simplistic, even deathly. Under pressure to choose, and the threat of death, Scott's least promising characters carry the burden of choice without its satisfactions or its costs: the saving, difficult, and therefore heroic choice is not to choose.

Although critics seem to follow Scott's lead as they take sides to map the oppositional structure of his novels, we might be well advised to consider his actual practice. Scott implied a choice between poetry and fiction, Jacobite and Hanoverian, a colourful past and a workable present, but *Waverley* itself begins with a notable failure to choose. Chapter 1, 'Introductory', opens promisingly, emphasising choice: 'The title of this work has not been chosen without the grave and solid deliberation which matters of importance demand from the prudent' (*WN* 1:3). However, the key term turns out to be 'not'. The author proceeds to run through alternative titles: 'Had I, for example, announced in my frontispiece, "Waverley, a Tale of other Days," must not every novel-reader have anticipated a castle scarce less than that of Udolpho [. . .]? Again, had my title borne, "Waverley, a Romance from the German," what head so obtuse as not to image forth a profligate abbot [. . .]?' – and he goes on, setting aside the 'Sentimental Tale', and the 'dashing sketch of the fashionable world' (*WN* 1:3–4). So what shall readers 'meet in the following pages'? '[N]either a romance of chivalry, nor a tale of modern manners'. Scott offers no preferred term. Rather, we will meet the substantially less defined 'characters and passions of the actors' (*WN* 1:5). Scott has chosen 'WAVERLEY, an uncontaminated name, bearing with its sound little of good or evil, excepting what the reader shall be hereafter pleased to affix to it' (*WN* 1:3). He offers a title that resists conventional oppositions and easy choices, but forces negotiation among vague 'characters and passions' on the part of a (probably very uneasy) reader.

This is no one-off by the 'maiden knight with his white shield' that the author here claims to be (*WN* 1:3). As Scott matured into the 'Author of *Waverley*', he came under criticism for repeating Jacobite plots. Reviewing *Redgauntlet*, the *Monthly Review* noted that Scotland 'has Jacobites, and freebooters, and Highlanders, and provosts [. . .] but [cannot] supply her votary with an endless variety of subject'.[12] If the author wrote *not* gothic or sentimental or fashionable tales, critics decided, he had cast himself inalienably as the writer of Jacobite plots, with their straightforward choices between Jacobite/Hanoverian, past/present, and so on. The Whiggish barrister and historical writer Andrew Bisset was sure that Scott's *Tales of a Grandfather* privileged authoritarian power – government and Jacobitism – to the neglect of Scotland's suffering Covenanters.[13] Scott, however, is always worth watching for his supposed flaws of commission and omission. In reality, the Covenanters received substantial attention (positive and negative) in *The Tale of Old Mortality* (1816) and *The Heart of Mid-Lothian* (1818). Furthermore, Scott knew what he was up to. In his 1827 *Chronicles of the Canongate*, Scott's authorial substitute, Crystal Croftangry, remarks: 'Now, the Highlands, though formerly a rich mine for original matter, are [. . .] in some degree worn out by the incessant labour of modern romancers and novelists' (WN 20:123). Yet Crystal continues with his Highland tale – and Scott, in the same vein, continues with Jacobitism. That is, Scott deliberately repeats apparent oppositions. But he never comes any closer to taking a side.

Critics who adopt a side proffered by Scott often lament that he himself fails in commitment. Why, they wonder, does he not render more positively the Jacobitism or the genre that he seems to prefer? Or could he please, as a reviewer of the tangled The Black Dwarf beseeches, at least tell his tales in chronological order – history and its biases of the moment might teach us when to identify with Jacobites, when to favour Covenanters.[14] The problem is only exacerbated by Scott's recursiveness. Immediately on Redgauntlet's publication, the Examiner moaned: 'it is a Jacobite tale, and we have recently had somewhat too much in this strain; not to mention that, in the Author of Waverley, it must necessarily lead to a repetition of himself'.[15] But this is perhaps the point. The author cannot change outcomes against the determinations of history. However, by centring stories on Jacobite history, and extending and adding to its narratives, Scott narrows in not on a choice between opposed terms, but on the randomness of reality and the impossibility of making any choice. Scott's Jacobite novels, then, constitute exercises in frustration. Scott knowingly repeats what cannot be changed – where a specific choice can make no difference. Repeating plots, and offering variations that can only resolve back into more of the same – the Jacobites will still lose – Scott orients his texts toward the moment of choice. With nothing to choose, choice itself carries the weight of Scott's texts. It is not the history of Jacobitism, its romance, or its political possibility that matter. Rather, Scott stresses the necessity and impossibility of relating oneself to a world of easy oppositions, fatal results, and no real choices.

Who can bear such a burden? We need a hero. But in historical novels, the hero has obligations to events.[16] The figures who anchor history, whether real or fictive, must act in line with expectations and known results. So who is left to manifest the struggle that is choice? The Waverley protagonist can seem passive to the point of weakness.[17] Even Scott's contemporaries recognised the phenomenon of the inadequate hero: the London Magazine remarked upon Redgauntlet's 'hero and heroine of the genuine Waverley stamp; a pair, like which we hope Heaven will never make so many as the Great Unknown does, or the world would shortly be peopled with Albinos'.[18] The characters around whom the Jacobite novels revolve typically prove incapable of recognising a choice even when it passes in front of them: Waverley misrecognises a militaristic gathering of the clans as a hunting party; Frank Osbaldistone of Rob Roy cannot see the Jacobitical wood for the trees of his own family drama. But it is in these wavering heroes, incapable of recognising oppositions yet stumbling toward choice, that the power of Scott's novels resides.

At first, Edward Waverley, Frank Osbaldistone, and Darsie Latimer (*Redgauntlet*) seem stuck at one extreme in an opposition often held to Scott's account. They are creatures of romance, insulated from the present with its necessities of choice. These young men drift along on a tide of unregulated reading and stories of the past. 'From such legends [Waverley] would steal away to indulge the fancies they excited' (*WN* 1:18); Frank, set to business, imagines himself a poet (*WN* 5:16–17); Darsie, the orphan who lacks a personal history, makes one up from romantic conventions, thinking himself 'the son of some India director, or rich citizen'– or English, at least (*WN* 17:2). Such are the 'dreaming boys'.[19] They occupy a fictional space loaded with expectations of heroism, and yet they have never been called upon to make a choice. Moreover, although contemporary readers of *Waverley* might maintain a hope of heroic decision-making through to the end of this, Scott's first novel, by the time they got to Darsie Latimer ten years later, they knew that such a protagonist could be no active hero. Waverley, Frank, and Darsie all are marked by the failure to choose – adrift in romance, they simply do not know what is going on.

Yet that does not mean they are set apart from history. In fact, because they are bound to romance, these unpromising young men fall subject to events. Waverley's wandering disposition takes him north of the Highland line, and there he encounters a strategic present. The would-be, and likely heroes of history – Donald Bean Lean in his French uniform, and Fergus Mac-Ivor, with his personal and national ambitions – meet Waverley on the ground of romance. Waverley, we know, is no hero, but Donald, Fergus, and Prince Charles himself treat him as such. They advance their plans through Waverley's desire to figure as hero. Similarly, Frank Osbaldistone, removing himself from the practicalities of business, opens a space for cousin Rashleigh to usurp him and manipulate his father's financial interests to force the Highlanders into the 1715 rebellion. Frank thus demonstrates the porousness of those apparently distinct terms, romance, business, and the serious stuff of history. As for Darsie, he falls into a history romantic for all its reality. Seeking the truth of his past, Darsie discovers that it is founded on an inheritance of story – both Wandering Willie's tale of Redgauntlets in hell, and his uncle Herries/Redgauntlet's report of the family's origins in bloodshed. The uncle, undeniably romantic when spearing fish from horseback in the gloaming, and threatening/rescuing Darsie not once but many times, yet bases his claim over his nephew (and thus his attempt to raise Jacobites to action in Darsie's name), on a legal claim of guardianship. History is a creative fiction, and romance may prove to be real history. Is choice, then, necessary?

Certainly, after all his insistence that there is a choice of genre at stake in

Waverley, Scott himself refuses to choose. He mocks Waverley's romanticism, tracking it from the hero's trivial interest in dress, through his mutually interchangeable love affairs, to his flirtation with Jacobitism. It is a short step from Waverley's sudden indifference to Miss Stubbs because of his fascination with himself as a 'young officer of dragoons, who wore for the first time his gold-laced hat, boots, and broad sword', to his disillusionment with Jacobitism because Fergus's sister, Flora, denies his suit – in both senses of the word (*WN* 1:25). Newly accoutred in 'the "garb of old Gaul," [. . . Waverley] looked at himself in the mirror more than once', yet just a few pages later he declares of love a feeling he will shortly apply to war: 'This then is an end of my day-dream!' (*WN* 1:214, 220, 236). And Scott equally punctures any investment in history. Mac-Ivor and Redgauntlet each see themselves as determined by the past, readied for this moment in history. But such a commitment to history depends on a presumption of history's trajectory and one's own merits that is inherently fictional. Posing as the result and the progenitor of history – although his family's claim to chieftainship is tenuous – Fergus is a politician. The moment we meet Fergus in all his deliberately understated performance as highland chief, Scott points out that: 'Fergus had a further object than merely being the great man of his neighbourhood, and ruling despotically over a small clan. [He . . .] had persuaded himself [. . .] that those who assisted [the Stuarts] would be raised to honour and rank' (*WN* 1:100). Fergus himself manifests the indeterminacy of history as he tries to manipulate it. We cannot truly choose either history or romance.

Yet history and romance, even romance as history, can choose you. Worse, giving over choice (however impossible that choice may be) proves deathly. Fergus, who would choose for others, is himself caught in the fictions that make up clan history. He dies romantically – and though we may die colourfully, we are still dead. On the eve of battle, Fergus sees the Bodach glas, that is said to bring defeat or death to his family, and presumes upon 'the truth, ascertained by three hundred years' experience at least' to foretell the worst. Waverley challenges: 'How can you, my dear Fergus, tell such nonsense with a grave face?' (*WN* 1:294–5). But Fergus is nonetheless captured, and dead shortly thereafter. In the first tale of *Chronicles of the Canongate*, 'The Highland Widow' (1827), Jacobite Elspat holds to her history, and decries her son's enlistment with a highland regiment. She drugs Hamish to keep him from returning to them, choosing for him. When soldiers arrive to arrest her son – but to save him from death as a deserter – egged on by his mother he kills a friend, and is therefore executed. Elspat henceforth remains fixed in the choice of that moment – in the deathly stasis of her role as the 'Highland Widow'.

And this is where being a Waverley hero reveals its advantages. Scott's protagonists well know that you can be hedged around by romantic and historical choices not your own. Waverley has plenty of time to think about it as he is hauled away from the melée (twice), and Darsie experiences the problem as he is dragged out of the quicksands (also twice). Yet choosing overtly only leads to death (Fergus) or exile (Hugh Redgauntlet) and may destroy those you love/exploit (Hamish, and Fergus's clan). Whether we choose or are chosen, we are trapped.

So what to do? At the heart of each Jacobite novel lies a gap, in which a secret lurks. Though plots imply bonny princes (*Waverley* and *Redgauntlet*), priests, and patriarchs (*Rob Roy* and *Redgauntlet*), the powerful heart of these novels is Scott's inadequate hero, incapable of filling any gap, and hardly worthy of a secret. When Waverley stands in front of Major Melville and Mr Morton to account to the government for his wavering conduct, the minister draws a moral distinction between those 'whom ambition, or hope of personal advantage, has led to disturb the peace' and 'youth, misled by the wild visions of chivalry and imaginary loyalty' (*WN* 1:173). Fergus chose, and must pay; but Waverley, though he has acted, has not chosen. Moreover, as a dreaming boy, who cannot tell romance from history and that history is romance, he does not offer much purchase for others to grasp. Much less can he be permanently chosen by anyone else. Better yet, he has one option not available to those, like Fergus, who are caught in the determinations of history or (as politicians) lack the full flexibility of dreamily creative romance: he can choose not to choose. Specifically, he can choose not to speak a choice. He can slide between systems while yet attaining a self.

All the silly sufferings of a Waverley hero prepare him for this moment of not uttering a choice. Repeatedly ill, Waverley finds himself in situations where he can understand nothing around him. Injured at the hunting party – not having enough wit to avoid a stampede of deer both visually romantic and violently actual – Waverley finds himself subject to the mysteries of Highland medicine. He can only watch: 'Edward, whom pain rendered incapable of expostulation, and who indeed saw no chance of its being attended to, submitted in silence' (*WN* 1:124). Rescued from arrest by a party of Highlanders – having been chosen – Waverley finds himself borne through bush and briar. And he finds himself again voiceless. Worse, this time Edward is thrown entirely in upon himself. His ear closed to Gaelic, his eye, too, is denied: 'while he laboured with the nail to enlarge the hole, that he might obtain a more complete view, a slight noise betrayed his purpose, and the object of his curiosity instantly disappeared' (*WN* 1:191–2).

Darsie Latimer also suffers through speechlessness. Kidnapped by his uncle, Darsie is injured and delirious. 'On seeing the physician', he says, 'it would have been natural to have appealed to him on the subject of my confinement [. . .] But the fever lay like a spell upon my tongue' (*WN* 17:161). Then, of course, Darsie becomes voiceless in the classic terms of romance: he is transformed into a girl who conventionally and actually lacks the possibility of communication. Dressed as a woman, with a riding mask that allows only the discourse of flirtation, Darsie finds 'mine is thickened with a plate of steel' (*WN* 17:204). With any attempt to speak recast by gender into misleading messages, Darsie, too, is thrown in upon himself. Literally falling into contact with his friend Alan Fairford – his dress makes him stumble into Alan's arms – 'he hesitated for a second or two to effect his purpose', and the opportunity is lost (*WN* 17:322). Scott's heroes seem further weakened by this inability to communicate. Yet each is progressively trained away from easy utterance toward inward thought and strategic silence.

In a powerful representation of what Judith Wilt observes as Scott's recurrent theme – 'gain through loss [. . .] expression through concealment' – Scott's Jacobite heroes learn to choose not to choose by what becomes a choice not to speak.[20] Waverley, having decided against rebellion, is happily relieved of the occasion to choose sides when he is separated in battle from his Highland cohort. Darsie, however, refracting Scott's growing emphasis on choice as he moves from one Jacobite novel to another, must choose, and he chooses to stay silent while plots crumble around him. Disinclined to believe 'that so many men of family and fortune were likely to embark in an enterprize so fatal', Darsie concludes that this uprising 'would fall to pieces of itself, and that his best way was [. . .] to remain silent' (*WN* 17:320). Under duress from his uncle, and others seeking to allay their own anxieties by aligning with him as a leader, Darsie insists that 'I suspend expressing my sentiments' (*WN* 17:348). As Wilt observes, in a Scott novel, 'That which you lay claim to, that shall you lose. Conversely, that which you hide from, hide from yourself, consent to lose, that shall you secretly [. . .] have at, if not in, hand.'[21] Managing not to speak, these heroes, unlike Fergus and Redgauntlet, lay claim to no opinion, and assert no self. They thus can live and be.

Still, it is a question how far any Waverley hero has a self to maintain. Here, it is worth considering what is held in abeyance when Waverley, Darsie, and even Frank Osbaldistone choose not to speak. Rather than having nothing to say, Scott's protagonists often seem overwhelmed by events and incapable of speech. Frank tells us, even before Rob Roy's wife summarily executes the traitor Morris, that the scene 'haunted my sleep for years afterward' (*WN* 5:267). Asked to speak and save the pathetic victim, he tries, but fails. Later, when the treacherous Rashleigh curses him on his deathbed, Frank does not respond, but rather closes down discussion and changes the subject. But the scenes that matter most may not be the ones that overwhelm Frank's sensibilities. Scenes where Frank's sensibilities, by contrast, require a choice not to speak, prove telling. *Rob Roy* begins with a classic choice against the father (and in favour of romance). Having lived the romance that is history, Frank (also following convention) achieves reconciliation with his father –

notably, through silence. Their exchange is limited to 'Francis – I am glad to see you', reaching a peak with 'my dear – dear son' (*WN* 5:312). These, says Frank, 'are scenes which address themselves to the eye and to the heart, rather than to the ear'. This novel, with its Jacobite context but a hero never remotely tempted to the cause, throws its emphasis on the ways in which the central figure progresses from being a bit of a vacancy into operating as a complex human subject, capable of recognising when not to speak.

In fact, the silence attained by the heroes of Scott's Jacobite novels is exacerbated by their move from inadequacy (having nothing to say) to superfluity (having too much to express, and the wisdom not to say it). Here, Scott sets the reductive determinations of history and romance against the associations accumulated by the experience of both. Eighteenth-century philosophers – Locke, Hume, Hartley, and Scott's own professor, Dugald Stewart – pointed to a self formed in the complexity of experience, through emotion and association.[22] Scott well understood this phenomenon. He even exploited it. For his notorious reformulation of George IV as Stuart prince, the author heaped up associations. A monarch swathed in tartan, surrounded by 'Highlanders', plied with Scott novels, and awash in whisky could easily be manipulated into acting as a Scottish groupie. But Scott set numerous alternative associations going for the locals during the King's jaunt to Edinburgh, and then gleefully toppled them all.[23] We live – we are most alive – he knew, amid the challenge of unpredictable associations. Character is formed, and strong character revealed, through the mind's inclusive capacity, and its ability still to function.

Thus Edward Waverley slowly layers associations one on another, and in so doing, moves from ignorance to clarity and into the uncertainty that is complexity. Loaded with romance and religious tracts (at Waverley-Honour), friendship and alcohol (at Tully-Veolan), Jacobitism and ambition (by Fergus), and caught in the web of love, midway through his novel Waverley begins to achieve the thought that arises from conflicting associations. He wonders whether he can marry Jacobite Flora and take her to England, or stay with Fergus and 'be whirled along by him' (*WN* 1:142). Then, a few pages later, and rejected by Flora, he realises 'inexpressible repugnance at the idea of being accessary to the plague of civil war' (*WN* 1:149). Quickly, he moves on: 'Reason asked, was it worth while [. . .]?' Darsie Latimer takes a more problematic route to an even more significant internal debate. This unknown orphan anticipates gaining knowledge of his past and therefore a precise identity, but as we might expect, experiences (real and fraudulent) construct a perplexed reality. Darsie is sure from the evidence (and wrong) that he must be English; he recognises not his uncle, but the abstraction that is the frown they share; that mark on the forehead is his only memory, however its meanings lie in the unpredictabilities of folk tale; he falls in love with a girl who proves to be his sister, but when that unrecognised sister presumes upon their relationship, he considers her a strange and forward woman. It is the difficulty yet achievement of association, even from such random and problematic data, that moves the vacant subject from ignorance to complexity and allows the wisdom of silence.

The importance not just of complex association but of consequent silence is heightened in Scott's novels by the vast range of characters who choose too easily, and chatter about it. Scott's heroes often compare unfavourably to their supporting cast: Frank Osbaldistone seems a dull dog when compared to Diana Vernon. Hedged about by conventions of gender, inheritance, and politics, Diana, nonetheless, knows and speaks her mind. But her choice is relatively straightforward. It is therefore not the important one – as is evidenced by her disappearance into marriage offstage (to Frank) and the fact that she is already dead at the time of the novel's telling. In *Redgauntlet*, Scott lays out the issues through a pattern of choosers, actors, and speakers against whom Darsie, with his confusions, complexity, and restraint proves to be the anchor of the text. Darsie is fortunate in his friends: Wandering Willie, 'Greenmantle' (his sister Lilias), Alan Fairford, Joshua Geddes, and – at one remove – Nanty Ewart, all choose and align themselves on his behalf. Yet Alan and Joshua are flung into frantic movement that makes no difference; Wandering Willie and Lilias sing, gesture, pass notes, and never manage to reroute Darsie's tale. It is the apparent non-choice that is a considered silence that matters.

Scott brings this point home in his *Tales of a Grandfather*. Notably, Andrew Bisset criticised the history Scott wrote for his grandson not for its sins of commission, but for those of omission.[24] A Scot who had gone south and would later align with radicalism, he wanted the author to make and utter a choice between sides. Evidently, Bisset's remarks caught Scott on the raw – or attacked what he considered a central importance of his text – for in his prefatory letter to the third series of tales (moving into the Jacobite period), the author responded peremptorily that he did not necessarily subscribe to Bisset's conclusions: 'I must not [. . .] leave it to be supposed that I have deserted my banners, because I have not at this time and place thought it necessary to unfurl them' (*MPW* 25:113). Scott insists that his is a silence with a reason – indeed, two reasons. First, choice is historically political, unthinking, and dangerous: 'Even in the history of this small and barren country of Scotland, men may read enough of its miseries, to make them regret how often they have been occasioned by the explosions of party spirit.' Second, that being the case: 'I have avoided [. . .] every attempt to prejudice your mind.' Scott wants his grandson to think for himself, hoping that he will come 'to perceive, that in political disputes [. . .] you are not to expect that either the one party or the other are to be regarded as infallible; and that you will remember that each particular action is to be judged of by its own circumstances' (*MPW* 25:111). Thus, Scott's riposte to Bisset is that he is not thinking in service of anyone's biases, but thoughtfully opening a space where new perspectives may arise.

And this is the true heroism of Scott's Jacobite novels. In tales of activity and colour, everything leads to the still, grey moment when a Waverley or a Darsie Latimer, at last understanding complex realities, nonetheless chooses not to assert himself. Alexander Welsh has noted that for a Waverley hero, 'actions and commitment [. . .] are so restricted that any activity depends upon other sources of energy', but Jane Millgate argues: 'That [Waverley's] choices are somewhat limited [. . .] should not distract us from their significance.'[25] Given the lacklustre progress of Scott's usual protagonist, in fact, it seems very strange to a reader when that hero accomplishes anything – perhaps especially the 'no speech' that we consider here. Typically, this is the moment at which we expect the hero to act and to do. Waverley has at last figured out his position with regard to rebellion; Frank embraces his father; Darsie knows who he is and what he wants. Yet we are used to these heroes doing nothing. All the more, we now expect them to say something – especially since they are often their own narrators. Nonetheless, they stay silent, anchoring novels of activity on that still, unspoken moment that is yet the turning point in their text.

Perhaps this is why Scott insists that such vague thinkers and unpromising dreamers are the heroes of his books. Waverley is a case in point. Structurally 'my hero' in the introductory chapter, the hapless Waverley is, however, set against the conventions of heroism by his author: for instance, because of his reading, 'our hero' has a 'dainty, squeamish, and fastidious taste' (*WN* 1:16). Yet Scott calls him 'hero' up to eighty times. And as Waverley piles up experience, he accumulates a heroism unknown to that 'hero of romance', Prince Charles, or the domineering Fergus Mac-Ivor. He approaches the condition Scott sketches out years later in *Redgauntlet*, after he himself has worked through associations based on novel writing, legal practice, and kings' visits: 'Those who follow the banners of Reason are like the well-disciplined battalion, which, wearing a more sober uniform, and making a less dazzling show [. . .] enjoy more safety, and even more honour, in the conflicts of human life' (*WN* 17:296). True heroism is not about action, and not necessarily about choice. It is about striving, struggling, stumbling – about learning the limits of the hero. True heroes are those who choose not to act, not to speak – not to pose like a hero, despite the weight of expectation they must carry. They choose not to dominate. That is, experience allows not dramatic action and public applause, but the quiet sacrifice of self to become one who can recognise the selfhood of others.

These Jacobite novels abjure the satisfactions of dramatic closure to embrace a different, more 'heroic' purpose. They are about losing the world of romance and history in the hard work of becoming a self. And such selving resonates through and beyond Scott's texts. Scott shows that as 'selves', we all live not in the past, in romance, or even in history, but in the present moment, where, by association, we are always being made. Scott firmly believed in the role of the reader.[26] And stories that challenge us by their repetitions of plot and multiplications of association are our stories. They operate in us. Scott's Jacobite novels serve as places of testing for his characters and for those who read about them. Furthermore, since circumstances will always change, and associations will always multiply, characters and readers both need to go through this process of becoming again and again in novel after novel.

This phenomenon of becoming, and its necessary repetition, is manifested by that most contentious, non-speaking scene of Scott's first Jacobite tale – the portrait of Fergus and Edward that hangs in Tully-Veolan. Here, the two 'heroes' sport highland dress in a 'wild, rocky, and mountainous pass, down which the clan were descending in the back-ground' (WN 1:361). But this is no portrait from history. Rather, it was 'taken from a spirited sketch', itself produced not from reality or even al fresco, but 'in Edinburgh by a young man of high genius'. From him, the sketch progressed to 'an eminent London artist'. Hanging at the end of the novel, made from ideas and impressions at different times and places, the painting is a site of association. It is insistently not about Edward or Fergus. Rather, it tests and constitutes those who view it in the repeatable moment of the reader's dubious gaze.

In these Jacobite novels, the conflicts of genre (history and romance) and clashes of mode (letter and journal in Redgauntlet) – all the confusions of interpretation that intrigued Francis Jeffrey but that increasingly annoyed many of Scott's critics – work to this end.[27] To read a Jacobite novel is to experience the vertigo of an Edward Waverley or a Darsie Latimer, captured and hurried off through events. It is to be beaten about with the characters, troubled in our own subjectivity, denied certainties – and thus transformed into Scott heroes. After all, as Scott insisted in the first chapter of Waverley, he wrote about men 'from the great book of Nature', in all their passion, complexity, and confusion. He wrote about us.

CHAPTER FIVE

History and Historiography

Catherine Jones

In a diary entry dated October 1831 Thomas Carlyle described Scott as 'the Novel-wright of his time, its favourite child, and *therefore* an almost worthless one'. Yet he wondered if there was not something in Scott's 'deep recognition of the worth of the Past, perhaps better than anything [the Author of *Waverley*] ha[d] *expressed* about it', into which Carlyle '[did] not see'.[1] This chapter explores the nature and significance of that 'deep recognition' by addressing Scott's handling of issues in Scottish history and historiography, focusing on the early to middle period of his career as a novelist. It analyses the ways in which he engages with different genres of historical writing of the ages of Enlightenment and Romanticism, paying particular attention to the canonical histories of David Hume and William Robertson, but also to minor historical genres, such as the memoir. Such works shaped Scott's understanding and interpretation of the relation of the past to the present, the progress of society from primitivism to civilisation, the poetics of distance, and the historical portrait.

On 25 May 1816 the Scottish record scholar and advocate Thomas Thomson wrote from Edinburgh to his friend and erstwhile contemporary at the bar Francis Horner, who had long been resident in London as a Whig Member of Parliament for St Ives, Wendover, and St Mawes, with news from the publishing world:

> Walter Scott has *covenanted* to write a popular History of Scotland, from the earliest period down to 1745, in four or five volumes 8vo, to be sent to press at next Christmas. It will be a very amusing book, I have no doubt – full of errors and mistaken views; but these he will gradually weed out in the course of successive editions, and I should not wonder at its becoming a favourite book in this country for ages to come. It will not, however, be a *good history*; it will rather be a collection of striking descriptions and characters, with little of true historical connexion. In some of its minute details, he will contrive to make the work extremely amusing.[2]

Thomson had first met Scott in the early 1790s, when the two men were studying law at the University of Edinburgh.[3] After qualifying as an advocate at the end of 1793, Thomson became part of Scott's circle of 'idlers' in the Outer House of the Court of Session, a group of young (briefless) advocates, who called themselves 'the Mountain' or 'the Montagnards', after one of the more extreme parties in revolutionary France.[4] Thomson, however, went on to build a solid practice at the bar; he also developed a reputation for legal antiquities, which led to his appointment on 30 June 1806 to the newly created office of Deputy Clerk Register, responsible for consolidating Scotland's archival base in Register House, Edinburgh, and overseeing the serial publication of her constitutional records.[5] In a letter to George Ellis of 7 April 1806, Scott declared that Thomson understood 'more of old books, old laws, and old history, than any man in Scotland'. Of his friend's new role in Register House he wrote: 'I expect many valuable discoveries to be the consequence of his investigation, if he escapes being smothered in the cloud of dust which his researches will certainly raise about his ears' (*Letters* 1:284–5). Thomson and Scott would both become engaged in significant editing projects over the ensuing decade. Among his official works, Thomson would produce the *Acts of the Parliaments of Scotland*, starting with the second volume, published in 1814, and concluding with volume 11 in 1824; the edition would carry the scientific handling of archives to new heights.[6] Scott, meanwhile, would not only forge a literary career as poet and novelist, but would also edit numerous memoirs and family histories, state papers, and pamphlets, as well as (with extensive historical annotation) the works of John Dryden, published in 1808, and of Jonathan Swift, published in 1814. Professional rivalry may well have led Thomson to distinguish in his letter to Horner between Scott's capacity to entertain with his stories of the past and the ability to perceive 'true historical connexion'. Horner, however, would give a more favourable assessment of the projected 'History', replying to Thomson on 30 May 1816:

> Scott's facility is wonderful; his own confidence in it perhaps still more so. But I dare say he will make an amusing history, and provided he writes one that becomes popular, he will do a real service to our countrymen; for a favourite history with the people must strengthen their attachments to the country. In the early days, while liberty and patriotism were aristocratic distinctions, he will be on their side; indeed, no historian, especially a poetic one, could fail to be right about Bruce and Wallace. But I fear he will be a mere Jacobite, when he comes down to the Reformation and the civil war.[7]

According to Horner, national history has the capacity to reinforce a love of country. Yet his comments also bring into focus the difficulty of the enterprise: as a Whig, Horner is poised to attack Scott's 'History' for its Tory or

'Jacobite' view of the early modern era. Only when treating such subjects as the medieval Wars of Independence, Horner suggests, will Scott be 'right'.

Scott had begun negotiating with publishers about the 'History' in 1814, securing an agreement with Archibald Constable and Longman two years later.[8] His correspondence with Constable about the work brings into focus the generic hierarchies of the period, in particular the distinction made by Hugh Blair, in his *Lectures on Rhetoric and Belles Lettres* (1789), between 'regular and legitimate' works of history, on the one hand, and those 'inferior subordinate species' of 'Historical Composition', such as annals, memoirs and lives, on the other.[9] Scott proposed to call the work 'Letters on the History of Scotland addressd [sic] to a family of young persons[.] By the Author of Pauls Letters from the Continent.'[10] Constable, however, thought this title 'quite unsuitable for a work of such importance' – that is, for 'legitimate' history. As a compromise, he suggested: '"A View of the History of Scotland from the earliest Records to the year 1745" in a series of Letters by Walter Scott Esq.'[11] Scott agreed, but insisted upon anonymity. 'When a man puts his name to so grave a matter as a History', he wrote on 26 October 1816:

> it should be something very different from the rapid and, I trust, animated sketch which I intend to furnish. Men would expect great depth of research and discussion of the disputed points, which is precisely what I intend to waive. I have not the least doubt that I will make a popular book, for I trust it will be both interesting and useful; but I never intended to engage in any proper historical labour, for which I have neither time, talent, nor inclination. [. . .] In truth it would take ten years of any man's life to write such a History of Scotland as he should put his name to. (*Letters* 4:280)

In his biography of Scott, J. G. Lockhart observes that 'if [Scott] ever wrote any part' of the 'History', 'the MS. has not been discovered'.[12] But the project had an afterlife not only as Scott's *Tales of a Grandfather* (1828–31), but also as Patrick Fraser Tytler's *History of Scotland* (1828–43). Tytler was the son of Alexander Fraser Tytler, Lord Woodhouselee, whose 'class of History' Scott had attended during his years as a student at Edinburgh University from late 1783 to mid-1786 and from autumn 1789 to 1792.[13] Aware that Tytler shared his father's deep interest in history, Scott prompted him to write a new history of Scotland that would make use of the Herculean labours of Thomson and others. Their conversation, as reported by Alexander Pringle of Whytbank, took place at Abbotsford in July 1823.[14] Scott had been considering what books to recommend as a course of reading in Scottish history to the young Duke of Buccleuch, writing to Lord Montagu on 17 July 1823:

> We are still but very indifferently provided with Scotch histories of a general description. Lord Hailles annals are the foundation stone and an excellent book

though drily written. Pinkerton in two very unreadable 4tos which yet abound in information takes up the thread where Hailes drops it and then you have Robertson down to the union of the Kingdoms. But I would beware of task work which Pinkerton at least must always be [. . .]. Laing is but a bad guide through the seventeenth century yet I hardly know where a combined account of these events is to be had so far as Scotland is concernd.[15]

Such reflections would have shaped Scott's conversation with Tytler. According to Pringle, Scott first explained to Tytler why he had decided to abandon writing a general history of Scotland, even though the project had been 'congenial' to him. Soon after commencing work on the 'History', Scott recalled, he realised that more was wanted than a 'popular romance', but that he did not have the time or inclination to undertake the research that would be necessary to compose a 'right history of Scotland'. Scott therefore proposed that Tytler take on the task.[16] In the Preface to the first volume of his *History*, Tytler claimed that he had 'anxiously endeavoured to examine the most authentic sources of information, and to convey a true picture of the times without prepossession or partiality'. Where he differed on 'points of importance' with earlier historians, he set out the grounds for his opinion in the 'Notes and Illustrations', printed at the back of each volume.[17] Tytler paid particular attention to the 'errors' of David Dalrymple, Lord Hailes's *Annals of Scotland* (1776–9).[18] But he also sought to respond to the challenges Scott's writing posed to 'legitimate' history.

Generic divisions remained. In an essay on 'History' published in the *Edinburgh Review* in May 1828, Thomas Babbington Macaulay suggested that while the best historians of recent times, such as Hume, had far excelled their predecessors in the art of deducing general principles from facts, they had fallen into the error of distorting facts to suit general principles. They had also given insufficient attention to 'the domestic history of nations', allowing the subject to suffer annexation into the territory of fiction.[19] Scott, meanwhile:

> has used those fragments of truth which historians have scornfully thrown behind them in a manner which may well excite their envy. He has constructed out of their gleanings works which, even considered as histories, are scarcely less valuable than theirs. But a truly great historian would reclaim those materials which the novelist has appropriated. The history of the government, and the history of the people, would be exhibited in that mode in which alone they can be exhibited justly, in separable conjunction and intermixture. We should not then have to look for the wars and votes of the Puritans in Clarendon, and for their phraseology in Old Mortality; for one half of King James in Hume and for the other half in the Fortunes of Nigel.[20]

In an *Edinburgh* essay on 'Hallam', published in September 1828, Macaulay elaborated upon the dichotomy between 'critical [. . .] history' and the 'historical novel', invoking a series of oppositions, each expressing a sense of breakdown and loss: reason and the imagination, the map and the painted landscape, the anatomist and the sculptor.[21] These polarities emerge out of the philosophy and aesthetics of the eighteenth century, but Macaulay's argument obscures the continuities between the so-called 'philosophical' or 'conjectural' histories of the Scottish Enlightenment and the Waverley Novels. Crucially, Scott combines in the processes of composition the faculties, perspectives and methods opposed by Macaulay.

In his autobiographical 'Memoirs', begun at Ashestiel in 1808, resumed around 1810–11, and revised in 1826, Scott describes how his sense of self and knowledge of the past developed initially through imbibing old songs and tales, through desultory reading, and, while attending the High School in Edinburgh, through disputation with a tutor at home – a young man 'bred to the Kirk' ('I with a head on fire for chivalry was a cavalier', he recalls, 'my friend was a roundhead. I was a tory and he was a whig – I hated presbyterians and admired Montrose with his victorious highlanders – He liked the Presbyterian classes, the dark and politick Argyle – so that we never wanted subjects of dispute'). With a powerful but capricious memory, Scott seldom failed to preserve 'a favourite passage of poetry, a playhouse ditty, or above all a border-raid ballad', but 'names, dates and the other technicalities of history escaped [him] in a most melancholy degree'. Yet he was able gradually to assemble in his mind much of what was 'striking and picturesque' in historical narrative, so that when he came to attend more to 'the deduction of general principles', he found that he was furnished with 'a powerful host of examples' in illustration of them.[22] In contrast, he gained formal understanding of the general principles of history at Edinburgh University through attending the lectures of Alexander Fraser Tytler (published initially as *Plan and Outlines of a Course of Lectures on Universal History* [1782], and later developed as *Elements of General History, Ancient and Modern* [1801]). The distinctively Scottish tradition of philosophical history would also have been explicated and developed by Scott's other teachers, in particular Dugald Stewart, professor of moral philosophy and author of *Elements of the Philosophy of the Human Mind* (1792–1827), John Bruce, professor of logic and author of *Elements of the Science of Ethics* (1786), and David Hume (the nephew of the philosopher), professor of Scots law and author of *Commentaries on the Law of Scotland, Respecting Crimes* (1797).[23] In addition, Scott would have had contact as a student with Robertson, who (among his other offices) was Principal of Edinburgh University from 1762 until his death in 1793.[24]

In their application of philosophical principles to history, the Scottish literati of the second half of the eighteenth century would contribute significantly to the development of modern historiography and the human sciences. On the one hand, Hume (in his *History of England* [1754–62]), and Robertson (in his three major histories, the *History of Scotland* [1759], the *History of Charles V* [1769], and the *History of America* [1777]), would try to find a way to reconcile philosophical and narrative elements in their accounts of major developments in history, while also emphasising the need for positive evidence and reliable sources. On the other hand, Adam Smith (in his *The Theory of Moral Sentiments* [1759] and *Wealth of Nations* [1776]), Adam Ferguson (in his *Essay on the History of Civil Society* [1767]), Henry Home, Lord Kames (in his *Sketches of the History of Man* [1778]), and John Millar (in his *Historical View of the English Government from the Settlement of the Saxons in Britain to the Revolution in 1688* [1787]) would apply the sociological speculations of Montesquieu to history, producing a conceptual framework to explain those major developments. Through the comparison of different societies, progress was shown to emerge from changes across economic, political, social and cultural spheres. Differences between peoples were explained within a historical scheme: from simple, rough and lawless to refined, polite and commercial societies.[25]

The gradual progress of mankind from primitivism to civilisation constituted the hallmark of Scottish philosophical history. Ironically, however, as Colin Kidd describes, '[t]he glory that was the polite, commercial and free Scotland of the late eighteenth century had arisen, not through the natural course of Scottish development, but in large part from an accidental acceleration brought about by the [Anglo-Scottish] Union [of 1707], and the subsequent assimilation of North British society to that of her more progressive neighbour'.[26] Those who were committed to the Enlightenment project tended to view Scotland's past before the Union as an age of feudalism and religious conflict from which they rejoiced to be delivered. Paradoxically, Scotland would become 'the historical Nation' by virtue of emancipation from her history.[27] For Scots historians, just as much as for English ones, the English parliamentary experience came to be considered as the normative standard against which to judge the successes and failures of institutions in other countries. 'British constitutional history and the history of England', Kidd observes, 'were one and the same. The usable past truly was a foreign country – England.'[28] Thus, Hume began his *History of England* as a *History of Great Britain*, [. . .] *Containing the Reigns of James I and Charles I* (1754), but adopted for the most part an Anglocentric perspective in which the history of Scotland and Ireland were treated in many ways as an adjunct to that of England.[29] The Scottish experience would enjoy a similar 'walk-on role' in Millar's *Historical View*.[30] Robertson, meanwhile, would paint a negative picture of Scotland's feudal backwardness in his *History of Scotland*, and welcome the Union as the moment at which Scotland acceded to British, and ultimately to European, historical norms.[31]

A strong tradition of commentary has explored the relationship between the intellectual programme of the Waverley Novels and Scottish philosophical history.[32] This commentary takes its cue from the last chapter of *Waverley* ('A Postscript, Which Should Have Been A Preface'), which frames the preceding narrative with a meditation on the modernisation of Scotland since 1745. Scott's analysis draws upon the general theoretical principles of Scottish philosophical history, and within that framework highlights the distinctiveness of Scotland's historical path. Yet Scott's relationship to philosophical history is one of disorientation as well as cooperation. Ina Ferris has argued that while the story of the progress of civil society and the British state – the official inscribed plot of history that culminates in the Glorious Revolution of 1688 – serves as the enabling assumption of the Waverley Novels, Scott 'novelises' (in Bakhtin's sense of the term) the historical genre, most notably in his concentration on obscure communities and minor events.[33] Furthermore, Scott incorporates into the Waverley Novels various linguistic forms of popular memory – song, tale, anecdote – and the languages of the cultural margins, which had been renounced from 'legitimate' history, with its elegant and elevated narratives of statecraft and warfare. By combining popular memory with a philosophical approach to history, Scott would profoundly transform historical writing in the nineteenth century.

Scott's command of the philosophical approach is particularly evident in the Highland and Lowland scenes in *Waverley*, which move across a range of topics of Enlightenment inquiry. After Edward Waverley's first meeting with Fergus Mac-Ivor, for example, the narrator offers some particulars of the Chief's 'character and history', describing, in the manner of Robertson, the state of the Perthshire Highlands around three centuries earlier when Fergus's ancestor had first set up a claim to be recognised as chief of his clan. Scott also plays with the speculative and comparative aspects of philosophical history. 'Had Fergus Mac-Ivor lived Sixty Years sooner than he did,' the narrator conjectures, 'he would, in all probability, have wanted the polished manner and knowledge of the world which he now possessed; and had he lived Sixty Years later, his ambition and love of rule would have lacked the fuel which his situation now afforded. He was indeed, within his little circle, as perfect a politician as Castruccio Castrucani himself.'[34]

Philosophical history is supplemented or countered in *Waverley* by forms of popular or folk memory, associated not only with Flora Mac-Ivor, in her role as Celtic muse, but also with such characters as 'the half-crazed simpleton' David Gellatley, who is the first person that Waverley meets at the manor house at Tully-Veolan (*WN* 1:58). When Waverley enters the village of Tully-Veolan, he adopts the stance of an 'enlightened' improver, as he observes the 'primitive' manners of the inhabitants. But Gellatley introduces a different register into the novel, singing, as he comes up to Waverley, 'a fragment of an old Scotch ditty'. The fragment 'False love', unbeknown to Waverley, is a vehicle of remonstrance: the heir to an English Jacobite family, newly signed on in the Hanoverian army, is being addressed as a faithless lover. 'David Gellatley's poetry', as Claire Lamont observes, 'is both a commentary on the action of the novel, and a measure of the growing maturity of its hero. And it is [. . .] an indication of the relative optimism of *Waverley*, despite Culloden in the background, that the poor foolish singer plays a valuable part in saving the family that protects him, and that the [. . .] young hero learns to listen and communicate with him.'[35]

As Waverley's private adventures intersect with the events of the Rebellion, Scott engages with John Home's *The History of the Rebellion in the Year 1745* (1802). Home had served as a volunteer on the government side during the Rebellion. The publication of the *History*, in Peter Garside's words, 'helped break something of a taboo in giving a formal account of its subject, made possible partly by its Dedication to George III. The *History* nevertheless broke new ground by incorporating recollections of Jacobite witnesses, and also comes to life [. . .] in those areas where Home had been personally involved'.[36] The *History* includes a particularly vivid account of the size and condition of the Jacobite army, as it lay encamped in the King's Park outside Edinburgh, which is given in the form of a report by a 'volunteer' (probably Home himself) to General Cope. Scott appears to be indebted to this report in his picturesque account of the Jacobite army assembling and marching out prior to Prestonpans ('The grim, uncombed, and wild appearance of these men', the narrator comments, 'created surprise in the Lowlands, but it also created terror': WN 1.229). It is likely that Home's narrative also informs Scott's account of the skirmish at Clifton, where details such as the shouting out of 'Claymore!' and the transitory state of the moonlight are common to both accounts.[37] Waverley last sees Fergus at Clifton in the moonlight with Evan Dhu and Callum Beg, 'defending themselves desperately against a dozen of horsemen, who were hewing at them with their long broad-swords' (WN 1:297). At such moments, as Robert Louis Stevenson suggests, 'we begin to have a sense of the subtle influences that modify and qualify a man's personality; that personality is no longer thrown out in unnatural isolation [as in the novels of Henry Fielding], but is resumed into its place in the constitution of things'.[38] The Waverley Novels could therefore represent 'a great enfranchisement' of the imagination for nineteenth-century novelists.[39] The Prestonpans and Clifton episodes highlight Scott's innovations.

In a digression on the philosophy of government in the first volume of his *History of Great Britain* (the section dealing with the reign of Charles I), Hume had argued that 'nothing will tend more to abate the acrimony of party-disputes, than to show men, that those events, which they impute to their adversaries as the deepest crimes, were the natural, if not the necessary result of the situation, in which the nation was placed, during any period'.[40] Like Hume, Scott sought to cool party passion. Accordingly, he emphasises the changes in society that have created a substantial discontinuity between the past and the present. Thus, after reporting the conversation between Waverley and Colonel Talbot, in which the Colonel describes Fergus as a fitting 'victim' for justice (the impending Carlisle assizes), the narrator comments: 'Let us devoutly hope, that, in this respect at least, we shall never see the scenes, or hold the sentiments, that were general in Britain Sixty Years since' (WN 1:340). 'Ah that Distance!' Scott wrote privately in 1826, 'what a magician for conjuring up scenes of joy or sorrow, smoothing all asperities, reconciling all incongruities, veiling all absurdness, softening every coar[se] ness, doubling every effect by the influence of the imagination' (Journal 127–8).

In The Heart of Mid-Lothian Scott engages with the minutiae of past and present Scots law, and with its broader philosophical 'map', as taught by Hume (the nephew of the historian).[41] The novel opens with the Porteous Riot, a train of historical events that culminated in the lynching of John Porteous, a captain of the Edinburgh City Guard, by a mob in September 1736. Distinguishing between rioting and treason, in his Commentaries on the Law of Scotland, Respecting Crimes, Hume had argued that the Porteous mob was a mob because it had one particular aim, to hang Porteous, and that it was not rebellion in that it did not challenge the state.[42] Scott, however, presents the scene in such a way as to align the activities of the mob with open rebellion, as identified and characterised by Hume (the levying of war against the King 'embraces all those risings, which though not aimed directly at the person of the King are however against his royal Majesty; that is against his Crown or royal dignity; against his prerogative, authority, or office').[43] The narrator uses, for example, the terms 'insurgents' and 'conspirators' to describe the participants in the Riot, and later identifies the root cause of the Porteous affair in the collision between, on the one hand, the state in maintaining its right to collect customs and excise duties, and using force to maintain that right, and on the other hand, the people in asserting their resistance to paying taxes and making known their sense of injustice.[44] Furthermore, the Queen regent and the government see the riot to be a challenge to their authority, and the people at large, including Jeanie, feel that the whole affair has a national political dimension, since 'the action, though violent and irregular', had become connected with 'the idea of ancient national independence' (WN 6:314). The novel intricately recreates the experience, at the individual and the collective level, of Scotland's loss of independence through the Union of Parliaments of 1707. 'I dinna ken muckle about the law', declares the 'rouping-wife, or saleswoman', Mrs Howden, 'but I ken, that when we had a king, and a chancellor, and parliament-men o' our ain, we could aye peeble them wi' stanes when they were na gude bairns – But naebody's nails can reach the length o' Lunnon' (*WN* 6:37).

Scott's use of dialogue and the Scots vernacular poses a challenge to 'legitimate' history. But there are also continuities of style and language between philosophical history and the novel, notably in Scott's detailed analytical presentation of the character of Queen Caroline. Portraits were a prominent feature of eighteenth-century historical narratives, such as Hume's, where they generally served as a post-mortem assessment of an important individual's virtues and vices.[45] Scott incorporates this feature of 'legitimate' history into the novel (although the portrait of Caroline serves not to conclude the narrative but as a prolegomena to Jeanie's interview with the Queen). Yet, arguably, the whole episode of Jeanie's relationship with the Duke and interview with the Queen – the culmination of her journey to London – belongs not to history, but to the world of magic, with its own wondrous logic.[46]

In *The Bride of Lammermoor*, which is set shortly before the Union of 1707, Scott combines a philosophical approach to history with forms of popular memory and Gothic fiction. The 'dismal' story of the ill-fated marriage of Janet Dalrymple, daughter of the eminent lawyer James Dalyrmple, first Viscount Stair, to David Dunbar of Baldoon in 1669, on which the novel is based, had been told to Scott many times, especially by his mother, Anne Rutherford, and by his great-aunt Margaret Swinton.[47] He was also familiar with a number of written versions of the tale, such as Robert Law's *Memorialls*, which Scott's friend Charles Kirkpatrick Sharpe had published from manuscript in 1818. In addition, the story had a basis in more public history, specifically the Gowrie Conspiracy of 1600 (the attempt by John Ruthven, third Earl of Gowrie, to murder or kidnap James VI: Ruthven and his brother were killed in this escapade, which some felt was an elaborate plot by James to have the Ruthvens murdered).[48] There are a variety of echoes of the Conspiracy in the *Bride*, and Caleb Balderstone specifically recalls the episode when he prepares lodgings for Bucklaw at Wolf's Crag.[49]

The Gowrie Conspiracy may be viewed as the opaque, imaginative centre of Robertson's *History of Scotland*. '[W]hether we impute the intention of murder to Gowrie, or to the King', Robertson observes, 'insuperable difficulties arise, and we are involved in darkness, mystery, and contradictions. Perhaps the source of the whole conspiracy ought to be searched for deeper, and by deriving it from a more remote cause, we may discover it to be less criminal.'[50] The obliquity and enigma of the Gowrie Conspiracy stand for the qualities that Robertson found in Scottish history as a whole; yet Robertson would reject a specious clarity, making the challenge posed by the past to his causal analysis the pivot of his work.[51]

Tytler, however, would take up the gauntlet thrown down by Robertson, to search deeper into the sources of the Gowrie Conspiracy, including in his account of the episode extracts from letters of the conspirators that he had unearthed in Register House.[52] Like Scott, Tytler would seek both to revivify the experiences of the past and to subject that past to rational understanding, as when he notes of the parchment bag found on Gowrie's corpse that 'such superstitious credit did both King and people give to the little bag of cabalistic words, that they insisted that no blood had issued from the wound till the spell was removed from the body, after which it gushed out profusely'.[53] Tytler's language and style shows the influence of Scott (the mob outside Gowrie House, for example, recalls the mob in *The Heart of Mid-Lothian*). Yet his *History* by no means met with universal acceptance. Summarising the critical response, Patrick Fraser would accuse Tytler of deliberate bias, and suggest that the last four volumes, instead of being denominated a history, should be described as a 'partial biography of Mary Stuart, of Regent Murray, and of Morton, interspersed with sketches of other grandees, and solemn denunciations of the coarse vulgarity and intolerance of Presbyterian ministers'.[54] Such attacks bruised Tytler, who prided himself on his objectivity. Scott, in the Waverley Novels, had succeeded in depicting a Scotland informed by many of the values they shared in a way that won assent from his readers. Tytler, trying to do the same on a factual plane, failed. But perhaps, as Michael Fry suggests, 'in a changed Scotland of bourgeois politics and sectarian religion, that synthesis was no longer possible'.[55]

CHAPTER SIX

Scott's Worlds of War

Samuel Baker

Throughout the last hundred years, and especially since the putative 'war to end all wars', and the Second World War, historiographical thinkers have campaigned to broaden the scope of a practice of history writing too long obsessed, in their view, with chronicling conflict. Rather than dwelling on strife, history, in this vision, should illuminate all aspects of human existence. In accordance with this historiographical project, modern considerations of Scott's historical novels have emphasised their enlightened engagement with matters beyond the merely political or military. Scott, we have learned, offers in his fiction histories of everyday life, of regions and local landscapes, of relations of production and consumption, of gender roles, and of the media he represents and utilises. With this multifarious agenda, it has been said, Scott's novels helped inspire the great nineteenth-century historians (Ranke, Michelet, Macaulay, Burckhardt) who set the parameters for their discipline's subsequent expansion. Welcome as this expansive account of Scott's achievement may be, however, it should not lead us to lose sight of the fact that war is a main topic of the Waverley Novels. Indeed, war can be recognised as *the* main topic of Scott's fiction, especially once one grasps that Scott, like most of his contemporaries, understood conquest, or the desire for it, to have shaped history so profoundly that politics itself might be said to be war by other means.[1] Although Scott helped broaden the idea of history to encompass more than war, he repeatedly depicted war – organised violence between distinct social groups – as the ultimate 'force', to quote the title of a more recent meditation on the phenomenon, 'that gives us meaning'.[2]

War, for Scott as an inheritor of the eighteenth-century sentimental tradition, is the main experience that quickens the understanding of life in those it spares, making immediate for them the stakes of cultivating their national community and their individual will. The novelist's mediation enables those unfortunate enough not to know war at first-hand to gain this experience at a distance. And since, of course, in many respects to know war up close is to be unfortunate, the displaced epiphanies of mediated war come to seem an improvement upon the old immediacy of conflict, especially when those displacements propose a future where war has become a thing of the past. War is not always what it seems, even or especially to its participants.

Scott's focus on armed conflict was urgent: he lived through the Napoleonic Wars, the most total wars known in his day. Scott's accounts of this experience evince the oscillation between realism and romance much noted in his work, and may well be said to heighten it. Scott urges realism when he argues, in an *Edinburgh Register* article written in 1809, that the 'safety' of Britain 'as a nation is unfortunately deeply implicated' in mustering a 'cool investigation' of Napoleon's power. He urges this, however, because he perceives Napoleon's successes as having given rise to the 'romantic delusion' that the French general was 'a demi-god at the head of an army of invincible heroes'.[3] Happily, Scott suggests, 'the spell flung around' Napoleon and his armies 'has been fortunately dispelled by repeated practical experiment,' that of individual Britons fighting individual Frenchmen. (These 'Cursory Remarks upon the French Order of Battle' strive to attribute Napoleon's successes to the single and simple tactical innovation of holding forces in reserve.) For Scott in his own wartime, the interplay of romance and realism explained the relationship of subjects to sovereign power, and did so most properly when the ability of individuals to claim or contest sovereignty was accurately weighed.[4] And this idea of individual responsibility coalesces in the author himself, as he weaves and dispels the charms of war that resound in the atmosphere of his historical imagination.[5]

Well before Walter Scott himself embroidered its legends, the Scott family was renowned for martial feats. For much of Scott's lifetime, Britain was at war, and many of his relatives and family friends served as soldiers. (A wonderful anecdote of Scott's early life, rich in allegorical implication, has him being taught to crawl by a soldier friend of the family who attracted him across the floor by pulling along it a shiny gold watch on a chain.)[6] Yet Scott himself never fought in a war. Subject as a child to illnesses, chief among them the polio that left him with a club foot, Scott, while enamoured of fighting, came to accept that his role in war would be as a commentator rather than as a participant. Meanwhile, he trained for another traditional family profession, the law. In considering Scott's relationship to war, it is important to consider the close if largely negative relationship between the law, a system for adjudicating or pre-empting conflict, which is premised on the state's monopoly over legitimate violence, and war, armed struggle between parties for whom (whether they have wished it or not) it is might that will make right. Many of Scott's narratives depict a relatively modern, law-governed society subsuming war within it. Yet while these tales may be narratives of enlightenment, they are also counter-enlightenment narratives. They justify the place of traditional warriors in modern society, explore how laws of military discipline, or even of literary and historical representation, can reserve legitimacy for violence in a modern culture, and extend the reach of the searing experience of armed conflict by virtualising it. They carve out retreats where violence rests, seemingly limited or latent – epistemic, ritual-istic, traditional, or historical – but nonetheless menacing in its potentiality, and sublime for those who apprehend it.

Once one grasps that the Waverley Novels find violence accomplishing this tactical retreat, one will better understand why, for instance, despite all of the ink spilled in defence of Scott on this point, it can, nevertheless, feel just of Mark Twain to have lain at Scott's feet personal responsibility for having inspired the cavalier Southerners to instigate the American Civil War.[7] That any failing of Scott's in such cases is part and parcel of a broader failing of the Enlightenment project, so slow as it has been to come to grips with war's romance, hardly allays the force of charges like that which Twain makes. Still, dialectical in this as in all things, Scott's fiction also transmits critiques of war, in general and in its historical particulars, that have reso-nated widely in subsequent centuries. Indeed, it is Scott's very ambivalence about war and its consequences that makes war narrative such a generative mode for him, a mode wherein worlds harmed or destroyed meet worlds pro-tected or created, as well as worlds that, because of the fortunes of war, never can or never yet have come to be.[8]

Scott's importance to the literary and cultural historiography of schismatic war in America suggests the wide impact his novelistic vision had in dissemi-nating the idea that a proper relationship to war might be decisive for the very possibility of making new worlds. Taking this broad view of Scott's achieve-ment, meanwhile, entails revising our idea of his own proper worldliness. Not the least of David Daiches's many contributions to Scott scholarship is an illustrated biographical study, *Sir Walter Scott and his World*, that patiently explores the variety of Scottish locales evoked by the author often called 'the Wizard of the North'. While it cannot help but touch upon scenes of conflict, this exploration is by and large a peaceful enterprise, as the idea Daiches presents here of the man and his works feels relatively settled (by contrast, for instance, with the divided Scott whom Daiches pictures elsewhere).[9] To unsettle this idea of Scott's achievement by tracing war in his work is to dis-cover the principle by which worlds bifurcate and multiply in his oeuvre. The border with England, and the social gulf within Scotland between Lowlands and Highlands, are only the most immediate lines of military struggle dividing the realms of Scott's imagination. Further worlds Scott brings into view when working in a military mode include the ancient world of imperial Rome; the medieval world of the Crusades, from the equivocally-conquered England of *Ivanhoe* to the to the holy land of *The Talisman*; late-medieval France as it was being consolidated by Louis the Prudent (*Quentin Durward* and *Anne of Geierstein*); and the worlds encountered in the imperial contact zones of India and America that provide settings for extensive (*Guy Mannering*) or brief but intense (*The Heart of Mid-Lothian*) offstage action. History, for Scott, is to a great extent the story of how Britain comes to manage the legacies of these other worlds. If this historical process works itself out through warfare, with its continual pacification on behalf of life and its compulsive repetition of scenes of death, it is ratified by writing, very much including Scott's own, that explains and illustrates the laws by which this process unfolds.

The other world most persistently shadowing Scott's own was the alternative realm of the Jacobites, and the cycle of violence most proximate to him – a living memory throughout his days – was the repeated rebellion of Stuart loyalists subjugated by Hanoverian Britain. For this reason, the story of the 1745 Jacobite rebellion provides Scott with a perfect starting point for the world-making craft of writing war fiction. In *Waverley* – a record not of chivalric glory, but of modern dutifulness – Scott traces his hero's proper regimentation into the modern British army, and therefore into the modern British society for whose standpoint that army would win the privilege of history-writing. Brilliantly, Scott refuses the romance of battle as a field for representing the virtues of British warfare. Instead, he visits his campaigners in their tents; and ironising their foibles, he provides notes, as it were, on styles of camp. He pointedly contrasts the glamorous but fatally undisciplined Jacobite muster, and its unstable mixture of Highland fabulists and effeminate French phonies, with the patient and modest mentoring afforded to Waverley, now a captured rebel, by the English Colonel Talbot. The Colonel's practical organisational skills demonstrate what enables the regular British forces to put down the inchoate attempts of the Jacobite rebels to conjure the return of their king.

In the novel's denouement, further stakes of the 1745 rebellion are established, but only evanescently, in the form of a series of icons of trauma that flash by the reader. Among these images are those that cluster around Waverley's Jacobite patron, Baron Bradwardine, who is pulled from the cave where he has hidden with his prized copy of Livy and returned to an estate whose signature Bear emblems are smashed before being somewhat improbably repaired to something close to their original state by his magnanimous English friends. Whereas these vignettes of the Baron's fate provide relatively pleasant images of antique and chivalric war emblems redeemed, such redemption is contrasted with the distasteful spectacle of Fergus Mac-Ivor's execution, and then the mention of his and his doughty clansman Evan Dhu's heads mounted on the gates of Carlisle. Scott handles these images gingerly, relating them second-hand or as if only in passing. That these occulted images constitute a reserve of martial experience for the reader is nevertheless suggested by another tableau in this closing series, the double portrait of Fergus and Waverley armed for battle.

If *Waverley* amasses a gallery of iconic images of war, Scott's second novel, *Guy Mannering; Or, The Astrologer*, experiments with showing war's effects indexically, acting at a distance, in a mode befitting a tale concerned with the putative influence of the stars on human affairs. This novel's first main protagonist is himself an English colonel in the British army, the eponymous Mannering, for whom visiting and revisiting Scotland becomes a way to work through the damage done to him and to his family by his military career in India in the mid- to late eighteenth century. *Guy Mannering* marks the début of the 'Author of *Waverley*', and with that début the task of locating, in the already crowded firmament of Scott's fictional creation, a new constellation. To that end, the novel brings forward what had been in *Waverley* muted themes of war's capacity for breaking hearts and homes, and makes of them main plot concerns. *Guy Mannering* is built around domestic disasters that befall families that depart, in one direction or another, from the golden mean of martial ardour. Initially, the novel foregrounds the Bertram family's attenuated fortunes. Having once 'made war, raised rebellions, been defeated, beheaded, and hanged, as became a family of importance, for many centuries,' they have 'sunk into subordinate accomplices', and would vanish altogether, losing their estate and last male heir, were it not for Mannering's work of restoration (*WN* 2:8). Then the novel hinges this restoration plot on the overcoming of the disaster that befalls Mannering's own house, in the crucial offstage sequence wherein Scott's protagonist ruins his marriage amidst the stresses of the Indian war by mistaking attentions paid by a young soldier – by the Bertram heir, it turns out – to his daughter for attempts to seduce his wife. The novel resolves this failure to reproduce domesticity in the imperial theatre of war through the removal of Mannering's once, and future, family back to the original, and more tractable, foreign territory of Scotland, where it can regenerate itself by regenerating the Bertrams.

It is on that more familiar Scottish ground that Scott lays out, in *Guy Mannering*, a narrative exemplary of the way in which his secondary worlds of war-making ultimately become subsumed into the primary world constituted by a pacifying narrative of British unification. The systematic manner in which Scott demonstrates this command of other worlds through the management of martial themes is epitomised by the choice of scenes he makes for the outset of the second volume of this, his second novel (the work charged with proving Scott's mastery of the second major genre he had taken up in the course of his second career as a romancer). At this juncture, Scott reintroduces his novel's second male lead, Harry Bertram – the suitor of Mannering's daughter – now grown to adulthood and travelling under what is, unbeknownst to himself, his second identity, that of the soldier of fortune Vanbeest Brown. The enlightened nobility of Bertram shines out as the young traveller shows himself well supplied with second-hand knowledge about the most prominent mark left by the ancient world on the modern British land-scape: Hadrian's Wall, the edifice that effectively divided Bertram's natal island in twain. Bertram walks into Scotland from Cumberland expressly so he can visit that ruin. When he arrives at the wall, Scott depicts Bertram 'scrambling up to a height which commanded the course of that celebrated work of antiquity' – commanding its course, it almost seems, in both space and time – and then gives him a speech in praise of the Romans that shows English to be no mere second language to the Scoto-Dutch adventurer (*WN* 2:118).

'What a people!' Bertram exclaims of the unifiers of the ancient world: 'In future ages,' he muses, 'when the science of war shall have changed, how few traces will exist of the labours of Vauban and Coehorn, while this wonderful people's remains will even then continue to interest and astonish posterity!' (*WN* 2:118). Bertram praises all manner of Roman constructions, but gives pride of place to their 'fortifications'. He associates Roman buildings with 'the grave, solid, and majestic character' of the Roman 'language' and compares them favourably to such 'modern labours' as those of the military engineers he cites, labours that, 'like our modern tongues, seem but constructed out of [Roman] fragments' (*WN* 2:118). To be sure, Scott ironises Bertram's enco-mium. Scott's younger protagonist's ability to commend the Roman art of war may legitimate him as a cosmopolitan hero fit to inherit a British estate, but the eager eloquence with which Bertram voices his praise of Roman warcraft is also requisite. His touchingly laboured speech belies his depreciation of British literary prowess, and underlines the local and global significance of the volumes of Shakespeare that Scott has just noted in his pockets. Bertram's speech thus fuses British literary invention with imperial ambi-tion and with the timeless Roman ethos of Stoicism which his brave words display – with that martial disposition which, no less ironically, proves him ultimately worthy of sympathy from Mannering, who is throughout depicted as a paragon of that soldierly ethos.[10]

When *Guy Mannering* works to overcome Britain's destabilising involve-ment in Asian conflicts by renovating its foundations in Roman military virtue, it manages distant worlds of war by redrawing their lines of connection through Britain's native land. Scott's third novel, *The Antiquary*, complicates this procedure by emphasising how arbitrary it can seem to read war into British landscapes and characters. In this novel – set in the early years of the war with revolutionary France, when Britain was only just finding its footing for that conflict – war inheres within symbolically rich but vague construc-tions that only the pedantic laird Jonathan Oldbuck, the antiquary of Scott's title, seems equipped to interpret adequately. Or, perhaps better, the novel's symbols seem cloudy until the novel has finished teaching its reader to see as Oldbuck does, at which point Scott reveals the novel's setting to be not simply a sleepy Scottish seaside community, but also the site of a threatened French invasion. In light of this denouement, Oldbuck can be seen to have displayed prescience at the novel's outset, when he immediately registers the merit of the young fellow passenger he befriends: 'Lovel', a British officer travelling incognito, who will eventually assume command of the forces assembled to meet the French threat. Even when Oldbuck mistakes this soldier for a player, his misprision hints at a deeper insight into the theatrical dimension of war. The magic of Oldbuck's antiquarian method inheres in its uncanny ability to strike at deep truths while committing obvious surface errors. Such magic, for instance, redeems the 'Kaim of Kimprunes' episode in chapter 4, in which Oldbuck, bringing Lovel to a recently-dug ditch he has mistaken for the remains of a ruined Roman coastal fort, feelingly evokes for his younger friend ancient seaborne invasions, the very type that it is Lovel's modern mission to fend off. As such episodes accumulate, they create a pattern whereby the antiquary's rage for meaning also proves to be an obsession with conflicts past and potential.

It is no surprise that the varied relationships Oldbuck bears to war in *The Antiquary* should recall Scott's own. Unable to serve in the conventional forces of his day, Scott, nevertheless, did enlist in the local militia mustered to stave off any French invasion of the region, and was said to greatly relish drilling to meet the French, at a time when a scenario such as that adumbrated by *The Antiquary* was actually expected to come to pass. Moreover, as a ballad collector and haunter of old ruins, Scott continually refined his knowledge of bygone struggles. By the time he was writing *The Antiquary*, Scott was also drawing on his interests in continental history and society, his avidity for serving as an armchair general, and his identification with the British state's fortunes to write directly about contemporary geopolitics, writing on military strategy, visiting Waterloo in the battle's aftermath, and publishing a poem (*The Field of Waterloo*) and a travelogue (*Paul's Letters to his Kinsfolk*) about what he registers as an inspiring but also profoundly unsettling experience. Scott snipes at Napoleon often enough in these texts, but also, like many British Romantic writers from across a wide political spectrum ranging from William Hazlitt's radicalism to Scott's own Tory leanings, he evinces a certain sympathy for Britain's arch-enemy, and late in his career he would invest heavily (both monetarily and libidinally) in bringing a monumental biography of the French general to the press.

Scott's military preoccupations were so pronounced that a popular theory of the Waverley Novels' authorship held that they were actually the work of his younger brother Thomas, an Army major serving in Canada at the time of their initial appearance. Such theories would have received a boost with the publication of the first series of *Tales of My Landlord*, designed by Scott as a departure from the *Waverley* line but quickly and correctly assimilated to it by his readership. *The Tale of Old Mortality*, the major work in this first series, echoes Scott's reflections on Waterloo while representing more directly than ever war and its remembrance on Scottish soil. Scott's central narrative in this novel concerns the Covenanters, Scottish Presbyterian rebels in the time of Charles II, and their struggle against episcopacy and other royal impositions on what they sought to preserve as their independent 'true church'. Characteristically, Scott identifies his protagonist here, the accidental insurgent Henry Morton, with a spirit of moderation and mediation, a spirit he shows in this instance tragically failing to win the day. Just before the Covenanters meet their Waterloo, as it were, at the Battle of Bothwell Bridge, Morton attempts to arrange a truce. He is hampered by the ardour for war of the royal forces, however, and then foiled altogether by the fanatical disarray of the Presbyterian zealots. Describing the battle that ensues, Scott pulls out all of the stops he had left in place when relating scenes of warfare in *Waverley* and its successors. Conveying at once the extensiveness and violence of the fighting and the fog of war that envelops it, he devises a new mode of military writing that would be much imitated in subsequent prose.

If *The Tale of Old Mortality* was partly inspired by Britain's victory over Napoleon in the Low Countries, it achieves a kind of chiasmus by associating Morton's eventual personal triumph with the Glorious Revolution that brought William of Orange across the channel to take the British throne. Escaping the field of Bothwell Bridge, and Britain entirely, Morton makes his way into exile on the continent and into William's service. He returns to Britain with William and Mary, putting his affairs back in order and tying up the loose ends of Scott's plot. The settlement brought about by the Glorious Revolution is thus experienced by Scott's readership as an achievement of personal integration, even amounting to the creation of a new kind of subject whose continental experiences enable him to both internalise and grow beyond the crises of sovereignty characteristic of the early modern era.[11] Any reader considering what would be entailed on a broader historical plane by such a project of post-war reintegration might well return full circle to reconsider the novel's opening frame. There the novel's supposed redactor, Peter Pattieson, encounters the memorialist of the Covenanters known as Old Mortality at work reinscribing the gravestones of obscure martyrs of that sect's struggle, and collects from him the stories that give rise to his narrative of Morton's life. Remembering the Covenanter cause, Old Mortality also perpetuates its partisans as individuals who, while they chose to support a party, might, like Morton, have made other choices had they been presented with them.

Scott meditates further on character building through war and remembrance throughout the rest of his *Tales of My Landlord*, most extensively in the campaign tale *A Legend of the Wars of Montrose*, where he offers what may be his most subtle critique of the difficulties inherent in integrating the various martial styles brought together in conflicts of the period.[12] The power of military action to build a world is felt no less tangibly, however, in novels like The Heart of Mid-Lothian that describe characters who fail to use the power at their disposal to properly knit subjects together with their sovereign state. The Heart of Mid-Lothian is usually celebrated for its success in rendering its heroine Jeanie Deans and her world-synthesising feat of winning Queen Caroline's clemency for her condemned sister. The aspects of The Heart of Mid-Lothian that readers find less palatable than this central sequence may owe their failure to please less to the shortcomings of Scott's craft than to the attentiveness with which he traces the consequences of men's martial failures. Scott's problematic anti-hero George Staunton, the father of Effie's lost child, is an energetic aristocrat who errs by channelling his taste for adventure not into lawful war, but into a life of crime.

Consorting with smugglers, Staunton becomes integrally involved in the Porteous riots, a series of real episodes of mob violence in Edinburgh in 1736. While readers have applauded Scott's taut dramatisation of the crisis of sovereignty that resulted from the mistakes of Porteous and other military authorities in the affair, they have underrated the significance of Scott's fictional elaboration whereby the natural-born officer Staunton both urges on and imposes discipline on the mob to his own ends – to mask an attempt to rescue Effie. Having been praised, or at least recognised, for his power to channel violence, Staunton can be blamed all the more for not finding a proper role within the state and its history. Even the staunch Cameronian Davie Deans, father to Jeanie and Effie, finally settles into a community for which Jeanie's husband, a Church of England pastor, provides the essential spiritual care. Thus more than in The Tale of Old Mortality, where the Covenanters are marked as a breed apart, in The Heart of Mid-Lothian Scott narrates the reabsorption of the Covenanter remnant into modern British society. Meanwhile, European exile, which in Old Mortality proved the making of Henry Morton, in The Heart of Mid-Lothian only seems to further enervate George Staunton and Effie Deans. It is thus overdetermined poetic justice that at the end of the novel, when Staunton departs the continent for the utopian island in the west of Scotland where he hopes to reunite with Effie and potentially (although unbeknown to them) with the son they have never known, a final failure of military command leads to his death. The doltish Duncan, Captain of Knockdunder, supposed to be policing the island, has been tolerating a band of outlaws that includes George and Effie's lost child, at whose hand Staunton dies in a botched robbery attempt.[13] For the lack of a commander with Staunton's abilities, the whole western colony is diminished, while Staunton's inassimilable son is lost in the New World.

Scott's treatment of illegitimate violence in The Heart of Mid-Lothian is only one example of his more general fascination with the subject. While mercenaries, irregular forces and outlaws figure significantly as early as his initial trilogy of Scotch novels, the problem of what constitutes a proper martial relationship to the state becomes a particular theme with, as Andrew Lincoln argues, *Rob Roy*, *A Legend of the Wars of Montrose*, and, I would add, *Ivanhoe*. Occupying with that last novel the fresh (for him) terrain of strictly English history, Scott follows tradition, if a tendentious strain thereof, by superimposing the story of England's most famous outlaw, Robin Hood, on the problem of English sovereignty in the wake of the Norman conquest. In the shadow of the Third Crusade, medieval Europe's grandest and most unified military undertaking to that date, Scott reveals an England whose plethora of power centres is leading it beyond civil war to anarchy.

Returning from the Crusade, Richard the Lion Heart does not immediately assert the absolute authority that might have been argued to be his by divine right. Instead, he resolves the situation by assembling an impromptu force of self-made men with whom to fight the Templars and Normans, who have ursurped the machinery of the state in his absence. Dwelling among his people in disguise, he falls in with Robin of Locksley (a.k.a. Robin Hood); with the convivial Friar Tuck; with his fellow crusader, the Saxon knight Ivanhoe; and, albeit indirectly, with Ivanhoe's Jewish ally and helpmeet Rebecca. Their re-conquest begins with the siege of Torquilstone where Richard, still in disguise, helps Locksley and his men rescue Ivanhoe from the usurping Normans and Templars who have captured him. The further rescue of Rebecca from a tribunal trying her on trumped-up charges of witchcraft simultaneously completes the rout of Richard's enemies. Scott's narrative thereby shows the achievement of English sovereignty to have been from the start, or from near the start anyway, not a matter of imposing rule, but of coordinating the fighting power of those subjects who most deserve the favour of the state.

Curiously, when Scott returned a few years later to trace Richard's earlier career, in the two novels *The Betrothed* and *The Talisman* that constitute his *Tales of the Crusaders* (1825), he begins the back story to Richard's triumphant return with a scenario of national consolidation through border war that hearkens back to his novels of Jacobite rebellion. *The Betrothed* does however lay more emphasis on a love plot or plots than most of those novels ever did– if 'love' is the proper term to name the desire for possession here enacted by a seemingly endless series of violent sieges, kidnappings, and rescues. The 'betrothed' of the title is Eveline Berenger, daughter of a Norman lord on the Welsh frontier. Early in the narrative, Eveline's father befriends a Welsh chieftain who, taking a fancy to her but learning that she is already promised to another Norman knight, lays siege to the castle of her father and kills him outside its gates. Eveline's betrothed, Sir Hugo de Lacy, rides to the rescue, but their marriage is postponed because he has committed to fight in the upcoming Crusade. During his absence, Eveline is protected by de Lacy's nephew, Damian. When Damian rescues her from another, outlaw member of the de Lacy clan who has abducted her, however, he is falsely accused of being an outlaw himself, prompting the King to send Prince Richard– the future Richard Coeur-de-Lion– to capture the fortress and set things right. Richard takes command of the situation; still, it is not he but a returning Sir Hugo who redeems Damian and concedes Eveline's hand to him, even while a Welsh minstrel-turned-assassin, trying to strike down Sir Hugo, the scourge of the Welsh, accidentally kills Eveline's abductor instead.

In contrast to *Ivanhoe*, whose love plot so notoriously privileges the laws of historical probability over the laws of desire when it marries off Ivanhoe to the Saxon princess Rowena rather than to Rebecca, *The Betrothed* matches up the fictional fortunes of love with the (putatively) historical fortunes of war. It, meanwhile, resonates with the Scotch novels' assimilation of Scottish spirit to the letter of the British law by showing the encounter with Welsh fancy to have been integral to the accomplishment of the Norman chivalry that Richard would eventually embody. If *The Betrothed* brings together love and war, and song and law, however, it does so brutally. Eveline, Sir Hugo, and Damian are so enmeshed in the battles that determine their fate that their characters lack the peace in which to elaborate private worlds, or, at least, to articulate them, and even if they could conjure the verve of a Rebecca, a Morton, or a Lovel, one wonders if the fustian in which Scott composes the novel could convey their individuality.

It is instead with *The Talisman* that Scott achieves an intimate analysis of the style of military leadership that his previous novels had shown bringing sovereignty into effect rhetorically, rather than simply by force of arms. Perhaps predictably, this analysis is elicited not by a heterosexual love plot that bares a hero's psyche, but by a study in homosocial bonding across a wider gulf between worlds than any yet treated by Scott: the gulf between the Christian West of Richard the Crusader on the one side, and Saladin the Saracen leader on the other. Richard's avatar in bridging this gap is Sir Kenneth, a Crusader eventually revealed to be a Prince of Scotland and the suitor of the English noblewoman Edith Plantagenet. As if parodying how his narratives of chivalry had, with *The Betrothed*, become mired in convention, Scott begins *The Talisman* with a bloody and pointless single combat fought between Sir Kenneth and a Saracen emir at a muddy oasis in the Holy Land. Fighting to a draw, the combatants call a truce, setting in motion a train of events that brings the Saracen, a skilled healer, to the bedside of King Richard of England, sick with a fever. Rising from his sickbed, Richard is able to restore order to the Crusader forces, which had been on the verge of mutiny – eventually with the help of Saladin, who is revealed to have been the Saracen noble healer who had fought Sir Kenneth and healed King Richard. *The Talisman* is peppered with violence, culminating in Saladin's cool beheading, in the course of a grand entertainment, of a Templar who has been conspiring against Richard. But, in the main, it finds Scott returning from the narration of military engagements to narrate, as he had in his initial novels, the camp life and personal relations of soldiers. Here, having returned all the way to the historical frontier of the Crusades, Scott locates in Saladin's ministrations to Richard the seeding of a paradoxical ethos in which one owes one's adversary healing, not only respecting but furthering the integrity of their world. The oldest military camp described in the Waverley Novels turns out to be an encampment of enlightenment, not barbarism.

In what was even for him an extraordinary elaboration of a metafictional conceit, Scott prefixed, to the first edition of the *Tales of the Crusaders*, an 'Introduction' that bears no direct relationship to the narrative that followed, but instead imagines a gathering said to be of all the parties 'interested' in the success of the Waverley Novels – but actually, of various characters from the novels – presided over by 'the Eidolon, or image of the author', with Oldbuck acting as secretary. The 'Author of *Waverley*' proposes to his characters that they apply to the Parliament for an Act of Incorporation, but is not able to make his case very effectively amidst their chatter and humorous hubbub. Affronted, the Author renounces his characters, and announces his intent to forsake historical fiction for the incredible but true story of Napoleon Bonaparte (thereby puffing the work in progress that he would actually soon publish). The promotional intent of this Introduction is obvious, of course; but Scott's *jeu d'esprit* makes it possible for him to insinuate some things in jest that he could never have said openly, in earnest. The true history, he suggests, of which his fiction is but the errant elaboration is the story of how Napoleon and his world came to be; and taking in hand the project of writing the life of that first maker of modern world war, he must lose his grasp of the inventions that have populated his art. *The Betrothed*, with its character-stunting plot of war and regeneration, seems to confirm that latter fear. But *The Talisman* dispels it, suggesting that the healing power of redeeming one's enemy's story can extend not only across the worlds which that narrative contains, but out into Scott's world, healing him as he finishes the task of confronting the pre-eminent warrior – or, better, perhaps, enchanter – of his day.

CHAPTER SEVEN

Scott and the Reformation of Religion

George Marshall

This chapter evaluates Scott's use of the events and the conflicting beliefs that marked the Reformation in Scotland. Historians increasingly accept the concept of 'the long Reformation', which is particularly applicable to the course of religious change in sixteenth- and seventeenth-century Scotland.[1] Instead of approaching the Reformation as a single historical event (in Scotland traditionally dated from the 'Reformation Parliament' of 1560), a 'long Reformation' captures the idea of a process, lasting at least a century, in which conflict over the nature of the church and of the Christian religion led to the development of a society that seems markedly closer to ours than does the medieval world. John Bossy offers a reason for this greater familiarity in his suggestion that until the seventeenth century 'Christianity' meant 'a body of people', but since then has indicated 'a body of beliefs'.[2] At the same time, in the words of Carlos Eire, 'the religion of immanence was replaced by the religion of transcendence'.[3] This watershed is simultaneously dramatised and analysed in four of Scott's novels: *The Monastery* (1820), *The Abbot* (1820), *The Tale of Old Mortality* (1816), and *The Bride of Lammermoor* (1819). These novels do not tell a sequential story, were not written in the chronological order of the events they narrate, and do not attempt to offer a systematic or comprehensive history of the Reformation in Scotland. Taken together, however, they reveal the characteristics of Scott's handling of religious issues – characteristics which would shape subsequent understandings of the place of religious belief in social history. Rather than being interested in theology for its own sake, and still less in ecclesiology, in these novels Scott shows how individuals define their religious beliefs in times of crisis. Despite his personal loyalties and prejudices, Scott was a dispassionate and thoughtful historian of religion, and his understanding of the Reformation, in particular, prefigures modern scholarly revisionism.

The relative familiarity of the world of the seventeenth century can be deceptive. Relating historical fiction to the mindset of people of the past is a hazardous undertaking, and authenticity in historical representations is notoriously elusive.[4] Modern readers of Scott cannot be confident that their own assumptions about religion mirror Scott's. Nor could Scott expect the past to reflect his present. As a Scottish Episcopalian, Scott was himself in a religious minority in Edinburgh, and even more so in Scotland as a whole. Although the violent religious-sectarian struggles of seventeenth-century Scotland had faded in the memory of some Scots of his generation and class, they remained contentious matters of debate. The educated classes disapproved of a clergyman who was 'enthusiastic' in his religious beliefs: the term 'moderate' expressed approval. The Episcopal Church by Scott's time showed a particular propensity for compromise; and in his expression of his personal religious views Scott consistently placed a high value on common sense and civic, as well as individual, virtue. In the sixteenth and seventeenth centuries, in contrast, varieties of Christian belief and modes of worship were sufficiently important for a substantial number of people to be prepared to die for them. It seems unlikely that either Scott or his associates would have emulated them. But this capacity for Christian martyrdom clearly interested him and, in general, he seems to accept that his characters say what they mean, whether or not he agrees with what they mean, and he makes it easy for the reader to spot the occasional hypocrite – hardly any in The Monastery, Moray and Morton in The Abbot masquerading as the champions of the reformed religion while trading monastic revenues, the odious Basil Olifant in The Tale of Old Mortality changing his religious views to accord most profitably with the climate of the day, and – most subtly – in The Bride of Lammermoor, Sir William Ashton, not a bad man but an ambitious one, avowing rather more enthusiasm for the reformed kirk than he really feels. What Scott did not do was ascribe major events to impersonal, determinist forces. As has come to seem natural for a novelist, Scott made outcomes contingent on the actions of individuals judging for themselves.

The Monastery narrates the lives of the community of one monastery (modelled on Melrose) and the people living in its vicinity: greater events take place at a distance. Through the use of fictitious narrators, Scott goes to considerable pains to define, and at the same time to obscure, his authorial position. The novel is introduced by a (fictitious) letter to the 'Author of Waverley' from Captain Clutterbuck, a half-pay army officer who has retired to a village near the ruined abbey of Kennaquhair. The account he gives of his meeting with a Benedictine monk is a crucial statement of 'where we are now', including potentially ironic references to the difficulties of maintaining impartiality in the writing of religious history. The struggles of the Reformation period are over and the neighbouring monastery is a ruin, more interesting to antiquarians than to surviving admirers of the reformers. Captain Clutterbuck insists that as 'a good Protestant' he could not undertake to help in the publication of anything 'written probably in the spirit of Popery' (WN 9:21). The monk, for his part, refers to Scotland as 'a land unhappily divided from the Catholic faith'. Each has his position. Yet there is clearly mutual respect, even friendship. When the monk wonders about Clutterbuck's 'heretical prejudices' he does so with a smile. The two have come a long way from the spirit of those ancestors who hurled insults and worse at one another in the sixteenth and seventeenth centuries. The Benedictine becomes 'my new friend' and 'the good father' (WN 9:15, 22). They share a love of antiquities: Clutterbuck, having confessed to the reader that this interest only took hold after he had failed at every other occupation that he had attempted, nevertheless demonstrates that he is a true scholar at heart by respecting the monk's superior knowledge even when it contradicts some of his own long-cherished ideas (WN 9:21–22). For his part, Clutterbuck, having travelled in Europe during his military career, has met many Catholics and professes to be comfortable with them. By 1820 Catholics were increasingly perceived as no longer constituting a political threat: the monk's admiration for the Hanoverian monarchy (WN 9:15) marks Scott's recognition of that point.

In his reply to Captain Clutterbuck the Author joins in the debate on impartiality in writing religious history. He does so in a teasingly self-deprecating way: 'I have buried myself in libraries, to extract from the nonsense of ancient days new nonsense of mine own' (WN 9:27–8). But on the Scottish Reformation, Scottish readers will take sides, as the author had found after the publication of The Tale of Old Mortality four years earlier (when the Reverend Thomas McCrie had denounced his representation of the Covenanters).[5] It seems reasonable to suppose that the main purpose of the two introductory epistles in The Monastery is to raise the question of partiality and impartiality in a jocular, self-deprecating, and sometimes slyly ironic, way in order to divert criticism. The Author and the Captain must 'arrange as we best can the manuscript of your Benedictine, so as to suit the taste of this critical age' (WN 9:30). Not, one notes, to tell the full truth, but a rather more modest ambition. And a final joke: 'You will find I have made very liberal use of his permission, to alter whatever seemed too favourable to the Church of Rome, which I abominate, were it but for her fasts and penance' (WN 9:30). Never mind about justification by faith, transubstantiation, pilgrimages, the cult of the saints, the Whore of Babylon: just consider the discomfort. Like the sexton, go for a 'kirk wi a chimbley on it' (WN 9:20). History repeats itself as bathos. But is Scott, here, laughing at his readers or at himself?

Having at the outset made his own impartiality an issue, Scott adopts a variety of techniques to avoid the sort of criticism that had greeted The Tale of Old Mortality. He also arms himself against accusations of being partial to Catholics by lacing the text of his novel with a mixture of irony and Protestant polemic. Readers with some knowledge of the brutality of the Reformation in England are likely to find some aspects of The Monastery baffling. In Scotland the monasteries were never formally dissolved, and there was very much less destruction of property than there had been in England and very little violence to individuals. Instead the monasteries were allowed to wither away, the mass – the main reason for their existence – having been proscribed by Act of Parliament. Protestant belief was spreading: Queen Mary was Catholic, as was the Regent, but some of the government and many of the nobility – including the Queen's half-brother – were Protestant. In 1560, unexpected even by John Knox, Protestants took control of Parliament, bringing about formally the last Protestant reformation in Europe and one carried out against the monarch's wishes. During the period in which *The Monastery* is set, the outcome was still uncertain. It was at one time common among non-Catholic historians to regard the Reformations in Scotland and England as inevitable, the replacement of an outdated religion by a more modern one; but this has been more generally challenged by recent historians.[6]

As James Anderson has argued, Scott's view of Roman Catholicism was influenced by eighteenth-century rationalist historians – rationalist yet with a prejudice against past societies – who 'all agreed that the Reformation was a good thing, and Popery a bad thing'.[7] *Tales of a Grandfather* gives a summary of the Reformation from a Protestant point of view but without acrimony (*MPW* 23:38–45). Scott's *Journal* gives slightly contradictory impressions. On the one hand, in February 1829 Scott expresses the hope that 'the Catholic superstition may sink into dust with all its absurd ritual and solemnities' (*Journal* 526). On the other, it is this very hope that led him to support Catholic emancipation, finding himself uncomfortably among the Whigs on the issue. Towards the end of his life he seems to have been more in the company of Catholics. He felt honoured at being asked to examine the papers of the late Cardinal Duke of York; and, during his tour of Italy in 1831–2, he was always happy to meet senior churchmen. In Malta he met the archbishop, a 'fine old dignitary of the Romish Church'; and he thought the octogenarian Bishop of Tarrantum 'still a most interesting man' (*Journal* 692, 694). At the monastery of Paestum the abbot, who was 'gentlemanlike and respectable', received Scott and his party with 'the greatest politeness' (*Journal* 705). Scott adds the comment that the Benedictines were 'the most gentlemanlike order in the Roman Church'. Any religious prejudice appears to have been moderated by the importance of being a gentleman. Clutterbuck's own Benedictine interlocutor is, of course, every inch a gentleman.

But by the early nineteenth century the passing of time and the gradual diminution of hostility to Catholics, at least among the educated classes, seems to have bestowed on monks, together with the ruins of their monasteries, an exotic attraction. Milton's visit to the monastery of Vallombrosa may not actually have occurred; but there was an abiding legend of it; and

Wordsworth certainly visited, as did Mary Shelley.[8] Such interest does not necessarily imply a softening of anti-Catholic feeling. Indeed, ruins could tend to confirm the received perception of Catholicism as irrational and mysterious. Nevertheless, public sympathy for the dispossessed French monks and secular priests who fled to Britain from the French Revolution may have helped change the way they were perceived, no longer as figures of power deserving to be overthrown but as fugitives in need of help, an understanding already suggested by the melancholy sights of the ruins of once great monasteries.[9] Given the widely held, and long-held, belief in the licentious lifestyle of monks assiduously promoted by the reformers and still widely held in Scott's day (by, for example, John Galt in *Ringan Gilhaize*, 1823), Scott is remarkably circumspect in describing the behaviour of the community in Kennaquhair. The monks here are not dissolute, though they have grown complacent and enjoy their material comforts. This picture has credibility. The Melrose community, in Anthony Ross's phrase, 'lived like members of a country club'.[10] Scott's reference in *Tales of a Grandfather* to the lives of monks, seems moderate and level-headed: 'though there continued to be amongst the monks many good, pious, and learned men, idleness and luxury invaded many of the institutions, and corrupted both their doctrines and their morals'. They had, in short, 'departed from the simplicity of their order' (*MPW* 23:33).

Scott is circumspect, too, in his treatment of the larger issues. His account of the 'Halidome' has elements of the idyllic, and makes the point that the tenants of the monastery were more prosperous than those on secular estates because they were less likely to be called for military service – a fact that acquires an ominous irony in the course of the narrative. Significantly, it is outsiders that bring conflict – the English army, the army of the Earl of Moray, and the pilgrim reformer Henry Warden. What the ordinary tenants make of it all is obscure. In a small scene, bordering on the comic, Scott demonstrates the impossibility of ever knowing. Lady Alice reads a book to the household, who listen politely, assuming it to be a volume of lives of the saints, while it seems that it is, in fact, an English translation of the Bible. The household servants remain blissfully unaware on the sidelines, not understanding a word of it, even though it is in the vernacular and therefore at the heart of the Reformation controversy.[11] When it comes to the particular, too, Scott does not hesitate to depart from his model, Melrose, and revise the course of history in the interests of making his story more dramatic. In its final years, Melrose did not actually have an abbot, in the sense of a head elected by the community, or even imposed on them by king or pope. By the time of the Reformation most Scottish monasteries were administered by a commendator, usually a royal appointment and designed to give a royal favourite an income.[12] As it happens, Melrose suffered from a particularly rapacious commendator who was in frequent dispute with a particularly feisty community. Such disputes would seem to have offered rich material for the historical novelist, but Scott chose instead to intensify the drama by giving the monks a slightly ineffective but kindly and hospitable abbot before, in the face of disaster, allowing them to elect one of their number better qualified to deal with an unprecedented situation. Moray is affronted when he learns that they have dared to elect an abbot without royal consent or (more importantly) his own. But Scott's plot is entirely credible. In 1562, even after the Reformation Parliament, and even though the abbey's finances were at that time being handled directly by the Crown, it was noted that an abbot of Melrose was present at a general chapter of the Cistercian Order in Cîteaux, presumably after having been elected, in defiance of the Crown, by his own community.[13]

The confrontation between the reformer Henry Warden and the newly elected abbot, Father Eustace, is intensely dramatised, to the point of theatrical (even operatic) exaggeration. By an extraordinary coincidence, the two are old friends who had studied together on the continent before pursuing their separate ways. Perhaps it is not so extraordinary, for history can offer similar friendships.[14] The meeting between the abbot and the reformer is, in effect, the climax of the novel, a set-piece in which each contestant states his case (WN 9:287–92). The narrator suggests that they had more in common than either would have admitted. This is a slightly mysterious observation. Does it mean simply that both would be prepared to die for their beliefs? Or that the fundamentals of Christianity could embrace both their beliefs? Or simply that their backgrounds and education are similar? Both have to find new religious identities in a rapidly changing and still fluid religious environment. Both could be said to be reformers. We are also advised that the monk has more of the head and the preacher more of the heart – a surprising statement. It perhaps means only that the preacher, being a convert, is the more zealous (notwithstanding that Father Eustace's zeal has throughout been acknowledged). But if it means that, in the author's view, Eustace's Catholicism is an intellectual stance, and that the preacher's is more emotional, then it is very surprising indeed. The more commonly held view is that the advance of Protestantism represented a triumph of intellect over emotion, of the transcendental over the immanent, of word over image, not the other way round. Whether or not Scott is subverting that view is unclear, and intriguing.

The next set scene, again verging on the theatrical, is the putative martyrdom of the new abbot and his monks. After the defeat of the army of the Halidome by Moray's Protestant army, the monks, with dignity and courage, prepare themselves for martyrdom. While the death-bell tolls, the entire monastic community, wearing vestments, and carrying incense and relics, emerges from the gateway and processes to the village, singing the *De Profundis*. Had the martyrdom occurred, Scott would have sacrificed historical credibility. At the dissolution of the English monasteries some monks in some monasteries stood firm and were hanged. Nothing similar happened in Scotland: so, in something of an anti-climax, Eustace, 'with skill and eloquence', negotiates with the enemy and secures terms that leave the monastery little worse off than it was before. It seems an unexciting ending, but in fact the story of *The Monastery* does not end there.

As a sequel *The Abbot* has some curious features. That only part of it reads like a sequel may be explained by that part having originally been intended as part of *The Monastery* and held over through lack of space. The details of these arrangements are given in the Edinburgh edition of the novel (*WN* 10:377–85). In its original, 1820, form, *The Abbot* began with an Introductory Epistle to Captain Clutterbuck, explaining that the new novel is based on the second part of the manuscript from which 'much [has been] omitted illustrative of the impulse of enthusiasm in favour of the ancient religion in Mother Magdalen and the Abbot' (*WN* 10:3). Thus Scott validates the link between the two novels and at the same time teases the reader with the admission that there is another, more authentic, text. He also opens up the possibility that there might be more than one point of view on religious issues. In his introduction to the 'Magnum Opus' edition of 1831, however, Scott adds a complication. He dismantles the frame of the 1820 text by admitting that Captain Clutterbuck is a fiction, designed merely to allow the author to express his own opinions; then promptly reinstates him by retaining from the 1820 text the second epistle addressed to the Captain indicating that he, the 'Author of *Waverley*', has had to make changes to the text of 'your friend' the Benedictine. So the framework is already back in place, together with the implication that there exists somewhere an alternative text. This is not so much reader-teasing as reader-baiting.

Once again, Scott's own religious views are an issue. 'We', he says, 'do not feel deep sympathy at this period with what was once the most powerful and animating principle in Europe' (*WN* 10:3). Yet the Catholics in *The Abbot* are for the most part sympathetically drawn. The Protestants, in contrast, are, with the exception of Henderson, less than attractive. Warden is, it is true, a good man, but a humourless one, who firmly declines to jest (*WN* 10:12). The Lady of Lochleven does not jest either, having adopted 'uncommonly rigid and severe views of religion' (*WN* 10:186). Moray and Morton, the great Protestant lords, are self-seeking, their religious views being shown as a mask for greed: the monastery has to be seized, not for the reformation of religion, but because Morton's brother has been promised its revenues. Father Ambrose, the new abbot, is as sympathetically drawn as his predecessor. His cool, rational address to the mob attacking the abbey is a high moment of the novel. Significantly, the mob is led by the 'Abbot of Unreason'. As with his predecessor, Ambrose's strength lies in his rationality, a quality that comes into use again at the very end of the novel when Mary's advisers are encouraging her to flee to Queen Elizabeth for protection. Ambrose tries to dissuade her. Reason tells him that England cannot accept two royal courts, and he knows that the Scottish queen is doomed. Of course, Scott's sympathy for his Catholic characters has to be interpreted in the context of the outcome of the Reformation. For him, the last abbot had sincerity and generosity, but his 'designs must be condemned, as their success would have rivetted on Scotland the chains of antiquated superstition and spiritual tyranny' (WN 10:101). It is probable that this represents Scott's own views and that it reflects the opinions of most educated Scots of his time; but one is free, perhaps, to wonder whether Scott was happier with the outcome of the Reformation than he was with the means by which it was achieved. Certainly, he is unequivocal about the destruction of monasteries and churches: 'there is no doubt that the humour of demolishing monuments of ancient piety and munificence [. . .] was both useless, mischievous and barbarous' (WN 10:62).

The Tale of Old Mortality, published four years before The Monastery, was Scott's first assay into the world of the Scottish Reformation, but it covers events that occurred a century after those recounted in the later novel – events which led, depending on one's point of view, either to the final triumph of the Reformation, or to its tragic betrayal, in the settlement of 1688–9. The early reformers, influenced by Calvin's Geneva, were looking for a church that was Calvinist in doctrine and Presbyterian in government, neither of which was acceptable to any of the Stuart kings. Charles I's determination to impose a prayer book and bishops on the Scottish Church was met with widespread opposition and the signing of the National Covenant in 1638. During the English Civil War, the Scots renegotiated this in the 1643 'solemn League and Covenant' for 'the preservation of the reformed religion in the Church of Scotland' and 'the reformation of religion in the Kingdoms of England and Ireland'. The Tale of Old Mortality follows the story of government repression and the defiance by the Covenanters, and their violent, extremist wing, the Cameronians.

The Covenanting movement has its origins in the reaction, expressed in the two Covenants of 1638 and 1643, against government determination to impose religious uniformity, a uniformity that, in the eyes of the most devout, amounted to no less than state-sponsored idolatry.[15] By the time of the restoration of the monarchy, Scott's chosen period for the novel, strict reformers were using the expression 'The Covenant' to embrace, not only the Covenants of 1638 and 1643 but also the various Covenants described in the Old Testament. The inclusion of the latter carried some implication of a special relationship between God and the nation, and even, among the most devout, the notion of the Scots as a chosen people, who must resist idolatry and be prepared if necessary for martyrdom. Scott is careful to differentiate the various shades of opinion among the Protestants: the Episcopalians, the followers of the 'indulged' clergy, the moderate Presbyterians, the extremists, and every shade in between. The Catholics do not feature at all in this novel, except as a distant bogey-man, the word 'papist' a catch-all insult.

The Covenanting movement was controversial territory for the novelist. For those of Scott's contemporaries who identified themselves with the Covenanters the only acceptable literature on the subject was hagiography. It is the Covenanters, not the early reformers, who have held the Scottish imagination, possibly because there were relatively few martyrdoms in the early Reformation period and no monarch of Mary Tudor's religious zeal. In the seventeenth century, in contrast, Covenanters were pursued with brutality by government forces in what were called, not unreasonably, 'the Killing Times'. For John Galt's narrator in *Ringan Gilhaize* the Covenanters were 'higher and holier' than the early reformers and this represented a strong popular myth.[16] Scott regards the Covenanters with a cooler, more dispassionate eye. He builds his story round the figure of Balfour of Burley, leader of the extremist group that assassinated Archbishop Sharp. That Balfour is an extremist is clear both to the protagonist Morton and to the reader from the language he uses, a language of violent rhetoric drawn from the Hebrew Bible. In case readers miss the point, Scott intrudes a mention of the 'stern fanaticism' of Burley, while Burley asserts that 'we are called upon [. . .] to smite the ungodly' (*WN* 4b:37, 43). A language of uncompromising aggression is joined by a complementary image when Morton encounters the Covenanter sitting, Bible in one hand, sword in the other. This image is reinforced by repeat showings – to Cuddie, to the little girl who sees him hiding in a cave, and in the recollections of Elizabeth Maclure. It encapsulates the character of the zealous Covenant while being but one step away from traditional icons and therefore ironically subversive of the Covenanter's claim to represent the true reformation of religion and the abolition of idolatry. Old ways of thinking are not so easily forgotten.

Burley's rhetorical style raises issues of category among the Covenanters. There were Covenanters who refused to condone violence; there were those who reluctantly took up arms in defence of their right to their religious beliefs; and there those who were prepared to use violence to destroy the religious beliefs of others.[17] Stylistically, Scott experiments with the use of Old Testament quotations, comically in the cases of Auld Mause and in Kettledrummle's sermon. Where one might wish to take issue with Scott is his failure to explain the theology that lies behind Burley's extravagant language. The Covenanters were not simply a persecuted group that had chosen to defy the government. Their views on the nature of the Christian faith and the government of the Church are unlikely to be palatable to most of today's readers, nor probably to many of the first readers of the novel, but they do have an internal logic that has to be taken seriously. The Covenanters' aspirations for the Church lie in the word 'idolatry'. The discrediting of the materialism of medieval piety and the replacement of a religion of immanence by one of transcendence meant the dismantling of all the outward symbols of the Church – prayers to saints, images, pilgrimages, liturgy, holidays, relics, and, above all, the Mass.[18] Opposition to these things contributed to a theology of idolatry; and, without this theology (explaining as it does why so many reformers saw the Reformation, not as an accomplished event, but as work in progress), there is a risk that Burley appears no more than a fanatic by temperament, eventually descending into madness as a result of persecution.

Morton, the one moderate in the novel, makes a plea for tolerance: 'I wish to have free exercise of my own religion, without insulting any other' (*WN* 4b:222). Morton's views may well be an anachronism.[19] Yet his declaration is given significance by the ironic framework of the novel, a framework that invites readers to think about the paradox between the extremists' ideals and their actions. The need for moderation is implied throughout. The final pages of the novel, in which the focus moves to the period immediately after the accession of William III, may confirm the reader's suspicion of centrist bias.[20] Another backward look at the Covenanters is found in the person of 'Old Mortality' himself, repairing tombstones in a vain effort to keep alive the memory of the covenanting martyrs, unintentionally confirming that the Covenanters belong to a sentimentalised past, treated as Protestant 'saints'.

The recognition of this and of signs of the beginnings of a more rational, more tolerant age comes in *The Bride of Lammermoor* (1819), in which Scott designs an unlikely combination of a critique of the religion and politics of the age with a private tragedy. Scott's use of historical fiction to display private struggle against, and related to, a background of great events, was never shown to greater effect than in this novel, where the Master of Ravenswood and the Lord Keeper face one another in a suddenly changed world. Money was, to a considerable extent, replacing religious doctrine as the substance of conflict. The framework within which the characters must interrelate is no longer that of civil war but rather one made up of law, economics, property, influence and corruption. It was hardly the ideal outcome of the religious settlement, but was nevertheless one that society, or at least those members of society that were comfortable with the Scotland of their age, could be grateful for. From 1689 onwards it was clear that the population of Scotland could not be coerced into a single religious faith: the age of denominations had begun.

In Scott's own day, the Church of Scotland had changed considerably. Those who felt strongly in opposing lay patronage as the method of

appointing parish ministers and who felt that the church had failed to maintain the ideals of the reformers had left the established church and formed
the Secession church in 1737. Although the Secession attracted labourers
and shopkeepers throughout Scotland, however, it made little headway in
Scott's social circles. At the same time, perhaps in reaction to the extremes
of the preceding century, the established church of the eighteenth century
was dominated by those who came to be known as 'Moderates'. Continuing
of necessity to pay lip-service to the tenets of Calvinism as expressed in the
Westminster Confession of 1560, most of the clergy, certainly most of the
clergy whom Scott was likely to know, took a fairly liberal view of doctrine
and assumed a church governance that respected education and property
rights. For Scott, an Episcopalian and of moderate and conservative outlook,
things must have seemed to have turned out well. At the Disruption of 1843
a third of the members of the General Assembly withdrew to form the Free
Church. Unsurprisingly, they included Scott's severe critic, the Reverend
Thomas McCrie, and the Reverend Henry Duncan, the anonymous author
of *William Douglas; or, the Scottish Exiles*, a novel published in 1826 to
counter what he saw as Scott's unfavourable portrayal of the Covenanters.
The Disruption would no doubt have given Scott, with his instinctive conservatism, cause for concern, for the event had some of the characteristics of
revolution. But the Disruption occurred some time after Scott's death and
there is no sign that he foresaw it. He was no proto-Victorian. Davie Deans
of *The Heart of Mid-Lothian* is a survivor from the days of the Covenanters:
he is anti-patronage, anti-toleration, and anti a great many other things, but
Deans is portrayed as comical, endearing, tiresome, and ultimately harmless.

Modern readers can see Scott as a man not so much of the Age of Reason,
as of the Age of Moderation. His mind is enquiring and ironic. He shows the
consequences of religious belief without troubling too much with the details
of its causes. 'Is there any once-great author less in vogue than Sir Walter
Scott?' asked *The Times Literary Supplement* in 2009.[21] Yet Scott's exploration of religious belief, conflict, tolerance and extremism, does suddenly seem
relevant to our world of today. 'Who would have expected theology to rear
its head once more in the technocratic twenty-first century?' Terry Eagleton
has asked.[22] The growing attention being paid to religion's importance in
society may adjust our reception of Scott's Reformation novels; and these
novels may even offer some guidance on how to live in a world in which the
desire to understand God can inspire, at one time, the greatest altruism and,
at another, the greatest cruelty: and in both the strongest determination. As
Scott repeatedly shows, those in positions of power ignore that determination
at their cost.

CHAPTER EIGHT

Romancing and Romanticism

Fiona Robertson

We meet as shadows in the land of dreams,
Which speak not but in signs –
ANONYMOUS (epigraph to Saint Ronan's Well, ch. 9, WN 16:80)

In chapter 1 of *Waverley*, Scott claims to have thrown 'the force of [his] narrative upon the characters and passions of the actors; – those passions common to men in all stages of society, and which have alike agitated the human heart' in all ages and cultures (*WN* 1:5). In his 1800 Preface to *Lyrical Ballads*, Wordsworth proposes 'to interest mankind permanently' through a poetics capable of suggesting 'the essential passions of the heart', tracing 'the fluxes and refluxes of the mind when agitated by the great and simple affections of our nature'.[1] One of these introductory statements has come to underpin the aesthetics of British Romanticism. The other, disconcertingly counter-historicist at the start of the first great historical novel, has puzzled many of Scott's readers. What might it mean to return to Scott as an analyst of the 'agitations' of 'the human heart'? To agitate is, from the Latin *agitare*, to set in motion, to move to and fro; to excite and to disturb. An inherently physical term, used by both Scott and Wordsworth to convey the errancies of emotion, agitation also characterises the years in which they were writing – years of political unrest; of social and aesthetic excitement; and of an intensified interest in the disturbing, from Gothic fictions of incest, murder, and haunting to scientific and quasi-scientific explorations of aberration and excess. When Scott seems separate from what we now call Romanticism, it is because he is no longer seen as *agitating* – formally, emotionally, politically, or personally. This chapter reasserts the importance of feeling in Scott's work, with special reference to his novels of the early 1820s; and reconsiders from this perspective his relationship to Romantic aesthetics.

According to Northrop Frye's influential 1963 formulation, 'the metaphorical structure of Romantic poetry tends to move inside and downward instead of outside and upward, hence the creative world is deep within, and so is heaven or the place of the presence of God'.[2] The association between

Romanticism and depth or inwardness continues to have great cultural power. In contrast, as Carlyle claimed in his review of the first six volumes of Lockhart's *Memoirs*, Scott 'was a genius *in extenso*, as we may say, not *in intenso*'.[3] The more he wrote, the less his writing seems to matter. In an aesthetics of diminishing return, Scott's interest in historical subjects and his move, in the 1820s, to tales set in medieval France (*Quentin Durward*, 1823) and Switzerland (*Anne of Geierstein*, 1829), India (*The Surgeon's Daughter*, 1827), the Holy Land of *Tales of the Crusaders* (1825) only seals his exclusion from Romanticism's inner circle, since, as Percy Shelley emphasises in *A Defence of Poetry* (1821): 'A poet participates in the eternal, the infinite, and the one; as far as relates to his conceptions, time and place and number are not.'[4] Like Aristotle in the *Poetics* and Sidney in *An Apologie for Poetry*, Shelley argued for poetry's superiority to the material details of history. Shelley's *Defence* also contends, however, that poetry (by which, following Plato, he meant 'every inventive art') 'awakens and enlarges the mind by rendering it the receptacle of a thousand unapprehended combinations of thought': 'The great secret of morals is Love; or a going out of our own nature.'[5] In these terms, Scott is a Romantic writer not only *in extenso*, but also eccentrically – that is, a writer always 'going out of' accepted norms and conventions, creating emotional connections (bonds of 'sympathy', in eighteenth- and nineteenth-century terminology) for his readers and his many re-writers. As in Shelley's 'Epipsychidion' (1821): 'Love is like understanding, that grows bright, / Gazing on many truths; 'tis like thy light, / Imagination!'[6]

At what point does 'many truths' become 'too many historical novels'? Scott exemplifies an eccentric Romanticism driven by range and difference; but the perception remains that his writing shies away from strong individual feeling, especially on the subject of love. Since 'Romanticism' has no necessary connection with the erotic, etymologically or conceptually, it is in theory possible to say that this perceived shortcoming is simply irrelevant. But all Scott's novels tell love stories. In practice, it matters whether or not readers are moved by them. Scott's reputation partly reflects his own expressed dissatisfaction with his portrayals of young lovers, from the poetry onwards, which tempts readers to dismiss them as formulaic and secondary, and to look for 'passion' elsewhere (in loyalty, kin, patriotism, conviction). According to biographical tradition, too, Scott seems relatively unscathed by erotic complication, largely because of his own presentation of his emotional life: one lost true love (Williamina Belsches) replaced by a marriage (to Charlotte Charpentier), which in his own words in a letter of 1810 to Lady Abercorn fell 'something short of Love in all its forms which I suspect people only feel *once* in their lives'.[7]

Williamina existed, but Scott also made her up, and she has been lastingly useful to him in protecting the secrecy that was necessary to him, creatively.

In this letter to Lady Abercorn ('with whom he had an epistolary flirtation', John Sutherland remarks),[8] Scott likens love to being 'nearly drownd'. In the *Journal*, too, in the weeks following Charlotte's death in May 1826 he describes dizziness, physical disorientation, and 'the hysterical passion that compels tears' as 'a terrible violence – a sort of throttling sensation' (*Journal* 149, 152). Scott's emotional vocabulary in passages like this is notably physical: overwhelming feelings are described in terms of near-death experiences. Critics recognise relatively few such extremes in his novels: the standard exception is the scene in *Rob Roy* in which Frank Osbaldistone chokes with tears as Diana Vernon rides away from him (*WN* 5:285). His letters tell a different story, though not openly; and, as in the 1810 letter to Lady Abercorn, his characteristic shift from aesthetic self-defence, to personal reflection, to emotional invitation, can be beguiling and revealing.

Most destructively of all for his literary reputation, some of Scott's best readers have deplored the lack of – or, worse, stylistic depletion of – passion in his writing. E. M. Forster criticised Scott for having 'a trivial mind and a heavy style', but his comments in *Aspects of the Novel* (1927) gather around one charge: 'think how all Scott's laborious mountains and scooped-out glens and carefully ruined abbeys call out for passion, passion, and how it is never there!'[9] Instead, Isabella Wardour (*The Antiquary*) speaks 'in accents which certainly chill the reader', while Caleb Balderstone (*The Bride of Lammermoor*) is one of Forster's examples of 'flat' novelistic character, with 'none of the private lusts and aches that must complicate the most consistent of servitors'.[10] In an essay on *The Antiquary*, Virginia Woolf likewise deplored the stylistic consequences of Scott's 'genteel' pen 'when, with a dismal croaking and cawing' his characters 'emit the astonishing language of their love-making'.[11] In some of the most influential analyses of Scott's writing, subsequently, it has been taken for granted that neither love nor the individualism of 'the Romantics proper', as Lukács calls them, matters much in Scott.[12] For Lukács, Scott's 'middling' heroes represent 'a renunciation of Romanticism, a conquest of Romanticism'.[13]

In much modern criticism, Scott remains poised between 'the Romantics proper' and more widely accepted conceptualisations of 'the Romantic Period'. Recognised as part of an ever-growing literary culture in these years – even as central to it in terms of productivity and readership – he is distanced from the individualism and concentration on feeling which now seem to characterise Coleridge, Keats or Shelley, and which in their own day promoted the creative personae of Charlotte Smith, Byron, De Quincey, and Laetitia Landon. However, it would be possible to construct a literary history of the Romantic period in Britain with sole reference to the works of Scott. An early love of folk tale and legend, imbibed in the impeccably authentic surroundings of a farm in the shadow of Smailholm, is overlaid with a fascination with Germanic diablerie and melodrama before settling into the more respectable forms of collecting and editing ballads and song. An intense engagement with the preservation of national tradition, especially during Britain's warfare with Napoleonic France, gives way to increasingly questioning, even ideologically riven, representations both of the public world and of the private aesthetic self, but also to a new formulation of the present as its own historical moment – something which, with a new degree of consciousness and design, was being shaped by the writer in an imaginably global present of reception and response, and leading to the more compart-mentalised forms of intellectual enquiry which, from the early 1820s, increasingly separated scientific, ethnographic, historical, philosophical, and auto/biographical writings.

In terms of Scottish writing in this period, Scott encompasses in turn the careers of Burns, Joanna Baillie, Elizabeth Hamilton, Byron, Galt, his own Lockhart, and Carlyle. Although the writings of the best-known British literary figures of the post-Napoleonic period are not usually categorised as 'historical fictions', the approaches to the historical and mythological pasts represented by Shelley's *The Cenci* and *Prometheus Unbound*, Keats's 'On First Looking into Chapman's Homer', and the two *Hyperions*, Hemans's *Lays of Many Lands*, and Byron's 'romaunt' *Childe Harold's Pilgrimage* and historical dramas *Marino Faliero* and *The Two Foscari* reflect a culture obsessively placing and relativising itself, only in part through the convenient medium of the recorded or imaginable past. Scott's non-fictional writings, meanwhile, chart the shifting preoccupations of the age, the earlier contextualising and editorial drive of the lengthy notes to the *Minstrelsy* and poems, as well as the editions of medieval writings and of the works of Dryden and Swift – all, in their different ways, explanatory and mediating enterprises – bifurcating into literary criticism, 'Secret Histories', and the apparently polarised historical ventures typified, in the late 1820s, by the *Letters on Demonology and Witchcraft* and the *Life of Napoleon Buonaparte*. Conceptually and in practice, Scott was not only what Hazlitt called Wordsworth, 'a pure emanation of the Spirit of the Age',[14] but also exemplary of the transitions of the age – its agitations.

1

Throughout the twists and turns of his writing life, Scott held to aesthetic principles which he stated explicitly, and publicly, in a number of writings of the early 1800s. Although they are not, now, generally included in histories of Romantic aesthetics, they were better known to nineteenth-century readers than some others which have come to supersede them. Indeed, their endorsement in later writings can make Scott's aesthetics difficult to see.

Nathaniel Hawthorne's Preface to *The House of the Seven Gables* (1851) begins: 'When a writer calls his work a Romance, it need hardly be observed that he wishes to claim a certain latitude, both as to its fashion and material, which he would not have felt himself entitled to assume, had he professed to be writing a Novel.'[15] The distinction between romance and novel looks back to Horace Walpole's discussion in the Preface to the second edition of *The Castle of Otranto* in 1765, and to many similarly inflected commentaries following Walpole. The association between romance and stylistic and imaginative freedom, however, owes most, for Hawthorne, to Scott, who had stated in the Preface to *The Lay of the Last Minstrel*: 'As the description of scenery and manners was more the object of the Author than a combined and regular narrative, the plan of the Ancient Metrical Romance was adopted, which allows greater latitude, in this respect, than would be consistent with the dignity of a regular Poem' (*PW* 6:1). 'Latitude' means freedom from narrowness, liberality of interpretation, tolerated variety of action or opinion. As Scott's immediate qualification – 'in this respect' – suggests, 'latitude' was not, and is not, an easy term to reconcile to a broadly conservative personal politics or to an imaginably conservative reading public. What the romance form seems to have represented for Scott is freedom from established rule; a kind of informality or irregularity; the freedom to write associatively, or experimentally, or idiosyncratically. We might now gloss this as 'to write creatively', to write with a capital R – Romantically. As Susan Stewart argues, the formal innovations of Romantic poetics mark an openness to difference and variety.[16] Although no Romantic period writer could seem further from Scott, ideologically or aesthetically, than William Blake – whose works Scott almost certainly did not know – Blake's address 'To the Public' at the start of *Jerusalem: The Emanation of the Giant Albion* (written 1804–7; published 1820), reflects on his poem's 'measure':

> When this work was first dictated to me I considered a monotonous cadence like that used by Milton & Shakespeare & all writers of English blank verse, derived from the modern bondage of rhyming, to be a necessary and indispensable part of verse. But [. . .] Poetry fettered, fetters the human race. Nations are destroyed, or flourish, in proportion as their poetry, painting and music are destroyed, or flourish.[17]

Blake's appeal to a national identity secured by artistic licence anticipates the closing sequence of Shelley's *Defence of Poetry*; but it also shares with Scott a resistance to the 'fettering' of art. Much of what subsequently comes to define Romanticism is suggested by Scott's little word, 'latitude'.

Scott's views on composition, too, may be set alongside Shelley's argument, in the *Defence*, that 'the mind in creation is as a fading coal': 'when composition begins, inspiration is already on the decline'.[18] Scott did not invent this idea any more than Shelley did, but he wrote about it at some length in the important final section of his review of Thomas Campbell's poem *Gertrude of Wyoming* (1809). This was a prominent article, leading the second number of the *Quarterly Review*: it was also Scott's first review of a contemporary work of literature. After discussing Campbell's poem, Scott reflects more generally on the extent to which poets should revise and refine their work. Writing anonymously, he castigates the carelessness of the poetry of one Walter Scott, only to spring to his own defence by asserting that the reading public prefers 'ruder' works which seem crafted in the first heat of imagination. '[I]n the irksome task of repeated revision and reconsideration,' he argues, 'the poet loses, if we may use the phrase, the impulse of inspiration; his fancy, at first so ardent, becomes palled and flattened, and no longer excites a correspondent glow of expression' (*MPW* 17:288). Scott states the superiority of 'the stamp of originality' over 'tame correctness', and writes from an author's perspective of the sinking of spirits which follows composition, the anxiety of re-reading 'the offspring of moments of enthusiastic feeling', then of doubting 'the faded inspiration' itself, as well as the words it has produced (*MPW* 17:289). Again one notes the physicality of this language.

The key aesthetic terms for Scott, then, are latitude, freedom, originality, and excitement. As the link to Blake is intended to suggest, these were not inherently or rigidly politicised terms. They are, however, exacting terms for aesthetic practice. For many Romantic writers, in all genres, writing experimentally and originally did not necessarily mean endorsing unconventionality in their characters or plots. Instead, the parameters of experimentation and originality were scrutinised in relation to the creative imagination itself, as they are in Coleridge's 'Dejection: an Ode', Shelley's 'Alastor', and Keats's 'Ode to a Nightingale'; and throughout Scott's novels, in which many characters – especially young lovers – are driven by imagination as much as by desire. In Scott's early novels, imaginative characters are predominantly characters who read widely, and errantly, in romance – Edward Waverley, Sophia Mannering, Frank Osbaldistone – and, throughout his works, female readers like Lucy Ashton have most to lose from their openness to fictional worlds. Whether the imagination is passive or active, a receiver or creator of ideas, is in Scott's writings, as throughout Romantic aesthetics, shifting and problematic. Scott discusses his own aesthetic practice most extensively in the multiplying paratexts of his novels – the prefatory/dedicatory/introductory epistles of his novels in their first-edition states, and the new introductions of the 'Magnum Opus' – but he also exposes in novel after novel the enchantments, and delusions, of imagination, especially in relation to love.

In this, too, he remained close to a dominant fashion in Romantic aesthetics which his own earlier writings had helped to promote. Scott was a key figure in the reappraisal and new dissemination of romance texts from the medieval and Renaissance periods, and, as in his appreciation of 'latitude', he recognised the freedoms romance materials offered in subject matter and style.[19] Tales retold or imagined anew in the medieval and Renaissance pasts introduced a heightened, sometimes consciously elaborate, sometimes implicitly critical, degree of decorative sensuousness to early nineteenth-century literature. Works such as Coleridge's 'Christabel' and Keats's 'The Eve of St Agnes' eroticised the medieval but also cast a cold eye on legerde-main, superstition, secrecy, and repression. When Scott turned, with *Ivanhoe*, to novels set in the more distant past and/or in more unfamiliar climes, he invited readers into more fanciful worlds, only to have them find, as Keats does at the close of 'Ode to a Nightingale', that 'The fancy cannot cheat so well / As she is famed to do, deceiving elf.' In *Kenilworth: A Romance* (1821), the dazzling pageantry of Elizabeth I's court is undermined by the pain and eventually the murder of Amy Robsart, countess of the Earl of Leicester. (Interest in Amy Robsart's story had been reactivated by James Mickle's imi-tation ballad 'Cumnor Hall' (1784), quoted at the end of *Kenilworth*: a letter of 17 November 1819 reveals that Keats planned a tragedy about Leicester.)[20] The elaborately decorated chambers in which Amy lives seem to her at first to have been 'the work of the great Magician Love' (*WN* 11:48), but they are emblematic of her fate just as Madeline's bedchamber is of hers in 'The Eve of St Agnes'. Images of the chase and kill drive the romancing of *Kenilworth*: 'shall we hunt in couples?', as Michael Lambourne asks (*WN* 11:29). The 'great Magician' is simultaneously 'love', the sinister alchemist and astrologer Alasco, the mechanists of the trap-door device by which Amy is murdered, and the 'Wizard of the North' himself.

2

'Thou hast destroyed her by means of her best affections', Anthony Forster tells Richard Varney when Amy Robsart lies dead (*WN* 11:390). Revisiting the question of 'passion' in Scott's work need not mean unearthing it in pre-viously unsuspected places; but, perhaps, following through the imaginative logic of E. M. Forster's and Virginia Woolf's comments, registering it as fra-gility, verbal falsity, inadequacy, and betrayal. In a series of essays written in the last months of her life, Laetitia Landon concentrated on the typical and atypical situations of Scott's female characters: his fondness for the situation 'of a father and daughter left dependant on each other's mutual affection'; women who fear their husbands, which 'says everything of misery that can fall to a woman's lot'.[21] Landon distinguishes shades of feeling and sugges-tion in Scott's depictions in ways which reveal how sensitively they could be read, and felt, by his contemporaries, quite independently of any instruc-tive or improving appeal to 'history'. *The Bride of Lammermoor*, she writes, 'haunted me for days and days. It is even now on my memory like a terrific dream.'[22] Brilliantly counteracting the male reader's invited choice between Rebecca and Rowena in *Ivanhoe*, she sees Rebecca's choice between Ivanhoe and Brian de Bois Guilbert as the really revealing one: 'His rich and fertile mind poured the materials of a new world into literature – but he insisted that it should take a conventional shape, and be bound by given rules.'[23] For Landon (as, in political terms, for Hazlitt), Scott's subversiveness depended on an apparently absolute adherence to convention. The emotional pressures of convention, however, are often the subject of his fiction of the 1820s, and, as in *Kenilworth*, they repeatedly reflect Scott's awareness of being caught in the web of his own magic.

In the early 1820s, Scott was writing more obsessively than ever before. He published ten novels in the years 1820–4, including his joint longest, *Peveril of the Peak*. Probably the busiest writing year of his life was 1821, with *The Pirate*, *The Fortunes of Nigel*, and *Peveril* – all 1822 – in hand. Actual and predicted sales figures peaked.[24] Imitators flourished, and historical fiction as a genre took on new life, especially in the United States.[25] Paradoxically, however, the years of Scott's greatest dominance of the literary marketplace were also the years in which his work was being, for subsequent generations, erased. Between 1818, when *The Heart of Mid-Lothian* reinvented the hero-inely heart, and 1824, when *Redgauntlet* signalled Scott's joint reclamation of his complex literary heritage and of his simplest personal fantasy, the literary world changed. Retrospectively, these seemed the years of Byron, Keats, and Shelley: concentrated, innovative, 'passionate', years. By 1820, in contrast, Scott had become established and marketable, amassing in his official ano-nymity the money to complete his architectural ambitions for Abbotsford and appearing to trade his creativity for a baronetcy. The novels of this period also become increasingly self-referential, so that as well as playing parts drawn from 'old plays' Scott's characters also reprise situations from his earlier works.

The move to *Ivanhoe*, and the novels which followed it, was a reasser-tion of Scott's 'latitude', but it also intensified his representations of the imagination under pressure. Throughout his life, he wrote analytically about the arcane, the occult, and about forbidden and disputed systems of belief, ranging from folklore and popular demonology to alchemy, divination, astrology, and the rituals of secret societies. He analysed superstition psy-chologically and socially: in *Quentin Durward*, for example, focusing on this unexpected factor in the character of Louis XI, and seeming, in his depiction of Louis's consultations with the astrologer Galeotti Martivalle, to wish to remove any suspicion that he had depicted that art with too much credulity in *Guy Mannering*. He returned repeatedly to chivalry as a code of practice and of belief: *Quentin Durward* is an extended reflection on the contradictions of courtly love, and unusual among Scott's fictions in juxtaposing the love stories of two countesses de Croye (the young heroine, Isabelle, and the middle-aged comic-grotesque, Hameline). Again, in this novel, Scott makes his young hero a reader of romances, a creature of imaginative 'enthusiasm', as in the scene in which Quentin listens to Isabelle singing, her figure 'being so partially and obscurely visible, as threw a veil of mysterious fascination over the whole' (*WN* 15:58: compare the unseen song-bird of Shelley's 'To a Sky-Lark', 1820: 'Like a high-born maiden / In a palace-tower', and the 'unseen musician' of the *Defence*).[26]

Questions of imagination, especially the 'overwrought' female imagination (the echo is from Keats's 'Ode on a Grecian Urn'), dominate *The Pirate*, the novel set in Orkney and Shetland in 1689 and indebted for much of its local detail to Scott's diary of his tour of the northern lighthouses in 1814. The close association between the 'dark heroine', Minna Troil – 'contemplative and high-minded', with a love of nature and of 'the solitary and melancholy grandeur of the scenes in which she was placed' (*WN* 12:21, 22) – and the 'extravagantly lofty' (*WN* 12:49) Ulla Troil, 'Norna of the Fitful-head', heightens the sexual tension Scott sets up between the two sisters, Minna and Brenda, the unloved son, Mordaunt Mertoun, and the pirate, Clement Cleveland. Laced with insistent, bizarre physicalities – the agricultural theorist Triptolemus Yellowley and his sister, 'Mrs Baby', Norna and her dwarf Pacolet, the bard Claude Halcro's obsessive recreations of his contact with 'the immortal John' (Dryden) – *The Pirate* is one of Scott's greatest eccentricities. Its centre, however, is entirely emotional, in that nothing is at stake except the feelings and fates of the four young lovers and the reconnection of the stories of Basil Mertoun and Ulla Troil. And although the schematic contrasts between characters – especially Minna and Brenda, 'Night and Day', tragedy and comedy, L'Allegro and Il Penseroso, the sublime and the beautiful – suggest aesthetic allegory, *The Pirate* considers love closely. Mordaunt's feelings flicker between Minna and Brenda; Minna's attraction to Cleveland prompts an extended narratorial discussion of how men and women come to be deceived in each other (*WN* 12:123–6); and Minna and Cleveland, Mordaunt and Brenda, converse. Minna Troil drew Scott into uncustomary intimacies of tone. 'Having a certain partiality for the dark Beauty' (*WN* 12:125), he analyses her feelings; and 'Reader, she was so', he asserts of her happiness, in the final paragraph (*WN* 12:390). Minna's vivid centrality in the sword-dance, 'most completely self-possessed, and in her own element' (*WN* 12:142), is charged, erotically, in ways Scott's heirs recognised and reinvented. Thomas Hardy developed the sexuality of this scene in Sergeant Troy's sword-play in *Far From the Madding Crowd* (1874); and

George Eliot's *Middlemarch* (1871–2), recasting the Troil sisters as Dorothea and Celia Brooke, carried forward Scott's enquiry into the place of female originality and passion in modern society.

As his novels progressed, Scott reinforced, not always to modern taste, their freight of literariness. In the process, however, he played another important role in the creation of the literature of his age. Contemporary literature is written into the Waverley Novels in chapter-epigraphs and numerous narratorial quotations and allusions, and in conversations between characters. Hazlitt noted Scott's habit of quoting 'almost every living author (whether illustrious or obscure) but himself'.[27] Wordsworth, Coleridge, Byron, Crabbe, and Burns are favourite points of reference; while in *Saint Ronan's Well* (published 27 December 1823; dated 1824) the heroine, Clara Mowbray, is described by others at the Well as 'the Dark Ladye' of Coleridge's ballad, and likened both to the Ancient Mariner and to 'Mat Lewis's Spectre Lady' (from 'The Gay Gold Ring', 1800) (*WN* 16:53, 54). Modern Scottish poets are particularly noted in this novel: Lady Penelope and Mr Cargill lament Scott's friend John Leyden, '[a] lamp too early quenched' (*WN* 16:205), while Clara is eager to buy '[Thomas] Campbell's new work' (*Gertrude of Wyoming*, hinting intertextually at her fate, but also recalling Scott's review of *Gertrude: WN* 16:217). The emotional climax of the novel, the confrontation between Clara and her brother John (that 'shudderingly fine scene' as Maria Edgeworth called it in a letter to Scott: *Letters* 8:142n.), is delayed by a skirmish over Burns ('honest' for Clara, 'a hobnail'd peasant' writing 'trash', according to John: *WN* 16:333). As in Jane Austen's *Persuasion* (1818) – which Scott also reviewed – sound and unsound judgements in modern literature are a constant preoccupation of its characters, and a measure of their emotional worth.

Saint Ronan's Well is Scott's only novel set in the nineteenth century (c.1809–11). In the 'Magnum Opus' introduction, he described it as an attempt 'to give an imitation of the shifting manners of our own time', after the manner of Frances Burney, Susan Ferrier, Maria Edgeworth, Jane Austen, and Charlotte Smith. This turn to 'women's' fiction and to contemporary society was unpopular with reviewers, and Scott's later comments present it as a failure. However, *Saint Ronan's Well* was innovative in its treatment of sexuality and social class. It tells the story of Francis Tyrrel, the supposedly illegitimate son who is actually the true Earl of Etherington, and his half-brother Valentine Bulmer, who has inherited the title. Seven years before the start of the novel, Tyrrel has been secretly engaged to Clara Mowbray and they have, once, given in to sexual temptation. Thinking she is marrying Tyrrel, Clara is tricked into a marriage with Bulmer instead; and although this marriage is not consummated, the play of suggestion, and Clara's mental state in the narrative present, invite readers to imagine that possibility. This is the plot as Scott wrote it, and as he tried very hard to have it published. He was persuaded, however, to obscure Clara's sexual relationship with Tyrrel, though he protested to James Ballantyne: 'You would never have quarrelled with it had the thing happened to a girl in gingham. The silk petticoat can make little difference.'[28] His original intentions are restored in the Edinburgh edition, along with overdue credit for thinking beyond the literary conventions governing female sexuality in his day. Eighteenth- and early nineteenth-century literature is strewn with seduced women, but of a lower social class. Richardson's gentry-class Clarissa is raped, and dies, a transfer of dishonour which prompted radical criticism in the 1790s.[29] Clara Mowbray is not raped, but consents; and she declines and dies years afterwards. Scott was interested in the legal complexity of Clara's situation. In Scottish law of the time she and Tyrrel are clearly married *per verba de futuro subsequente copula*, and her marriage to Bulmer, additionally, is non-binding on the grounds of gross fraud.[30] But this legal framework is, just as importantly, a means by which Scott could explore a peculiarly tainted love-triangle and its wider emotional and social effects.

The predatory atmosphere of *Saint Ronan's Well* reminds us how often Scott's novels deal explicitly with sexual threats to women (see the forced marriage of Lucy Ashton, the Torquilstone episode in *Ivanhoe*, and the pressures on the Alices of *Peveril of the Peak* and *Woodstock*) and, usually implicitly, with problems of sexual ensnarement faced by men. In the novel's early, more socially satirical chapters, the most striking portrait is that of Lady Binks, formerly Rachael Bonnyrig, 'who, during the last season, had made the company at the Well alternately admire, smile, and stare, by dancing the highest Highland fling, riding the wildest pony, laughing the loudest laugh at the broadest joke, and wearing the briefest petticoat of any nymph of Saint Ronan's' (*WN* 16:50). She has succumbed, calculatingly, to Sir Bingo and has forced him to marry her, a sour contrast to the separation of Clara and Tyrrel. Throughout the novel, men continue to be pursued – Bulmer by Lady Binks, and Tyrrel, 'this Unknown' (*WN* 16:33), by Lady Penelope Penfeather (a suggestive portrait of the over-attentive patroness).

A predatory association of a different kind serves to demonstrate the links between literary allusion and passion in Scott's work. The title-page of *Saint Ronan's Well* has an epigraph quoting Wordsworth's 'Hart-Leap Well' (from the 1800 *Lyrical Ballads*):

> 'A jolly place,' said he, 'in times of old!
> But something ails it now: the spot is curst.'

Scott asked for this 'motto' to be inserted just before he completed the novel, in a letter of November 1823 to James Ballantyne (*Letters* 8:123). Part One of 'Hart-Leap Well' describes 'Sir Walter's' ruthless pursuit of a 'poor Hart' which dies in one desperate last attempt to escape him. He builds a pleasure-house in the Hart's honour, where he brings his paramours. In Part Two, the present-day narrator records time's and nature's erasure of this monument to cruelty. At the geographical and symbolic centre of *Saint Ronan's Well*, on the road between the old and new towns, is the 'Buckstane', 'a large rough-hewn pillar of stone, said by tradition to commemorate the fall of a stag of unusual speed, size, and strength, whose flight, after having lasted through a whole summer's day, had there terminated in death, to the honour and glory of some ancient Baron of Saint Ronan's, and of his staunch hounds' (*WN* 16:76). Waiting to intercept Clara, 'Tyrrel lay on his breast near the Buckstane, his eye on the horse-road which winded down the valley, and his ear alertly awake to every sound which mingled with the passing breeze, or the ripple of the brook' (*WN* 16:80–1). Much later, the terrain of 'Hart-Leap Well' is repeated in Clara's escape from Shaws-Castle: even Clara's footprints in the wet soil recall the three hoof-marks of Wordsworth's poem (*WN* 16:356–7). Scott's transposition of Wordsworth's tale reflects his understanding of its resonance in a wider Romantic ecology, for the Hart is also the Heart, deval-ued by Sir Walter's sexual dalliance. It also fundamentally redirects what has seemed to many readers a concentratedly economic account of the swerve of wealth and patronage away from the 'Old Town' of Saint Ronan's, on its own steep slope, towards the sham elegance of the 'New Town' of the spa. Scott sets up the contrast between the two settlements in great detail, but destroys it with a pen-stroke, just as John Mowbray orders the demolition of the new town perhaps, but not clearly, because he associates it with his sister's unhappiness (*WN* 16:372).

Although it may seem overdetermined by local legend, by novelistic convention, and by a poem which haunted a new 'Sir Walter' as he built his pleasure-house, Tyrrel's wait by the Buckstane is vividly rendered and (since he is poised like a hunter) ambiguous. It is one of the emotional still-points of the novel, contrasted to the social hubbub Tyrrel has just left and to the dys-functional, strained conversation he is about to have with Clara. Reinstating feeling in Scott's works is partly a matter of registering the sudden intensity of moments like this. It also calls for a reconsideration of what we think of as 'intense' in Romantic-period writing more generally. Wordsworth claimed of *Lyrical Ballads* that 'the feeling therein developed gives importance to the action and situation, and not the action and situation to the feeling'.[31] In practice, these qualities are not easily separable. Wordsworth himself frequently occupied Scott's emotional territory, as in his 'Lament of Mary Queen of Scots on the Eve of a New Year', the poems from the two Scottish tours of 1803 and 1814, the poems on the river Yarrow 'visited' and (with lines on Scott) 'revisited', and *The White Doe of Rylstone* (1807–8, published

1815). Hemans wrote many poems directly inspired by Scott: 'Dirge of the Highland Chief in "Waverley"'; 'An Hour of Romance' (written while reading *The Talisman*), 'The Heart of Bruce in Melrose Abbey', 'A Farewell to Abbotsford' (lines presented to Scott in 1829), and 'The Funeral Day of Sir Walter Scott'. Keats echoed *The Lay of the Last Minstrel* in 'The Eve of St Agnes', and cited Scott repeatedly in the letters and poems written during his Scottish tour of 1818.[32] Scott became written into the texts of Romanticism just as he shaped an understanding of contemporary literature by quoting extensively from it in his works, setting it constantly in dialogue with his own imagined situations and characters. In all the different ways this chapter has explored, Scott was at the heart of Romantic aesthetics.

CHAPTER NINE

Monarchy and the Middle-Period Novels

Tara Ghoshal Wallace

After a mortifying imprisonment and a rough Highland rescue, Edward Waverley arrives in Edinburgh weary, dazed, and unsure of his future. He is met by Fergus Mac-Ivor, who bears him off to 'meet a friend whom you little think of, who has been frequent in his enquiries after you'. That friend, of course, is Charles Edward, who forestalls Fergus's introduction, declaring: 'no master of ceremonies is necessary to present a Waverley to a Stuart'. It is an iconic encounter, displaying in full the Stuart charm and its effects: within moments, 'Waverley, kneeling to Charles Edward, devoted his heart and sword to the vindication of his rights' (*WN* 1:205, 206). This is the kind of scene to which readers point when asserting Walter Scott's 'enthusiasm for the Stuart family', his fascination with 'the romantic House of Stewart', his 'admiration for the Stuart monarchy', and his sympathy 'born out of the seductiveness of Stuart charisma'.[1] At the same time, however, critics recognise that Scott sees beyond the Stuart allure to the flaws that resulted in multiple failed monarchies. Scott's Stuart royals manifest childish irresponsibility (Charles II in *Woodstock* and James VI and I in *Fortunes of Nigel*) or a narcissistic obsession with personal needs (Mary in *The Abbot*) that puts their subjects at risk.[2] As he constructed these multivalent Stuart figures, Scott would surely have been mindful of failed or troubled monarchies in his own time, which had seen the executions of Louis XVI and Marie Antoinette, the madness of George III, and the scandalous 1821 trial, for adultery, of George IV's wife Caroline. His representations of Stuart monarchs gesture, therefore, not only toward his own novelistic history, but also toward the state of the historical context within which he wrote.

On 21 November 1558, in her accession speech at Hatfield, Elizabeth I articulated her doctrine of the prince's two bodies, 'one body naturally considered' and another 'body politic to govern'. Thirty years later, in the famous Armada speech at Tilbury, she exultantly reiterated her double identity: 'I know I have the body but of a weak and feeble woman, but I have the heart and stomach of a king and a king of England too.'[3] She thus claimed for herself an integrated duality which allows a monarch seamlessly to merge mortal and spiritual selves, two genders, as well as self and nation. As Ernst Kantorowicz puts it, the 'composite' of ruler and realm was 'transferred from "head and members" to the head alone [. . .] was reduced to the king alone, that is, to his "two bodies"'.[4] The Stuart monarchs who succeeded Elizabeth furthered the ideology of incorporation. James VI and I, in his first speech to Parliament in 1603, deployed the marriage metaphor to assert his supremacy: 'I am the husband, and all the whole island is my lawful wife; I am the head, and it is my body.'[5] Charles I, on 21 January 1649, invoked both theological and legal authority when rejecting the right of the House of Commons to pass judgement on him, specifically citing the incorporation of judicial and royal power, so that 'no learned lawyer will affirm that an impeachment can lie against the King, they all going in his name'.[6] And in 1659, the Duke of Newcastle reminded Charles II: 'Monarchy is the Government In cheefe of the whole body Politick, In all its partes, & Capaseties by one person only So that if eyther the whole Body Poleticke bee under Any pretennce goverened in cheef by more then one severally Itt is no monarchy.'[7] In Scott's novels, Stuart monarchs make visible the strains imposed by this ideology, and fail, ultimately, to integrate (or, conversely, to separate effectively) their mortal, personality-ridden selves and the public, infallible self crucial to effective royal rule.

Scott's Stuarts articulate with mordant humour the dangerous slippage between the monarch's two bodies. In *The Abbot*, when Mary bestows her purse on her page Roland Græme she assures the Protestant chaplain at Lochleven that 'it contains only these two or three gold testoons, a coin which, though bearing my own poor features, I have ever found more active against me than on my side, just as my subjects take arms against me, with my own name for their summons and signal' (*WN* 10:238). This resonant remark reveals how carefully Scott registers the implications and effects of the monarch's dual identity. As simulacra for royal power, the coins, disjoined from the physical body they represent, can be deployed not only against the authority claimed by the Queen's person, but can also challenge the very idea of a composite royal identity. Indeed, the ideology itself enables Mary's enemies to construct a dichotomy to legitimate their opposition. If the body politic can be separated from the material body, then deposing Mary cannot be considered rebellion against royal authority, especially if that authority can be transferred to other material assets bearing the Queen's imprint – coins, or her child James. Separating the temporal and political bodies of Mary, the Regent, Moray, and his supporters move to vest (or reinvest) royal power in coins and offspring, which can in turn be deployed against the original form. The division of body and legitimacy establishes a state in which, as Doctor Lundin sarcastically notes, there are 'two sovereigns in the land, a regnant and a claimant – that is enough of one good thing [. . .] so if we lack government, it is not for want of governors' (*WN* 10:243). Such fragmentation culminates in the battle of Langside, as the narrative voice sardonically observes: '"God and the Queen!" resounded from the one party; "God and the King!" thundered from the other, while, in the name of their sovereign, fellow subjects shed each other's blood' (*WN* 10:363).

In *Peveril of the Peak* (1822) Scott returns to the darkly absurd ramifications of the two-bodies ideology. When Sir Geoffrey is charged with involvement in the Popish Plot, Charles II laments his own powerlessness to intervene: 'I can scarce escape suspicion of the Plot myself, though the principal object of it is to take away my own life' (*WN* 14:328). In case the reader misses the risible but real threat to which Charles alludes, Scott provides a dialogue that demonstrates how deeply the illogic of the dichotomy has taken root among the followers of Titus Oates. Inflamed by the acquittal of the Peverils, the mob mutter their suspicions about the King:

> 'It is the device of the Papist whore of Portsmouth,' said one.
> 'Of Old Rowley himself,' says another.
> 'If he could be murdered by himself, why hang those that would hinder it?' said a fourth.
> 'He should be tried,' said another, 'for conspiring his own death, and hanged *in terrorem.*' (*WN* 14:429)

Interestingly, in the fictional plot against Charles II, Scott inverts the historical rationales invoked to incarcerate Mary and execute Charles I in the name of royal authority. When Buckingham conspires with Christian to stage a palace coup which would overthrow Charles II and install Buckingham as 'Lord Lieutenant of the Kingdom', the Duke insists on the sanctity of Charles's person even while he denies the legitimacy of the King's body politic. Where the London mob would kill the person in the name of the Crown, Buckingham insists on protecting 'Rowley's person' while moving against the King (*WN* 14:448–9). Like his father and his great-grandmother, Charles II becomes a victim of an ideology originally constructed to consolidate and assert royal power.

Scott's novels move beyond the monarch's personal danger to the more complex political nuances of the ideology that incorporates king and nation. Much of the first volume of *Peveril* engages with the consequences attendant upon Charles the king-in-exile evolving into Charles the king. The refrain of Charles's ingratitude to loyalists is taken up by both the Countess of Derby and Sir Geoffrey. The Countess, admonishing Lady Peveril to 'Put not your faith in princes', recounts what she considers Charles's betrayal of the memory of her husband, executed in his cause (*WN* 14:54). Sir Geoffrey dismisses the Countess's reluctance to draw him into her conflict with the King because 'an his Majesty will grant warrants against his best friends, he must look to have them resisted' (*WN* 14.71). Neither acknowledges that Charles now embodies legal authority in the land, and that the embodiment works mutually: if the King stands for law, he must also take a stand against those who flout the law, no matter how loyal they had been during the Civil Wars. Charles's determination to merge his former exiled, supplicant body with the royal body politic strikes the old Cavaliers as the basest kind of disloyalty. By clinging to an outdated relationship with the man and asserting proprietary rights over the King's policies, they deny, albeit unconsciously, the ideology of royal power for which they had fought.[8]

Defying Charles's warrant against the Countess of Derby, Sir Geoffrey gathers an armed cavalcade to escort her safely out of reach. When his park-keeper Lance Outram, though cheerfully obedient to his master's call, wonders why, after twenty years of 'wishing for the King – and praying for the King – and fighting for the King – and dying for the King' they should immediately 'get into harness to resist his warrant', the steward Whitaker berates him for not understanding that during the Civil War, 'we fought for the King's person against his warrant' because the Parliamentary forces had made the 'proclamations, and so forth, always [. . .] in the name of the King and Parliament' (*WN* 14:72). The dizzying twists of such reasoning lie beyond Lance's comprehension, but he stands ready to engage in further hostilities against the Puritans who seem to have staked a claim on a piece of the monarchy. So quickly do barely contained hostilities break out in Restoration England that the Popish Plot serves as both the cause and symptom of an unstable realm. The Earl of Derby, echoing Dryden's *Absalom and Achitophel* (frequently invoked in *Peveril*), tells Julian Peveril that 'Old England, who takes a frolicsome brain-fever once every two or three years [. . .] is now gone stark staring mad on the subject of a real or supposed Popish Plot [....] and is as furiously unmanageable as in the year 1642' (*WN* 14:157). Amid an engulfing political agitation Julian finds that 'a man's life may depend on the society in which he travels' (*WN* 14:221). The Popish Plot, in challenging the coherence of the royal body, has led to instability and danger everywhere in England.

Like *Peveril*, *The Abbot* notes the perils of journeying through a realm fractured by the separation of monarch and royal authority. Scott points again to the violence lurking just under a fragile and dubious peace brought about by suppressing rather than incorporating opposition forces. Roland's first moments in Edinburgh demonstrate the volatility that abruptly dissipates the façade of prosperous urban bustle, when he becomes embroiled in a street fight between Leslies and Seytons. The brawl, as much as the battle at Langside and the dangers of travel through 'this unhappy and divided realm', belies the Reverend Henderson's lecture to Roland about the peace and unity achieved by separating Mary from her crown (*WN* 10:231–4).

Interestingly, the violent outburst in the opening pages of *The Fortunes of Nigel* (1822) seems to be entirely apolitical. Rather, Scott ascribes these frays to class divisions between aggressive apprentices and their targeted customers. Like the Edinburgh magistrates in *The Abbot* who eventually disperse the feuding Leslies and Seytons, civil authority in London exerts only tenuous control over a turbulent populace. The London in which James holds court is so dangerous that Heriot must travel with armed guards when he goes to see the King, 'for such was the state of the police of the metropolis, that men were often assaulted in the public street for the sake of revenge or of plunder' (*WN* 13:61). Thus, Dalgarno's boast to Nigel that unlike in Edinburgh, 'Here, sir, no brawling in the street is permitted' (*WN* 13:136) takes on the same ironic colouring as Henderson's characterisation of peaceful Scotland under Moray. Indeed, Dalgarno's fiction about peaceable London is immediately contradicted by the duel between the blustering Captain Colepepper and the irate Citizen (*WN* 13:146–7).

Although Scott articulates in *Nigel* no direct connection between urban violence and a splintered royal authority, he begins the novel with a reference to the gap between an integrated royal body and a united polity. Even though the division between Scotland and England has been 'happily terminated by the succession of the pacific James I', the King's failure to mitigate 'the mutual hatred of two nations [. . .] spreading from the highest to the lowest classes, as it occasioned debates in council and parliament, factions in the court, and duels among the gentry, was no less productive of riots and brawls amongst those of the lower orders' (*WN* 13:19–20). In other words, the union of two kingdoms in one king's body has not effected a cohesive body politic. Mindful of rivalries and grievances between his English and Scottish subjects, the historical James VI and I attempted to establish a formal union of the two nations, in part by constructing an analogy between his physical body and the island he ruled. Writing to the House of Commons in May 1604, he urged them 'to procure the prosperity and increase of greatness to me and mine, you and yours, and by the away-taking of that partition wall which already, by God's providence, in my blood is rent asunder, to establish my throne, and your body politic, in a perpetual and flourishing peace'.[9] The historical James failed to bring about this union. Scott's representation indirectly but unmistakably attributes this failure to the fissures in James's own character and his inability to fashion a coherent centre of power and authority in the body of the monarch.

No one claims that James is one of the Stuart monarchs about whom Scott harboured romantic illusions. Critics cite Scott's stated animosity toward James and his jaundiced view of the Jacobean court.[10] At the same time, they recognise in Scott's portrait a triumph of complex characterisation; Scott's James remains a vibrant figure who compels readers' engagement even as he decisively fails to earn their respect.[11] In James, Scott finds the perfect vehicle to explore the unstable hybridity of the King's two bodies, and the consequences when the King fails to perform the integrated self required by ideology. The reader's very first glimpse of James makes explicit the duality which undermines the King's authority. Among the dichotomies present in the King's chamber are valuable artefacts made unattractive 'from the manner in which they were presented to the eye', as well as a mixture of scholarly folios, 'light books of jest and ribaldry', speeches to Parliament, notes regarding international diplomacy, and 'a list of the names of the King's hounds' (WN 13:66). The contradictions visible in accoutrements, the narrator tells us in a long analytical paragraph, are 'mere outward types of those which existed in the royal character, rendering it a subject of doubt amongst his contemporaries, and bequeathing it as a problem to future historians' (WN 13:66).

In Scott's novel, these doubts and problems are connected with James's disconcerting habit of laying bare the machinery for staging royal power. Stephen Greenblatt, extending Kantorowicz's thesis about the King's two bodies, points out that power becomes 'manifested in those signs of secular worship – bowing, kneeling, kissing of rings – that European rulers increasingly insist upon': 'kingship always involves fictions, theatricalism, and the mystification of power'.[12] In Nigel, James's method of constructing and enforcing signs of power falls ludicrously short of mystification. For example, Richie Moniplies describes what seems like a burlesque of ritualised respect when he recounts the right way to supplicate the King – 'I suld have held up my hand to my brow, as if the grandeur of the King and his horse-graith thegither had casten the glaiks in my een' (WN 13:47) – but James provides his own unconscious parody as he coaches Heriot on how to 'deliver a Supplication, as it suld be done in the face of Majesty', from shading the eyes to kneeling 'as if ye would kiss the hem of our garment', to placing the petition 'reverentially in our open palm' (WN 13:71). After he waxes ridiculously ecstatic over the recovery of his gems, James has to resort to asserting his body politic, admonishing Richie: 'Take heed, sir, you are not to laugh at us – we are your anointed Sovereign' (WN 13:349–50). A monarch who must provide subjects with detailed instructions on performing 'signs of secular worship' can hardly advance the mystification that underpins his power.[13]

Through much of the novel, James remains 'the perplexed monarch, whose ideas of justice, expedience, and convenience, became on such occasions strangely embroiled' (WN 13:73). Too poor to honour his debt, too timid to defy Buckingham's machinations to appropriate Nigel's property, James has to be prodded to assert royal power on Nigel's behalf. Interestingly, when Lord Huntinglen urges him to exert his authority, James's language enacts a shift from simulacrum to real, from 'I will do what I will, and what I aught, like a free king', to 'I am a free King – will do what I will and what

I should' (WN 13:114, emphasis added). Driven to act like a king, James can, at least momentarily, become one. But even here, his vacillations, his 'piteous state of uncertainty', and his fear that 'Steenie [Buckingham] and Baby Charles' will interrupt his moment of self-assertion, attest to the needy, anxious man who cannot overcome his own nature in order to inhabit an integrated kingly body (WN 13:115). James's awkwardness in performing majesty – his inability 'to veil over or conceal his own foibles' – can work in his favour (WN 13:109); but he is repeatedly compromised by scenes in which the ignoble man attempts to assume royal dignity, as when he encounters Nigel at Greenwich: 'The poor King was frightened at once and angry, desirous of securing his safety, and at the same time ashamed to compromise his dignity; so that [. . .] he kept making at his horse, and repeating, "We are a free King – man – we are a free King – we will not be controlled by a subject. – In the name of God, what keeps Steenie?"' (WN 13:305–6). James's language may reach for regal identity, but the troubled man always breaks through the performance.

Unlike James, Scott's Queen Mary seems to glory in her gift for performing both monarch and woman, while simultaneously foregrounding the tension between the two entities by consciously and visibly inscribing the strain on her own body. Mary's first appearance testifies to the multiple self-presentations of a monarch Judith Wilt calls one of Christendom's 'most enigmatic figures'.[14] The scene begins as a duel of sarcastic barbs between Mary and Margaret Douglas, but abruptly changes in tone as Mary demonstrates her control over her dual persona, 'suddenly changing her manner from the smooth ironical affectation of mildness to an accent of austere command' and calling upon 'the full majesty of her rank' (WN 10:189). Only moments later, she struggles out of 'a strong fit of hysterical affection' to proclaim 'it is over – and I am Mary Stuart once more' and to stand 'like the inspired image of a Grecian prophetess, in a mood which partook at once of sorrow and pride, of smiles and of tears' (WN 10:191). This is the kind of passage that, unsurprisingly, provokes readers to declare that Scott's 'idealization of Mary Stuart was a romantic dream that superseded his historian's scepticism and sense', and to assert that 'Scott had that romantic devotion to Mary Queen of Scots which few of his countrymen can escape'.[15] Such evaluations, however, overlook passages which call attention to Mary's very unromantic performativity. For example, the admiring description of the Grecian prophetess is followed by a reminder of Mary's theatricality; as she mourns the beauty 'destroyed by sorrow and by fear', 'she again let her slender fingers stray through the wilderness of the beautiful tresses which veiled her kingly neck and swelling bosom, as if, in her agony of mind, she had not altogether lost the consciousness of her unrivalled charms' (WN 10:191). Scott packs into this vignette the layers of manipulation and effect that constitute the problematics of her character. Even as it reveals how Mary deliberately draws attention to the majestic and the sexual duality in her body, the narrative voice succumbs to her seductive arts. Performance and artifice in this case become part of the allure: as Greenblatt argues, 'one of the highest achievements of power is to impose fictions upon the world and one of its supreme pleasures is to enforce the acceptance of fictions that are known to be fictions'.[16]

Mary's performance and its effects become less attractive later in the novel. Scott puts in the mouth of the smitten George Douglas a parody of his own textual capitulation to Mary's charms: 'I had planned the escape of the most beautiful, the most persecuted of women [. . .] the most injured of queens [. . .] the most lovely of women' (WN 10:282). George's hyperbolic language effectively undermines the rapturous endorsement of the earlier narrative voice, and when Mary responds to Margaret Douglas's passionate accusation that she has lured the impressionable young man to folly, her complacency – 'The Queen cast a not ungratified glance on a large mirror, which [. . .] reflected her beautiful face and person' (WN 10:284) – signals narrative disillusionment. The Queen's systematic deployment of her sexualised body to attract followers is most evident when she displays herself to the gathered forces at Niddrie. While 'the unadorned beauties of the lovely woman' and her subsequent performance of modest withdrawal captivates the troops, the reader is privy to her disingenuous mortification: 'Mary flung herself into the nearest seat, and still blushing, yet half smiling, exclaimed, "Ma mignonne, what will they think of me! – to shew myself to them with my bare feet hastily thrust into the slippers – only this loose mantle about me – my hair loose on my shoulders – my arms and neck so bare"' (WN 10:347). This rather unseemly catalogue of the feminine body parts she has exposed serves to highlight her performativity when she subsequently appears 'before her assembled nobles in such attire as became, though it could not enhance, her natural dignity' (WN 10:347). Unlike James, Mary smoothly changes her behaviour from unbridled exuberance to 'winning courtesy' as the occasion demands (WN 10:347). While Mary skilfully enacts the duality recommended by James Melville, who claims to have counselled her to 'bend up her spirit by a princely and womanly behaviour'[17] the reader nevertheless registers the artifice behind both spontaneity and dignity.

Moreover, The Abbot provides a darker view of Mary's narcissism. As she dwells on her grievances, she abrogates her royal responsibilities. Certainly, the Queen evokes sympathy when she reminds Roland that she has been manipulated by others 'since I was stretched an orphan child in my very cradle, while contending nobles strove which should rule in the name of the unconscious innocent' (WN 10:293), but even here her language reflects her tendency to depict herself as perpetual victim. The final chapters of the novel emphasise Mary's need to construe all tragedies as part of her own story. Gazing on the dying George Douglas, Mary places herself in the role of chief sufferer: 'thus has it been with all who loved Mary Stuart! [. . .] they looked on the wretched Mary, and to have loved her was crime enough to deserve early death!' (*WN* 10:366). Mary repudiates the Abbot Ambrosius's reproach that she is 'too much occupied with her own sorrows to give one thought to ours', but the reader sides with Ambrosius, especially when Mary tells Roland: 'I would not again undergo what I felt' when the Seytons and Hamiltons died at Langside (*WN* 10:368).[18] The Mary represented in *The Abbot* consistently perceives herself as the romantic heroine of a tragic tale; her theatrical self-presentation as persecuted Queen and victimised woman destablises Scott's supposedly romanticised portrayal.[19]

Mary performs for targeted audiences. Roland, Margaret Douglas, her troops, her rebel nobles, all become audiences for her theatricalised selves. Her tactics are congruent with a dictum laid down by James in his directions to his son Henry: 'a King is as one set on a stage, whose smallest actions and gestures all the people gazinglie doe beholde: and therefore although a King be neuer so præcise in the discharging of his office, the people, who seeth but the outward part, will euer judge of the substance by the circumstances'.[20] Charles II, in *Peveril*, makes explicit the strategic need for royal theatrics when he cuts short a dispute with Buckingham because 'we must not forget (as we have nearly done,) that we have an audience to witness this scene, and should walk the stage with dignity' (*WN* 14:326).

In the morally askew world of the Restoration court, public perception matters so much that Buckingham can swallow the 'insult' when Charles rejects his proffered suit to Princess Anne 'because I thought no one knew it', but must seek vengeance when the repulse becomes known (*WN* 14:445). Power and self-respect reside in reputation more than in deeds, in credible fiction rather than in reality. The Charles II of *Peveril* has fully internalised Newcastle's directive 'to be courteous and civil to everybody [. . .] the putting off of your hat and making a leg pleases more than reward or preservation'.[21] Despite narrative condemnation of his lax morality, his cowardice, and his indolence (all of which are pointed out at various points in the text), Charles retains his undisputed claim as the most charismatic, and perhaps the most skilful performer among Stuart monarchs. In *Woodstock*, Scott considers Charles's apprenticeship as royal actor. Here, in his final portrait of a reigning Stuart monarch, Scott produces a narrative about the making of the King's two bodies, imagining how Charles II evolves into the consummate performer and charismatic monarch readers have encountered in *Peveril of the Peak*. *Woodstock* presents a Charles who, despite his many limitations and weaknesses, learns to reconcile, or at least to manipulate, the desires of his private and public selves. In rewriting Charles, Scott provides a palimpsest that retains traces of earlier representations of Stuart monarchs and those who engage with them; Charles II's intertextual body in *Woodstock* contains (in both senses of the word) the performative world constructed by Stuarts.

Charles enters *Woodstock* as a decidedly dichotomous self, his dangerously recognisable body disguised first as a gypsy woman and then as the Scottish page Louis Kerneguy. Unlike Henry Seyton in *The Abbot*, Charles in female guise is both inept and intimidating: Alice Lee instantly places the gypsy among the 'Denaturalised women [who] had as usual followed the camps of both armies during the Civil War', noting that her clothes 'were indifferently adjusted and put on as if they did not belong to the person by whom they were worn', and that she walks 'with prodigious long unwomanly strides'. Fully conscious of his strange appearance, Charles seeks to deflect her suspicious hostility by claiming an Otherness defined by race rather than gender, enjoining Alice to 'Look on my swarthy brow; England breeds none such' (*WN* 19:198–200). Discommoded and disempowered by this doubly alien body, Charles quickly abandons it, telling Albert Lee he had been 'a libel on womanhood' (*WN* 19:229). In his first appearance as Kerneguy, Charles appears equally unnatural and cartoonish, a parodic Scottish churl (*WN* 19:213–14). This time, however, Charles succeeds in modifying rather than discarding a borrowed identity and transforms himself overnight into a well-spoken and charming guest. The transition is simultaneously startling and credible, so smoothly calibrated that the re-formed Kerneguy seems to have assimilated the rough youth rather than become a wholly different self. Charles, in other words, has learned to incorporate multiple identities and to pitch his performance according to his audience.[22]

At Woodstock, Charles is caught between the desires of the 'body naturally considered' and 'the body politic to govern', between the lustful man determined to seduce Alice and the sovereign charged with shielding his subjects from harm. In *Peveril*, the struggle is brief and comic, as the King encounters insuperable impediments to possessing Alice Bridgenorth; confounded by Buckingham's rivalry, Julian's protective presence, and Alice's spirited resolution, he abandons the attempt, for reasons more social than moral. In the end, he merely regrets that 'so much beauty should be wedded to so many shrewish suspicions' and exits the game (*WN* 14:331–2). When Scott rewrites this scene in *Woodstock*, he makes it a conflict as fraught as the political contest between Cromwell and Charles, converting it into a crucial rite of passage, during which Charles experiments with multiple combinations of the King's two bodies.

Charles's desire for Alice ensnares him in a series of specious arguments with himself, rationales which in *Peveril* are assigned to the hypocritical Christian and the repulsive bawd Chiffinch. Christian, justifying his plan to prostitute Alice Bridgenorth's body, argues: 'Will men say I have ruined her, when I shall have raised her to the dazzling height of the Duchess of

Portsmouth, and perhaps made her mother to a long line of princes?' (*WN* 14:303). In *Woodstock*, Charles embraces this 'profligate logic', convincing himself that the Lees would be honoured to have royal blood flowing in their bastard heirs (*WN* 19.252). When the 'private' self embodied in Kerneguy fails to seduce Alice, Charles enlists his public body to aid his private desire, in the mistaken assumption that no loyal (and ambitious) maiden can resist a monarch's importunities. In his determination to possess Alice, Charles deploys his whole arsenal of weapons of seduction, from majesty to bribery to self-pity. But he has made a fatal miscalculation: once confronted by the person of the King, Alice occludes the private, desiring body of the man. She insists on kneeling and kissing his hand. She remains standing in his presence, although 'the lover entreats – the King commands you' to sit, because, she argues, 'the King [. . .] cannot abrogate the subject's duty, even by express command'. Like Alice Bridgenorth in *Peveril*, she strategically places herself under Charles's protection, guarding herself from the man by empowering the King, confidently declaring, 'What can I fear from the King of Britain [. . .]?' (*WN* 19:285–6).

But Alice Lee has more to accomplish than her own safety. Taking on the role of Ambrosius in *The Abbot*, of Heriot and Huntinglen in *Nigel*, and of the Duke of Ormond in *Peveril*, she has to teach Charles how to play his own kingly role. If her representations in the seduction scene show him that he has 'placed his own interests more in collision with the gratification of his present passion than he had supposed' (*WN* 19.288), her subsequent intervention to prevent his duel with Everard finally brings home to him the duties of a sovereign. Charles accepts Everard's challenge after his inner debate between 'Wisdom' and 'passionate Folly' (*WN* 19:295) ends in yet another capitulation to reputation; he frets more about the sarcastic barbs of Villiers and Wilmot than about endangering a life which others have died to save. Deliberately rejecting his political identity, Charles opts to inhabit the body of a private gentleman who would be shamed by refusing a challenge. Whereas Elizabeth had risked her life for a national cause – 'to lay down for my God and for my kingdom and for my people mine honor and my blood even in the dust'[23] – Charles chooses to venture his body and the future of the monarchy for the sake of private honour. When the duel is interrupted, Charles once again splits his two identities: he rebuffs the Reverend Rochecliffe by asserting his position as Head of the Church of England and he appeals to Alice as a man who would find it 'too shameful' to retreat from a challenge (*WN* 19:307–9). But when Alice, determined at all cost to protect the royal body, incurs Everard's misapprehension and anger, Charles at last embraces fully the duality of the King's bodies. Man and Sovereign collude to save Alice's happiness and test Everard's principles, achieving 'such complete self-possession as indeed became a prince' (*WN* 19:312).[24] The results vindicate Charles's decision to reveal his identity: re-enacting Waverley's response to Charles Edward, Everard kisses the royal hand and vows to 'rescue your person [. . .] with the purchase of my own' (WN 19:315). Charles, incorporating both the gentleman and the monarch, evokes sentimentality even in the level-headed nationalist Everard Markham.

It is this integrated King's body that arrives in London on 29 May 1660 'over roads strewn with flowers', pausing 'in kindness perhaps as well as policy' to acknowledge old friends. The final vignette, when Charles reverently seeks Sir Henry's blessing and the old Cavalier dies after 'one exhilarating flash' (WN 19:417), indeed seems to press Woodstock towards what Nicola J. Watson calls 'an emergent genre of national romance'.[25] But behind this moving moment lurks the memory of Charles's encounter with Major Coleby in Peveril. Coleby, like Sir Henry, dies moments after Charles notices this forgotten old royalist, leaving his careless monarch 'dreadfully shocked' but still as 'exceedingly perplexed' (WN 19:412–13) as his grandfather about how to exert his royal authority to help other supporters in distress. The ideal embodiment that Charles II seems to have attained at the end of Woodstock is always marked by the traces of old canvases and manuscripts, which haunt this royal body as persistently as the royalist 'ghosts' haunt the Parliamentary Commissioners attempting to reconfigure the royal property at Woodstock.

Scott refused to provide a synthesis for the vexed dialectics surrounding Stuart monarchs, insisting instead on their conflicted identities, which occupy multiple and contested positions not available to the tidy impulses of romantic readings. Mary Stuart's self-proclaimed (and performative) split between queenly dignity and womanly passions in The Abbot remains unresolved, as does James VI and I's unkingly timidity and his lofty notions of royal prerogatives in The Fortunes of Nigel. The figure of Charles II, in Peveril of the Peak and Woodstock, gestures towards both his biographical and literary ancestors: consummate performer, amoral rogue, gracious sovereign, penitent sinner, Scott's Charles II is both palimpsest and pentimento.

CHAPTER TEN

Scott and Political Economy

Alexander Dick

Few critics today would agree with Thomas Carlyle that Walter Scott's outlook was entirely 'economical', though some might concur with Walter Bagehot that the Waverley Novels 'contain a good deal of political economy of a certain sort'.[1] Scott was born and raised among Edinburgh's burgeoning professional class, sympathetic to tenets of Adam Smith and his followers. But Scott was also a landowner who agreed with Burke, Wordsworth, and other Tories that unrestrained capitalism harmed Britain's agricultural heritage and folk cultures. Britain had thrived since 1688 because the commercial middle class did not abandon their respect for landed property, aristocratic privilege, and manly virtue. Critical consensus has it that by staging imaginary encounters between commerce and romance Scott's novels helped to inculcate this Toryism further into the nineteenth century.[2]

But this consensus assumes that political economy was a discrete coherent discipline with widely known, incontrovertible principles and a clear commitment to commercial expansion and middle-class hegemony. In fact, the period between 1802 and 1832 was less the 'coming of age of political economy' than a tortured adolescence.[3] There was little, if any, agreement about where value came from, how money works, or how far commerce should grow. Should government encourage free trade or protect domestic agriculture? How much control should the state exert over finance, employment, and wages? Was population growing or falling? When was the right time to marry, have children, leave home, and die? The Waverley Novels are not entirely 'economical'; nor was Scott prima facie a political economist. Nevertheless, there is much to be learned about the historical and, indeed, ongoing importance of Scott's writing when it is read in an economic context.

The Progress of Society

Scott's interest in political economy came in many respects from a broader interest in history and, in particular, the relations between rank, work, and education that, in Scottish Enlightenment philosophy, was understood to be the key to social progress. The influence of the Scottish Enlightenment on the Waverley Novels was profound, and has been the subject of extensive discussion.[4] Scott's family was connected socially with the circle of 'moderate intellectuals' surrounding Adam Ferguson, then Chancellor of Edinburgh University. Scott was also a member of the Speculative Society, one of the many academic clubs in Edinburgh, where he read papers before William Robertson and Dugald Stewart.[5] As a student, Scott attended Stewart's lectures 'on Politics Proper, or the theory of Government', part of a general course, published as *Outlines of Moral Philosophy* in 1793, which put the issues of rank, property, and trade alongside theories of perception, abstraction, sympathy, ethics, and rights. With expertise across the fields of the arts curricula, the Scottish academicians trained members of the Scottish kirk, bar, and civil service, under separate jurisdiction from England under the terms of the 1707 Union.[6] The heart of their curriculum was the study of the relation between the Church, the State, and the Public, sometimes called 'philosophical history'. From accounts of eminent world leaders, the historians derived general principles of governance and management that also extended into aesthetics, literature, and rhetoric.

Scott later reread many of his teachers' works. This rereading is especially evident in the chapter on 'The Progress of Civilization in Society' that opens the second series of Scott's *Tales of a Grandfather*, the history of Scotland he wrote for his grandson, published between 1828 and 1831. Like Ferguson's *History of Civil Society*, Scott's 'Progress' encompasses the development of human government from hunter-gatherer groups to the domestication of animals to the establishment of feudalism and the modern state. Scott's account of the transformation of society was meant to justify the unification of the Scottish and English states between the accession of James VI and the Act of Union, the events that bookend the second series of *Tales of a Grandfather*. But most of the opening chapter is devoted to what would have been readily identifiable, in 1828 (when Scott wrote it), as political economy: the division of labour, the development of barter, exchange, coinage, and money, the growth of trade, and the separation of society into professions and classes (*MPW* 23:226–9).

Towards the end of the chapter Scott recounts the inventions of writing and printing. It is a rare self-reflexive moment in the *Tales*. With the discovery of writing, Scott notes, 'a barrier is fixed against those violent changes so apt to take place in the early stages of society, by which all the fruits of knowledge are frequently destroyed' (*MPW* 23:230–1). Writing is a form of preservation. The invention of printing, by contrast, means accessibility and dissemination: 'the admirable invention of printing enables the artist to make a thousand copies from the original manuscript, by having them stamped upon paper, in far less time and with less expense than it would cost to make half a dozen such copies with the pen' (*MPW* 23:232). Scott's main example of the success of print is the Bible which, 'became so numerous, that every one above the most wretched poverty could at a cheap price, possess himself of a copy of the blessed rule of life', and thus led to the 'happy Reformation of the Christian Church'. Whereas most of the 'Progress' emphasised the way a healthy commercial state requires social inequality, Scott's account of the growth of print reveals a more liberal perspective:

> the printing-press is a contrivance which empowers any one individual to address his whole fellow-subjects on any topic which he thinks important, and which enables a whole nation to listen to the voice of such individual, however obscure he may be, with the same ease, and greater certainty of understanding what he says than if a chief of Indians were haranguing the tribe at his council-fire. Nor is the important difference to be forgotten that the orator can only speak to the persons present, while the author of a book addresses himself not only to the race now in existence, but to all succeeding generations, while his work shall be held in estimation. (*MPW* 23:233–4)

This passage points to a significant ambiguity in Scott's economic history. On the one hand, Scott underlines the importance of property and rank as the stabilising force of commerce. On the other, Scott claims that the invention of money and the acquisition of wealth by those with the right combination of tenacity and know-how had led to the emergence of a distinct intellectual class who could rival the power of the aristocracy. Why would Scott do this?

The answer lies in the story of how political economy disentangled itself from Scottish moral philosophy and the controversies about education, property, and governance that ensued. The first and most important writer to downplay significantly the involvement of the state in economic affairs was Adam Smith. Smith's argument in his *Enquiry into the Nature and Causes of the Wealth of Nations* that the division of labour produced forms of understanding and civility independent of the hierarchical state was not his only point, but it certainly became the most controversial. Ferguson argued that the accessibility of print would encourage intellectual specialisation and accelerate social alienation. Stewart by contrast taught that the expansion of print since the Reformation had encouraged philosophers to overlook their differences in languages and fields and thus fostered interest in the 'species in general' within the 'republic of letters'.[7] The controversy surrounding this market-driven republic of print came to a head again during the Revolution debates. Edmund Burke, an ardent follower of Smith, claimed that the resentment of an ungoverned and disenfranchised public intellectual class had, like paper money unbacked by specie, spread the democratic ideals that caused the French Revolution. Economic liberty would only be socially cohesive if it were accompanied by a 'love of country' including the tastes and ideals of its anointed, and propertied, leaders. Thomas Paine insisted, again *pace* Smith, that only the complete separation of the economic and political spheres and the enfranchisement of a free press would produce a truly enlightened education system.[8] These disputes continued to be part of the broader economic conversation through the diverging economic mandates of the *Edinburgh* and *Quarterly* reviews, in both of which Scott was involved.[9]

The turning point came with the debate over the Corn Laws.[10] Through the war, English farmers had enjoyed high prices, healthy rents, and easy credit. With the anticipated end of hostilities and banner harvests in 1813 and 1814, the price of corn began to fall. Defenders of price controls urged that a sudden drop in the price of corn would devastate the agricultural sector and, in turn, the village bankers who had supported them. Others urged Parliament to import cheaper European corn, which would reduce prices and take considerable pressure off the correspondingly high wages of manufacture and trade. The protectionists won: in March 1815, Parliament passed the Corn Law. Unfortunately for the farmers, an abysmal harvest produced massive shortages, bankruptcies in the financial sector, and eventually riots in the streets.

The 'distresses', as they were called, spurred a profound change in the character of economic discourse. Economic writers had hitherto argued that since the health of the economy was based on the productivity of land for which farmers and statesmen alike were responsible, the blame for fluctuating prices should be placed on traders and consumers. After 1815, many economists argued that this model did not take into account either changes in the value of land over time or the effects on prices of large government programmes like the parish poor laws. Rents, wages, and profits, they insisted, were all determined by natural forces that the state could forestall but never control. This determinism was enshrined in David Ricardo's *Principles of Political Economy* (1817), particularly in the law of diminishing returns.[11] Consumer demand required the cultivation of less-arable lands, making production more expensive, driving up rents, increasing wages, and reducing profits. Fluctuations in prices are inevitable; prosperity is not. Over the course of the 1820s and especially after Ricardo's death in 1823, his fellow economists mounted a campaign of popularisation that would make 'classical political economy' orthodoxy. Countless economic handbooks were published, including J. R. McCulloch's *Discourse of Political Economy* (1824) and James Mill's *Elements of Political Economy* (1827), alongside manuals for women and children, such as Jane Marcet's *Conversations on Political Economy* (1816) and Richard Whateley's *Money Matters for the Young* (1833), and fictionalisations, such as Harriet Martineau's *Illustrations of Political Economy* (1832–4).[12]

Many writers were troubled by the new economic principles.

Parliamentarians like William Huskisson, otherwise sympathetic to market principles, feared that a sudden fall in the price of corn would have deleterious effects on Britain's social institutions.[13] Though hardly averse to commerce, Samuel Taylor Coleridge and Robert Southey were mortified by the irreligious attacks on national property. Property was not land per se, but the idea of national unity. The bone of contention between the political economists and their Romantic critics was not commerce but language. Whereas the economists believed that language conveyed universal truths to free individuals, the Romantics believed that understanding was the domain of an élite intellectual.[14] Scott was less antagonistic to the market, but he agreed that writers should hold a special place within it, a place enshrined in bardic traditions and threatened by economic populism. This is the running argument of Scott's prefaces and introductions: the 'Author of *Waverley*' is the force behind the trade in books or as the head of a company of printers, publishers, and editors. Authors are labourers and entrepreneurs, but their appreciation for the value of land, family, and civility also provides the moral and cultural understanding that will keep the forces of capitalism in check.[15]

The Population Problem

The role of the writer in society was also at issue in one of most controversial economic concerns of the period: population. The relation between the health of a nation's economy and the size of its population was a well-established maxim during the eighteenth century. Hume and Smith believed that an increase in population was a sign of thriving commerce. For others, however, the idea that human population would outstrip food production contradicted basic Christian dogma. It was also so far in the future that idealists like Godwin and Condorcet were persuaded that it in no way impeded human perfectibility. It was on this point that Thomas Robert Malthus's *Essay on Population* (1798) staked its claim. The possibility that population growth, which increased exponentially, would outstrip food production, which increased arithmetically, was for Malthus inevitable and immediate. All value was reducible to the human need to eat and reproduce. The only things that would check unlimited population increase and compel human kind to lawful civility were the natural checks of war, misery, and vice.[16]

Malthus's *Essay* provoked strong reactions. Christian economists regarded the population principle not as a challenge to divine providence but as one of its surest signs.[17] Others believed that its central premise was irreligious, so much so that Malthus, himself an Anglican divine, spent the rest of his life trying to soften his original claim. To subsequent editions of the *Essay*, Malthus added stocks of statistical evidence to support his contention that consumption and population would always delimit production. He also introduced the concept of 'moral virtue' to ameliorate the grim prospects his data foretold and argued that it was the responsibility of teachers and ministers to inculcate such self-restraint.[18] Malthus was surprised by attacks on the *Essay* by Robert Southey (in the *Analytical Review* in 1804) and William Hazlitt, who claimed that the population problem could be overcome through education,[19] but he was less sympathetic to Wordsworth's promotion of parish poor relief and Shelley's insistence that the 'calculating' pragmatism of his political economy would stultify the human imagination, encouraged as it was by erotic love and promoting future social reform.[20]

Unlike Wordsworth and Shelley, Scott knew Malthus and seemed keen to promote his views. In 1811, he suggested to Murray and Ellis that they should invite Malthus to become the economic reviewer for the *Quarterly*.[21] Scott understood the effects of population theory in the Highlands. While it is tempting to attribute the Highland Clearances to cultural prejudice, they found a good deal of intellectual justification for their actions in the writings of Malthus and other economists. McCulloch, for instance, believed that massing Highland farmers and their livestock into enclosed farms had turned an unproductive, indolent, and dangerously overpopulated region into a productive, industrious, and self-regulating one.[22] Scott was more ambivalent. In an 1806 letter to Lord Dalkeith (later the 4th Duke of Buccleuch), he wrote that 'the dismission of the superfluous population who occupied the estates of the Border Chieftains' during the reign of James VI was not a forced emigration (except in a few minor instances) but a result of the clans' inefficient feudal economies of vassalage and land-sharing (*Letters* 1:329):

> The frequent civil wars, and the unsettled state of the country must have greatly retarded the progress of those causes of depopulation which have operated with such rapidity in the Highlands where there was nothing to balance the Landlords natural desire to make the most he could of his property except the pride of some individuals & the compassion of others. (*Letters* 1:331–2)

In 1817, Scott took the Malthusian line that the poor relief was 'a sad quagmire [. . .] into which [. . .] millions of cart loads of good resolutions have been thrown without perceptibly mending the way' (*Letters* 4:494). Scotland's poor were unlikely to be an encumbrance because they were 'less populous' and the distances between farms and villages in rural Scotland made the drunkenness and indolence of the English countryside next to impossible. The situation was different in the cities and the 'manufacturing districts' where business owners routinely speculated on outlandish prospects and promised 'extravagant wages'. When these businesses failed, the 'loss fell on the nation together with the task of maintaining a poor renderd effeminate and vicious by over wages and over-living and necessarily cast loose upon society' (*Letters* 4:496). Scott's solution was to tax manufactures, though he doubted that this would meet much approval.

Another instance of Scott's Malthusianism is 'On Planting Wastelands' (1828), a favourable review – for the *Quarterly* – of Robert Monteath's *The Planter's Guide and Profitable Planter*. One of Scott's chief concerns in the review is the mass importation of Scotch Fir from Canada to the Highlands, a trade conducted in close proximity to the emigration of Highland farmers to Canada, in many instances on the same boats in opposite directions. Scott's statements that the Scotch Fir is 'very prolific' and 'easy to raise in immense quantities', though it is an 'inferior variety' and 'mean-looking' to the native Highland Fir sounds very much like contemporary anxieties about the growth of unproductive human populations.[23] A number of Scott's novels address the population question. The 'ominous Malthusian language of population and resources' haunts the narrator's implicitly pessimistic description of Fergus Mac-Ivor's estate in *Waverley*: 'he crowded his estate with a tenantry, hardy indeed, and fit for the purposes of war, but greatly outnumbering what the soil was calculated to maintain'.[24] The fourth volume of *The Heart of Mid-Lothian*, in which Jeannie Deans and Reuben Butler are resettled in the 'ominously' empty village of Roseneath, betrays a troubling Malthusian subtext. Such a resettlement can only take place once the Highlands are cleared 'without undue violence of its former occupants, inhabitants themselves imagined as no more native than the Deanses and the Butlers'.[25] The Highland repopulation is not the consequence of a utopian scheme – Charlotte Sussman indicates that such schemes were published regularly in the 1810s – but rather by the advent of the theory of labour value in which people are moveable commodities.[26] The final paragraphs of the novel also represent the story of unwanted Highland émigrés in the career of the Whistler, Effie Deans's unwanted child, who prompts a more disruptive side to Scott's engagement with Malthusianism. Like Fergus Mac-Ivor, whose clan operates on an archaic economy of centralised distribution and gift exchange, the Whistler represents an archaic 'general economy' that the 'restrictive' Malthusian economy of population control and labour value was intended to suppress.

The Bullion Controversy

The difference between old and new concepts of value was also a part of Romantic-period debates about money and finance. In some respects these debates were extensions of the financial revolution that began in the late seventeenth century with the establishment of the national debt, the opening of the Bank of England, and the spread of paper credit. Historians have long understood the effects of these changes on British society, most importantly the emergence of a new kind of autonomous subject whose capacities extended as far as his manners – and credit– allowed.[27] Nevertheless, the state retained considerable influence over finance: coins were still minted under the auspices of the crown; Parliament controlled wage levels and levied taxes; the courts prosecuted forgers and fraudsters whenever possible.[28] The Bank of England, one of many metropolitan and country banks extending loans and making investments (for profit), was responsible for holding the nation's gold and silver reserves and for lending to the government. The idea that an institution like the Bank of England could on its own sustain a nation millions of pounds in debt is to a large degree reflective of the persistence of old associations between the very idea of 'credit' and aristocratic prestige.[29] Scott himself faced financial ruin twice in his career because of his own and his publishers' rather grandiose notions of how much literature should be worth and their subsequent failure to meet both the demands of the reading public and the standard of aristocratic privilege.[30]

In 1797, these arrangements were put under duress by the suspension of cash payments: in response to a shortage of metallic currency and to corresponding threats of a French invasion, Parliament allowed the Bank of England to renege on its 'promise to pay the bearer' of any note the equivalent value in silver or gold. One- and two-pound notes were issued for the first time, and for the next 24 years good coin was scarce. In 1810 the Commons Committee on the High Price of Bullion demanded a 'return' to gold convertibility within two years. Its report had wide support – hundreds of pamphlets were published – but there was enough dissent both in and out of Parliament that none of its motions carried. For the government, the suspension was a war effort: the paper currency would be sustained not only by Britain's commercial prowess but also by its nationalist faith.[31] By and large, arguments surrounding the suspension fell along party lines. 'Bullionists' advocating a return to the 'ancient standard of the realm' were mainly Whigs, radicals, merchants, traders, and stockbrokers. 'Anti-bullionists' who argued that finance could expand as far as commerce required were primarily farmers and bankers. In other respects the divisions were less clear. Ricardo, whose arguments in favour of the gold standard were the blueprint for the eventual resumption of cash payments, conceded that gold was not in itself the standard; it was a commodity like any other, and a symbol of economic confidence.[32] Radicals like William Cobbett and Thomas Wooler claimed that paper money was tantamount to state-sanctioned forgery, the whole mandate of which was to undermine the sincerity and crush the confidence that existed between honest people.[33] Coleridge agreed with bankers like Thomas Coutts and Thomas Smith, industrialists like Thomas Attwood, military men like Colonel Robert Torrens, and agriculturalists like Sir John Sinclair that the standard of value was an 'idea' produced by collective or national fellow-feeling. But they disagreed on whether this idea was the consequence of social civility, the productivity of land, or the ancient constitution.

Scott was anti-bullionist by disposition: he did not believe that gold could ensure the stability of finance any more than he believed that commerce could thrive without a strong state. Many of Scott's works from the period point toward these anti-bullionist convictions. The plot of *Rokeby* (1813) hangs on the search for a cask of gold which is ultimately never found. The treasure-hunt motif appears again in *The Antiquary* (1816) in which the German 'illuminatus' Dousterswivel dupes the debt-ridden Sir Arthur Wardour into thinking that a trove of gold is hidden beneath his chapel, Saint Ruth's. Two caskets are found, but neither ultimately is the legitimate property of Sir Arthur. They have been put in place by Edie Ochiltree, the old beggar, and Lovel, the young hero of the novel who is later revealed to be the long lost son of the melancholy Earl of Glenallan. Sir Arthur's fortunes are finally restored when his son Reginald is able to procure guarantees of solvency from a London agent. The restoration of the fortune by paper endorses the views of the novel's titular antiquary, Jonathan Oldbuck, whose flights of historical fancy are presented, like the paper money he trusts, as true manifestations of ancient communal ideals.[34]

As *The Antiquary* also hints, Scottish and English finance operated on different principles. Scotland had two national banks: the Bank of Scotland and the Royal Bank of Scotland. Their competition, which kept fees low and interest down, coupled with a relatively small but literate population, meant that through the eighteenth century Scotland benefited from a surprisingly stable and open financial system. Although cash payments were suspended in Scotland only days after they were in England, the Scottish 'free banking' system made it perfunctory.[35] While the 1826 crash devastated the banking and finance sectors throughout Britain, it did not have the same long-term, political consequences as the suspension of cash payments. New self-regulating economic policies, in particular the gold standard and cash payments, were firmly in place. For many, the cycle of boom-and-bust, inflation and deflation, speculation and atonement was the natural state of business.[36] In order to extend this sense of normality, Parliamentarians offered to extend the gold standard system to Scotland. The outcry in Edinburgh was loud and immediate.

In February and March 1826, Scott published in the *Edinburgh Weekly Journal* three letters that would become the *Letters of Malachi Malagrowther*.[37] The main target of his polemic was the English drive toward centralisation. The suspension of Scottish currency contradicted the spirit of the Union, he declared, which enshrined the financial autonomy of the two countries. The English gold standard was mere 'innovation'. Scottish banking was built on public accountability, what Scott called a 'republic, the watchful superintendence of the whole profession being extended to the strength and weakness of the general system at each particular point; or, in other words, to the management of each individual Company'.[38] The medium of this security was publication: 'every Bank throughout Scotland is obliged to submit its circulation, twice a-week in Edinburgh, to the inspection of the Argus-eyed tribunal'. Because their bankers had to publish records of their solvency, Scottish citizens could trust their bankers in a way that English citizens could not:

> The public have, in this manner, the best possible guarantee against rash and ill-concocted speculations, from those who are not only best informed on the subject, but, being most interested in examining each new project of the kind, are least likely to be betrayed into a rash confidence, and have the power of preventing a doubtful undertaking at the very outset.[39]

Conservative attacks on the gold standard were based on conventional and paternalistic ideas that the state knew best. Scott's point, by contrast, was that the Scottish banking system was more modern than the English precisely because it was not based on the state, statehood being one thing Scotland did not have.

In their defence of Scottish free banking, the *Letters* occasionally slip into a jingoistic and anti-modern mode. Scott hints that Scots might take up arms to defend their financial liberty, such as the moment when he alludes to the magically-numbered '45' Scottish Members of Parliament or refers to the government as 'the enemy'. Initially, Scott claims that the 'body politic' in Scotland is healthy and thus is in no need of 'physic' as the English quack economists seem to think. As Scott famously put it, a nation that cannot grow wheat must eat oatcakes; a nation that uses paper has no need of gold. By the third letter, this same body is being encouraged to lift the blazon for the 'auld cause'. This is a clear example of the paradox in the *Letters* between economic modernism – a currency needs no inherent value to operate successfully – and archaic nationalism – the banking system symbolises the independence of the Scottish people.[40]

In a letter to John Wilson Croker, who had criticised Scott's nationalistic defence of the banking system as fantastic and backward, Scott made this warning: 'The restless and yet laborious and constantly watchful character of the people, their desire for speculation in politics or any thing else, only restrained by some proud feelings about their own country, now become antiquated and which late measure will tend much to destroy, will make them, under a wrong direction, the most formidable revolutionists who ever took the field of innovation.'[41] The complications of finance also character-ise Scott's nine-volume *Life of Napoleon*, originally planned for *Constable's*

Miscellany in 1825 but not published until November 1827. Scott's assessment of Revolutionary France's experiment with paper credit, the *assignat*, as essentially pragmatic, prepares for an assessment of Napoleon which is far more sympathetic than many contemporary treatments. In Scott's extended contextualisation, Napoleon's demagoguery becomes a foil for a practical economy based on the judicious circulation of public opinion.

The slippage from self-reliance to retribution reflects a decline in Scott's confidence also apparent in the literary works he completed in 1826 and 1827. *Woodstock*, which was finished about the time he was writing *Malagrowther*, is the last of three historical romances (the others are *Redgauntlet* and *The Talisman*) about disguised kingship. While *Woodstock* retains a faith throughout in Charles's kingly disposition, it also betrays anxieties about the viability of monarchy at a time when they were outpaced by more abstract notions of individual faith and political expediency. Ultimately, what saves Charles is the regard that others have toward him, the people's recognition of his right to rule. By contrast, the characters in the *Chronicles* struggle to identify with a gold-standard economy that is foreign and alienating, but also seemingly inevitable. In 'The Highland Widow', for instance, Elspat MacTavish, the embodiment of doomed Jacobitism, flees to the countryside after the death of her husband at Culloden. Her son, Hamish, who she hopes will become a true clansman, joins a Highland regiment and at one point sends his mother a five-guinea coin, the proceeds from his enlistment. Elspat mistakenly tries to interpret the coin not as a medium of exchange but as a story: she 'remained gazing on the money, as if the impress of the coin could have conveyed information how it was procured' (WN 20:82).

For Elspat, the coin is a talisman or even a tale, with a provenance based in war, heroism, and communal power, much as it would be to an antiquarian. Her attempt to read the coin defies the economic insistence that it is merely an abstract unit of account. Indeed, it even defies her narrator, the prim and nostalgic Mrs Bethune Baliol, who sheepishly explains: 'The moral principle which so naturally and so justly occurs to the mind of those who have been educated under a settled government of laws that protect the property of the weak against the incursions of the strong, was to poor Elspat a book sealed and a fountain closed' (WN 20:83). Elspat is 'antiqued' by her own story: her effort to connect monetary value with a heroic past is ensnared within the tale's seeming modernity, symbolised in turn by the gold coin.

Scott's writing throws modern and archaic economies into relief. Suddenly, paper, that most modern of commercial instruments, becomes an antique and the gold coin ('the ancient standard of the realm') becomes a beacon of a relentless modernity. It is not surprising that money should be the thematic heart of his most complex fictional works, not only *The Antiquary* and *The Chronicles of the Canongate* but also *The Heart of Mid-Lothian* and *Rob Roy*.

That Scott understood this tension, and others related to questions of population, governance, and value is a testament to his perceptiveness on economic affairs. But it also indicates the vibrancy of political economy in Scott's day and its interconnectedness with literary works.

CHAPTER ELEVEN

Late Scott

Ian Duncan

1

Two events, towards the end of 1825, announce the last act of Scott's career. On 20 November he began writing a journal, which he would keep, bar a few interruptions, until five months before his death. December brought the nationwide financial collapse that would ruin him, as became clear in the new year of 1826. Scott spent the remainder of his life writing books to pay off his debt – fifteen published volumes of fiction, a nine-volume *Life of Napoleon*, thirteen additional volumes of Scottish and French history, and miscellaneous other works, including the 'Magnum Opus' edition of the Waverley Novels. At the same time he was writing every day in private, reflecting on his situation, conduct and feelings, as well as on passing events. Critical assessment has split Scott's late career between the journal and the published writings, deprecating the last few novels as his weakest, blighted by overproduction, distress and illness. The idea of a 'late style', applied by Theodor Adorno to the perverse yet heroic rejection of organic form by Beethoven in his last years, would seem to have little bearing on works so utterly in thrall to physical and economic necessity.[1] Critics have found, in contrast, that the journal's private address secures a contemplative depth, a psychological and moral stronghold, from which its author is able to recon-stitute himself as his own greatest literary achievement.

Scott evidently expected his journal to be published. 'I have deprived my family and the public of some curious information by not carrying this reso-lution [of keeping one] into effect', he announces (*Journal* 1). He crafts the journal as a kind of posthumous writing, one that will come fully into its own – in the transaction of reading – after the author's death. The early entries show him arranging himself for posterity in a series of set pieces, such as essays on the literary characters of Thomas Moore and Byron, through which he triangulates his own authorial persona. As the clouds gather, Scott's self-fashioning assumes a resolutely ethical cast: 'Of all schools commend me to the Stoicks' (*Journal* 25).[2] Losing control over everything else in his life, including the plot, Scott reasserts authorship over the domain of his own character.

This chapter makes a case for the quality and interest of Scott's later fiction. It examines works which develop aesthetic and ideological questions already well established in Scott's writing and those which strike out in new directions, with a sometimes startling experimental thrust. Certainly, the late novels exhibit a powerfully revisionist concern, one which cannot simply be ascribed to their author's increasing conservatism. The two strongest (by general consent), *Woodstock* (1826) and *The Fair Maid of Perth* (*Saint Valentine's Day*, 1828), revisit key topics and situations from the earlier work. In *Woodstock*, Scott recombines his great political themes of revolution and sovereignty in a story set during the English Civil War, two years after the execution of Charles I. How can sovereignty be reimagined after the dismemberment of the king's sacred body? The proximity of the disaster forestalls the Humean solution – custom – with which Scott usually settles the question of legitimacy in a post-revolutionary era (as in *Waverley* and *Redgauntlet*). Oliver Cromwell himself appears as deus ex machina to oversee an interim solution: performance. Given the cue to act like a king, the deconsecrated heir, Charles II, eventually rises to the occasion – while even Cromwell, king for a day, lays aside his fanatic's and usurper's rigour and dispenses grace.[3]

The Fair Maid of Perth returns to Scotland as the conventional site of 'uneven development' in Enlightenment philosophical history: specifically, to the juxtaposition of cultivated Lowlands and wild Highlands, familiar from *Waverley* and *Rob Roy*, as the arena for an anthropological clash of values. Here we view distinct kinds of society – patriarchal clans, the feudal court, the civic and guild community of the town – contending in the same historical moment. The story sorts them into residual, dominant and emergent formations according to their command of the techniques (moral as well as practical) of violence, rather than any more exalted quality. (The pacifism of the Fair Maid qualifies her for her domestic destiny, far from designating any utopian horizon.) For the tale's gore-soaked climax Scott combines two of his signature topoi, warring Highlanders (see *Waverley*, *A Legend of the Wars of Montrose*, *Rob Roy*) and the chivalric tournament (*Ivanhoe*). The duel between rival clans, staged before court and citizens, recalls the tartan-clad pageantry the author had arranged for George IV's 1822 state visit – except that this is really an 'exterminating feud':

> For an instant or two the front lines, hewing at each other with their long swords, seemed engaged in a succession of single combats; but the second and third ranks soon came up on either side, actuated alike by the eagerness of hatred and the thirst of honour, pressed through the intervals, and rendered the

scene a tumultuous chaos, over which the huge swords rose and sunk, some still
glittering, others streaming with blood, appearing, from the wild rapidity with
which they were swayed, rather to be put in motion by some complicated
machinery, than to be wielded by human hands. (WN 21:369)

Scott's description reveals the genocidal policy behind the spectacle in the
scene's decomposition from a set of individually motivated 'single combats'
– the conventional heroic action, we might suppose, of a Waverley Novel
– into an indiscriminate industrial technology, a 'complicated machinery'
which harvests human lives. As a vision of the state's management of primitive violence it is more devastating than any of the ideological exposés aimed
against Scott by his critics.

Anne of Geierstein (1829), ostensibly a sequel to Quentin Durward (1823),
veers outward, to far Gothic reaches of improvisation. A strong historical
thesis – the ascendancy of absolutist Realpolitik (personified by Charles XI)
over the break-up of feudal chivalry (represented by Charles of Burgundy)
– had articulated the quest-romance plot of Quentin Durward. Here the
extension of the theme (Charles is trounced by the Swiss Confederacy) is
dislocated by hair-raising narrative swerves and abysmal plunges which simu-
late the logic of a dream or nightmare rather than historical analysis.[4] The
opening episode provides an emblem of what is to come: paralysed by vertigo,
the hero clings to a ledge over an alpine chasm, attracting the attention of
a passing vulture as well as the eponymous Maiden of the Mist. In the most
surprising of these plot-swings, the hero's father sinks through the floor to
find himself in the hands of the Vehmgericht, a subterranean secret tribunal
which exerts an obscure and (it appears) arbitrary sway over events – much
like the novel's author.

Scott's last completed novels were published as a set, the Janus-faced Tales
of My Landlord, Fourth Series (1831). One of them, Castle Dangerous, looks
backwards and inwards, superimposing the beginnings of Scott's career in
Border minstrelsy over its imminent dissolution, in the figure of an enchanted
archive which is also a mass grave and rubbish dump. The other, Count Robert
of Paris, looks forwards and outwards, to a post-national arena of world history
and a Lamarckian experiment in anthropological science fiction. Count
Robert, in particular, rebukes the traditional view of late Scott with its display
of an audacious expansion of the author's imaginative reach at the end of
his life. Before a more detailed consideration of these strange and unsettling
works, this chapter addresses the most widely read of the late works of fiction,
the short story 'The Two Drovers'. Its masterful technical and thematic concentration would appear to set this tale apart from the weird extravagance
of the novels. Like them, however, it undertakes a disconcerting return to
earlier ground – in this case, the national theme of Waverley and Rob Roy.

Matching if not excelling any recent analysis of the psychology of national identification, 'The Two Drovers' is Scott's most scathing treatment of the predicament of an 'organic', 'archaic' or 'residual' cultural identity under the pressure of modernisation.

2

'The Two Drovers' appeared in *Chronicles of the Canongate* (1827), the first work of fiction Scott began after his ruin. The *Chronicles* followed closely upon Scott's polemical intervention in national politics, the *Letters of Malachi Malagrowther*, which, as discussed in Alexander Dick's chapter, denounced a proposed Westminster reform of Scottish banking on the grounds that it would undermine the institutions through which Scotland had been able to maintain a distinct national identity within the Union. Such measures, Scott commented privately, 'are gradually destroying what remains of nationality and making the country *tabula rasa* for doctrines of bold innovation' (*Journal* 113). In the absence of an independent state, culture supplies the substance of a national identification which is the only bulwark against modern anomie and its political consequences. 'The Two Drovers' provides, through the techniques of fiction, an impressively sceptical analysis of this Romantic cultural nationalism.

Scott's tale narrates the clash – tragic in the Hegelian rather than Aristotelian sense – between the rival moral codes of a modern, legal and commercial national society and a kinship-based traditional culture. The conflict lays bare the paradox or doubleness of modern national identity, framed by a historical condition of uneven development: the objective inauthenticity of the 'imagined community' as a construction or invention and its subjective authenticity as a structure of feeling. 'The Two Drovers' reveals the tragic production, rather than mystical persistence, of a 'primitive' residue of identity within the new, imperfectly unified – ethnically and culturally heterogeneous – eighteenth-century British state.

The two drovers are a Highlander, Robin Oig M'Combich, and a Yorkshireman, Harry Wakefield, whose professional association in the common network of markets and trade-routes opened up by the Union brings them to acknowledge one another as friends. One day, however, a dispute over grazing rights escalates into violence. Wakefield strikes Robin Oig with his fist, and Robin, humiliated and enraged, stabs Wakefield with his dirk. The English judge who presides at the ensuing murder trial instructs the jury that Robin's act stems from cultural difference, not moral turpitude: both men '[acted] in ignorance of each other's national prejudices' (*WN* 20:143). Englishmen are accustomed to settle their quarrels with fisticuffs but Highlanders, with their clannish pride of rank, fight with weapons and consider it a shameful degradation to be struck by the hand. Robin Oig acted upon a coherent (if 'mistaken') code of honour, the product of his Highland origins. The judge invokes the anthropological principle of cross-cultural analogy licensed by Scottish Enlightenment conjectural history:

> Amongst [the Highlanders'] mountains, as among the North American Indians, the various tribes were wont to make war upon each other, so that each man was obliged to go armed for his own protection [. . .] Revenge [. . .] must have been as familiar to their habits of society as to those of the Cherokees or Mohawks. (WN 20:145)

The judge glosses the case as a tragedy of uneven development – the violent recalcitrance of a primitive mentality not yet pedagogically assimilated into the new national order. The law defines the act as murder, all the same, and the judge regretfully sentences Robin to death.

The judge's explanation, which lasts for ten pages in the 1827 edition, makes up a rather ostentatious coda to the narrative of the drovers' conflict. This supplementary position appears to grant it privileged authority, like an editorial postscript, at the same time that it shows up such authority as excessive – as though Scott, the master story-teller, tacked on a gloss because he mistrusted the capacity of his tale to make sense by itself. This seems unlikely. The very conspicuousness of the explanation prompts us, rather, to question its credentials as an account of what we have been reading. The judge, after all, is an actor in the story rather than an authorial medium set outside it; he himself belongs to the historical condition he is analysing. Nor (we begin to see) is English justice a transcendental principle in the historical formation of the modern British state. Scott reinforces the point by placing the narrator too, at the same moment, within the threshold of the tale:

> My story is nearly ended. The unfortunate Highlander stood his trial at Carlisle. I was myself present, and as a young Scottish lawyer, or barrister at least, and reputed a man of some quality, the politeness of the Sheriff of Cumberland offered me a place on the bench. (WN 20:142)

The narrator's sudden materialisation as a Scots advocate in an eighteenth-century English court of law radically historicises his earlier confident pronouncements on national character (applied to Wakefield as well as Robin Oig), made in the register of an objective ethnography, as well as the judge's subsequent appeal to an Enlightenment discourse that claims a universal knowledge through and against its recognition of local cultural variation.[5]

The judge is obliged to make that universal claim in order to pass sentence on the man whose subjective difference he has scrupulously acknowledged, in the classic ethical and political dilemma of a liberal philosophy. He defines 'the pinch of the case', the point at which cultural difference must cede to a universal standard, accordingly:

> But, gentlemen of the jury, the pinch of the case lies in the interval of two hours interposed betwixt the reception of the injury and the fatal retaliation. [... T]he time necessary to walk twelve miles, however speedily performed, was an interval sufficient for the prisoner to have recollected himself; and the violence which with which he carried his purpose into effect, with so many circumstances of deliberate determination, could neither be induced by the passion of anger, nor that of fear. (WN 20:144–5)

The judge appeals to a universal structure of human subjectivity, an objective moral ratio between passion and reason, given credibility by its mapping onto the categorically objective coordinates of time and space: 'the time necessary to walk twelve miles'. The judge's disposition within rather than outside the tale should challenge us, however, to turn back a few pages and re-read the representation of the 'pinch of the case' – the account of Robin's state of mind during 'the time necessary to walk twelve miles' – in Scott's narrative. In order to avenge his broken honour, Robin has to retrieve his knife from another drover to whom he has given it for safekeeping:

> When Robin Oig left the door of the ale house, seven or eight English miles at least lay betwixt Morrison and him. The advance of the former was slow, limited by the sluggish pace of his cattle; the last left behind him stubble-field and hedge-row, crag and dark heath, all glittering with frost-rhime in the broad November moonlight, at the rate of six miles an hour. And now the distant lowing of Morrison's cattle is heard; and now they are seen creeping like moles in size and slowness of motion on the broad face of the moor; and now he meets them – passes them, and stops their conductor. (WN 20:139)

The phrase 'English miles' reminds us of the residual currency, well into the eighteenth century, of the pre-Union Scots mile, still conditioning local perceptions of time and space. Even as it affirms the judge's objective coordinates ('six miles an hour') the narrative undoes them: more drastically, by a sudden abandonment of the prevailing convention of a past-historic, third-person narration for a sudden plunge into the present tense. This irruption of an 'archaic' convention (connoting epic *furor*) at the very 'pinch of the case' dramatises the irreducibility of Robin's subjectivity to the moral ratio pronounced by the judge. What the judge calls 'passion' does not decay with the passage of time as an opposite and superior principle, reason, reasserts its natural sway. Passion, instead, constitutes itself a kind of reason. The passive construction, at the same time, generalises this subjectivity. It is not, idiosyncratically or pathologically, Robin's, so much as the expression of a cultural mentality.

Scott represents, then, the specific density of a cultural mentality which is inaccessible to, and resistant to, the mandate of Enlightenment reason. But the story does not make this simply the case of a primordial identity that proves recalcitrant to the artificial modernity supposed to subsume it. After all, what constitutes that density, that resistance? Early in the tale the narrator describes the psychological and anthropological roots of Robin's sense of self, his 'pride of birth', which 'was like the miser's treasure, the secret substance of his contemplation, but never exhibited to strangers as a subject of boasting' (*WN* 20:126). Scott's phrase, 'the secret substance of his contemplation', accords strikingly with cultural theorist Slavoj Žižek's account of 'the Thing' that constitutes the occult core of national subjectivity:

> What is therefore at stake in ethnic tensions is always the possession of the national Thing. We always impute to the 'other' an excessive enjoyment: he wants to steal your enjoyment (by ruining our way of life) and / or he has access to some secret, perverse enjoyment. [. . .] The basic paradox is that our Thing is conceived as something inaccessible to the other and at the same time threatened by him. [. . .] What we conceal by imputing to the Other the theft of enjoyment is the traumatic fact that *we never possessed what was allegedly stolen from us*: the lack ('castration') is originary, enjoyment constitutes itself as 'stolen', or [quoting Hegel] it 'only *comes to be* through being *left behind*'.[6]

Scott's tale dramatises this logic at several points. The tension between Wakefield and Robin acquires its 'national' gravity in the taunts exchanged between the Highlander and the boors in the Cumberland tavern, which elaborate, very precisely, contending fantasies of 'the theft of enjoyment', as each party accuses the other of devouring – locust-like – its resources. When Robin asks Morrison, a Lowland Scot, to return his dirk, Morrison offers to back him in his quarrel – with the following remarkable explanation of how a local identity becomes 'national': 'Ye ken Highlander and Lowlander, and Border-men, are a' ae man's bairns when you are over the Scots dyke' (*WN* 20:139). In other words, you are 'Scottish' – abstracted from an array of regional identifications – once you are across the Border, out of Scotland, in a foreign country.

Robin's 'pride of birth', likewise, accrues its value on condition of its alienation. His consciousness of the point of view of strangers has made it 'the secret substance of his contemplation'. The perverse pleasure-principle that the judge will generalise into a national principle of honour becomes a motive – acquires ethical energy, flares into action – once it is despoiled:

> The treasured ideas of self-importance and self-opinion – of ideal birth and quality, had become more precious to him, (like the hoard to the miser), because he could only enjoy them in secret. But that hoard was pillaged, the

idols which he had secretly worshipped had been desecrated and profaned. Insulted, abused, and beaten, he was no longer worthy, in his own opinion, of the name he bore, or the lineage which he belonged to – nothing was left to him – nothing but revenge (WN 20:139)

With a noteworthy tact, Scott's representation of Robin's 'Thing' respects its negative structuration as well as its subjective reality. The metaphor of the 'miser's hoard' does not specify an order of value based outside the general economy of commercial society – historically prior to it, for example, the flower of an organic community. It denotes, rather, a peculiarly negative inside of the general economy, since its value is conferred through the miser's act of withholding the very tokens of that economy (gold, money) from exchange and circulation.

The judge invokes the law's universal authority in a transcendental register: 'The law says to the subjects, with a voice only inferior to that of the Deity, "Vengeance is mine"' (WN 20:146). This solemn ventriloquism exposes its necessary arbitrariness, the source of its authority in the state's monopoly of violence. 'Englishmen have their angry passions as well as Scots', he concludes, 'and should this man's action remain unpunished, you may unsheath, under various pretences, a thousand daggers betwixt the Land's-end and the Orkneys' (WN 20:146). In an extraordinary, apocalyptic reversal, the judge envisions Great Britain – the multinational modern state – as united not by law or reason but, spontaneously, organically, ecstatically, by the obsolete, aboriginal passion ascribed to the wild Highlander. From Robin Oig's representing that embarrassing anomaly, a vengeful savage in civil society, it now seems the entire society is poised to revert, in a moment, to bloody barbarism – unless the law engross that violence to itself.

3

If 'The Two Drovers' returns with a vengeance to Scott's national theme, Count Robert of Paris directs critical attention to that theme's scientific basis, as expounded by the judge in the story: a universal human nature. Scott had claimed this key tenet of eighteenth-century moral philosophy as the scientific basis of the historical novel. He opens Waverley with a declaration that the 'passions common to men in all stages of society' have regulated his story: he reads 'from the great book of Nature, the same through a thousand editions'.[7] Scott invokes what anthropologists would later call a 'monogenetic' historiography. A unified human nature, founded on the principle of descent from a common origin, governs the ideology of unified development and a universal history which particular peoples or nations must join on the path to modernity.

Late eleventh-century Constantinople, the setting for *Count Robert of Paris*, is about as far away from eighteenth-century Scotland as Scott could get, and doubly cut off from the path to modernity, first by the schism between western and eastern Christianity and then by the Ottoman conquest. The cast of characters includes Greeks, Turks, Normans, Varangians, Africans, Scythians, a bluestocking princess, a ferocious warrior-countess, a seditious philosopher nicknamed 'the Elephant', a real elephant, a tiger, a mechanical lion, and an eight-foot-tall captive orang-utan. Scott, it seems, has defini- tively abandoned his commitment to the characterology, national territory and 'prehistory of the present' that should constitute (in Lukács' phrase) 'the classical form of the historical novel'.[8] *Count Robert* occupies, instead, a new imaginative space, the imperial cosmopolis or world-city, and makes it the conjectural arena for a new kind of history: the natural history of man.

Why should a romance set in Constantinople be called *Count Robert of Paris*? Constantinople is the Paris of a Europe at the last crossroads between Classical antiquity and the Middle Ages: the analogue, that is, of Paris after 1830, the decadent capital of a once progressive Enlightenment, its his- torical promise broken by the modern cycle of revolution and restoration. (The novel opens with a meditation on the futility of artificially restor- ing empires.) David Hume had called the grand project of Enlightenment the 'science of man', the foundation of all branches of secular knowledge; eighteenth-century Scottish philosophers turned to history as the discipline which would realise that project, in histories of manners, institutions, and modes of social, political and economic organisation. The claims on an as yet unwritten 'history of the species man' made by two of those philosophers, Lord Kames and Lord Monboddo, questioned the science's central principle: the universality and immutability of human nature. Kames surmised that humans devolved into separate species after Babel, Monboddo that the mys- terious great ape, the orang-utan, was a race of humanity lacking only the artificial acquirement of speech. Post-Napoleonic Paris, reclaiming its role as world capital of the human sciences, now issued a more formidable set of challenges to the orthodox model of human nature. Jean-Baptiste Lamarck revived Monboddo's orang-utan hypothesis in a general assault on the fixity of species. The hospitable reception of Lamarck's work in Edinburgh's scien- tific circles in the late 1820s provoked Charles Lyell to issue a high-profile refutation in the second volume of *Principles of Geology*, published just a few months after *Count Robert of Paris*.[9] Ailing as he was, Scott kept his fiction open to the intellectual currents of the age – including those that were disin- tegrating the philosophical foundation of his art.

Exploding the monogenetic model of history, *Count Robert of Paris* offers fantastic glimpses of a multiplicity of human developmental forms and paths. A band of Scythians provokes the conjecture of a demonic genealogy. The

Anglo-Saxon 'foresters' (refugees from *Ivanhoe*) 'made a step backwards in civilisation, and became more like to their remote ancestors of German descent, than they were to their more immediate and civilized predecessors' (*WN* 23a:209–10). Scott's play with these ideas extends to perverse jokes, as when the Crusaders, wishing to return across the Bosphorus without breaking their vow 'never to turn back upon the sacred journey' (*WN* 23a:253), ride their horses backwards onto the transport barges in what the narrative calls a 'retrograde evolution' (*WN* 23a:255). 'Retrograde evolution' is only one among several morphological possibilities in Scott's Constantinople, where the boundaries between culture and race, race and species, and human and non-human species shift and blur.

These mutations and dissolutions condense around the novel's most spectacular figure, the giant orang-utan. Invoking the creature's ambiguous status in late-Enlightenment natural philosophy, Scott sets him in a murky no-man's-land between human and animal species-being.[10] The orang-utan's appearances provoke strange rhetorical disturbances, as though his uncertain identity corrupts the text around him – nowhere more so than in a hallucinatory sequence mid-way through the story. Count Robert, invited to dinner at the imperial palace, is startled by the ramping of the Emperor's mechanical lion, and smashes its skull with a blow of his fist. After the banquet (he has been drugged), Robert awakens to find himself in an underground dungeon menaced by a tiger – a real tiger, not a mechanical one. Once again he reacts by smashing its skull. The creature appears more like an effect in a magic-lantern show than a zoological specimen: 'he gazed eagerly around, but could discern nothing, except two balls of red light which shone from among the darkness with a self-emitted brilliancy, like the eyes of a wild animal while it glares upon its prey' (*WN* 23a:161). This apparition generates the voice of a fellow prisoner, who tells Robert that his eyes have been put out with red-hot irons. The mutilation of eyes or tongues, recurrent throughout the novel, marks the victim's removal from fully human status. Deprived of the organs of speech or vision, he is reduced to a mere body, to 'bare life', the condition of a beast or slave. The episode culminates in the entrance of the grotesque figure of the orang-utan, who understands orders given in Anglo-Saxon and babbles his own strange language.

What logic moves this bizarre narrative sequence, with its delirious transitions, contrasts and transformations? Mechanical animal versus living animal, eyes without a body versus a body without eyes, the man bereft of the endowment of humanity (vision) versus the animal that may possess it (speech): these recapitulate the historical set of conjectures about the essential quality distinguishing humans from animals which informed the emergent science of man, from the Cartesian account of the animal as machine, through the empiricist abstraction of a vision-based cognition, to the Romantic investment in language as the uniquely human property. 'In our culture,' writes the philosopher Giorgio Agamben, 'man has always been thought of as the articulation and conjunction of a body and soul, of a living thing and a *logos*, of a natural (or animal) element and a supernatural or social or divine element.' Instead, Agamben proposes, we might think of man 'as what results from the incongruity of these [. . .] elements, and investigate not the metaphysical mystery of conjunction, but rather the practical and political mystery of separation'. He asks: 'What is man, if he is always the place – and, at the same time, the result – of ceaseless divisions and caesurae?'[11] At the end of its author's career, *Count Robert of Paris* undertakes the critical work Agamben calls for, bringing the techniques of fiction to bear on those 'divisions and caesurae' that govern the category of the human. Disarticulating man, Scott also disarticulates the 'classical form of the historical novel' that he is famous for having established.

4

J. H. Alexander points out that 'Scott's last three extended fictions' (comprising the unfinished *Siege of Malta* as well as *Count Robert of Paris* and *Castle Dangerous*) all 'had their origin in narratives known to him from his childhood or early youth'.[12] That origin's gravitational pull is felt most insistently in *Castle Dangerous*, which reaches back to the matter of Scott's first literary success, the chivalry and minstrelsy of the Scottish Border. Unnervingly, this romantic superstructure of cultural memory and youthful fancy keeps disintegrating into a ruinous, labyrinthine, rubbish-strewn terrain, a material substrate of death and waste, which – far more than the flickering, unstable plot – provides *Castle Dangerous* with its imaginative continuity.

Even more than is usually the case in Scott, the various quests and missions on which the characters set out keep getting interrupted, blocked and diverted. One of these thwarted expeditions sends Aymer de Valence on a night-ride through Douglas Town, where an eerie shadow-warrior challenges him and vanishes into the darkness. Aymer's pursuit of the apparition leads him to an underground vault of the ruined church (one among several downward plunges in the tale) and an uncanny denizen named Lazarus Powheid. Feeding his fire with 'relics of mortality', Powheid combines the role of local antiquary, the curator of cultural memory, with that of sexton, disposing of the dead as so much rubbish. The ancestral shades, he explains, languish in purgatory, since their intercessory rites have been abolished by their foes; unable to move on, they haunt the earth, a kind of spectral waste matter.

The scene seems emblematic of the story, like the enclosed allegorical places that show up at crisis points in Spenser's *The Faerie Queene*. It shares attributes with the eponymous castle itself, which becomes, through a condensation of symbolic functions, something like the allegorical place or representation of Scott's art at the end of his life. Douglas Castle is the very topos of romantic chivalry and the Debatable Land, repeatedly taken and retaken by the Scots and English, and now the occasion of a gallant wager of love and arms. More than a token in a chivalric game or military strategy, the Castle is also important for what it contains, in the dual character of archive and dump. In its former character it holds a legendary treasure for Border antiquaries and poets, the book of Thomas of Erceldoune – better known as Thomas the Rhymer, who, intimate with 'the gifted people, called the Faëry folk, [. . .] united in his own person the quality of bard and of soothsayer' (*WN* 23b:37–8). Scott imagines a benign version of the black book of the ancestral warlock Michael Scott in the very first of his romances, *The Lay of the Last Minstrel*. The Rhymer's verses, mediating between human and faëry realms, join together 'forgotten minstrelsy', ancestral origins, and 'prophecies concerning the future fates of the British kingdom' (*WN* 23b:41). The Rhymer himself is the archetype of the wizard-like minstrel, custodian of the nation's past and future, whose final avatar is Walter Scott.[13]

The castle is also an anti-archive – the site of the 'Douglas Larder', an obscene midden and mass grave:

> Douglas caused the meat, the malt, and other corn or grain to be brought down into the castle cellar, where he emptied the contents of the sacks into one loathsome heap, striking out the heads of the barrels and puncheons, so as to let the mingled drink run through the heap of meal, grain, and so forth. The bullocks provided for slaughter were in like manner knocked on the head, and their blood suffered to drain forth into the mass of edible substances; and lastly, the quarters of the cattle were buried in the same mass, in which were also included the dead bodies of those in the castle, who, receiving no quarter from the Douglas, paid dear enough for having kept no better watch. This base and ungodly abuse of provisions intended for the use of man, together with throwing into the well of the castle carcasses of men and horses, and other filth for polluting the same, has since that time been called the DOUGLAS LARDER. (*WN* 23b:35–6)

It is the scrambling of categories – human and animal, food and filth – that makes the Douglas Larder 'a never to be forgotten record of horror and abomination': not the massacre of captives (standard practice in these wars). While the archive is a source of cultural origins and purpose, of meaning and making – a symbolic magic activated by being remembered, recited, read – the dump is the reverse. It decomposes the distinctions of culture, and culture itself, into undifferentiated waste.

Scott relates this nauseating vision of the antithesis of art in the fourth chapter of *Castle Dangerous*. Its association with death, specifically with the author's death, becomes insistent as the tale proceeds, culminating in the extraordinary envoi of Jedidiah Cleishbotham's 'Introductory Address', which Scott wrote last. Here the masquerade of author-functions definitively breaks down and Scott contemplates, via the cases of Cervantes, Fielding and Smollett, his own looming mortality. Like the *Journal*, but to more disturbing effect, Scott's last romance also poses itself as a kind of posthumous writing.

CHAPTER TWELVE

Afterlives

Nicola J. Watson

On 21 September, 1832, Sir Walter Scott died on a sofa in the dining-room at Abbotsford, ending over thirty years of astoundingly prolific literary production. Scott's death did not, however, put an end to his celebrity, cultural reach, or profitability. The death of those occurred sometime between the two world wars, when Scott ceased to be identified as important in either high or popular Anglophone culture, though his reputation lasted longer, and to an extent survives, in Eastern Europe. That is not to say that he actually ceased to have cultural importance. Arguably, anglophone and, certainly, European culture's continuing sense of history as a living heritage materialised within story, place, building and artefact still stands on the now invisible foundations and within the shadowy frames and moods established most influentially by Scott.

1

On the news of Scott's death, London's Covent Garden staged a theatrical spectacular in his honour. The main item on the programme for Monday, 22 October 1832 was a stage adaptation of *Waverley*, followed by an afterpiece, Sheridan Knowles's *The Vision of the Bard*, a 'masque' conceived and performed 'in honour of the Genius of the Minstrel of the North'. In the opening scene a bard, accompanied by the Geniuses of Scotland, England, Ireland, and Scottish Song, supported by the Spirit of the Mountains and allegorical figures of Fancy and Immortality, paid homage at Scott's tomb at Dryburgh Abbey. This framed a series of eight elaborate tableaux drawn from Scott's poetical and fictional works: 'Loch Katrine' from *The Lady of the Lake*, in which Fitz-James encounters Ellen Douglas; 'The Cavern of Derncleugh' from *Guy Mannering*, showcasing Meg Merrilies and plenty of Highlanders in tartan; 'The Sea-shore' from the episode in *The Antiquary* in which Edie Ochiltree and his companions are nearly drowned by the rising tide; 'The Pass of Aberfoil'(*sic*) from *Rob Roy*, featuring more Highlanders; the interview between Jeanie Deans and Queen Caroline in 'The Royal Gardens' from *The Heart of Mid-Lothian*; 'The Lists at Templestowe' from *Ivanhoe*; Old Mortality in soliloquy in a 'Ruined Abbey'; and finally the interior of Kenilworth castle, a scene featuring Queen Elizabeth, the Earl of Leicester, Varney, Raleigh, Tressilian, and a line-up of Yeomen of the Guard. The Bard's vision concluded 'with the representation of / A JUBILEE, / supposed to be given at Abbotsford, / in commemoration of Scotia's Minstrel, / at which the Various Characters in his Dramatic Works are assembled / In Honour of His Memory!'[1] A playbill for a later performance amplifies: 'A View of Abbotsford (the residence of the lately deceased Poet) Painted expressly by Mr Stanfield, to which celebrated place will be introduced in commemoration of Scotland's Immortal Bard, a Pilgrimage of the principal dramatic characters his genius has created by the whole company, in imitation of the honours paid to Shakespeare in the celebrated Jubilee.'[2]

Further details about this final scene are provided by reviewers. The *Theatrical Observer* (23 October 1832) commended 'the last scene where by a pretty conceit [. . .] posterity are supposed to be engaged, in 3364, paying a tribute to the still cherished memory of Scott, by celebrating a Jubilee at his mouldered tomb', a confusion of place which would undoubtedly have annoyed the scene-painter. *The London Literary Gazette* noted: 'The whole closes with a jubilee, in which all the characters reappear and are grouped with many others at Abbotsford, which is seen in ruins, as if centuries had elapsed – the effect of which is surpassing.'[3] It would have been easy to confuse the representation of Abbotsford in ruins with the ruins of Dryburgh Abbey, site of Scott's grave and partial inspiration for Abbotsford; and such a confusion was over-determined by the way that the masque effectively conflated this imaginary Jubilee with the protocols of the Shakespeare birthday celebrations derived from David Garrick's original Stratford Jubilee of 1769, imagining it taking place not on the multi-centenary of Scott's birth, but of Shakespeare's – the Shakespeare birthday celebrations did indeed culminate at Shakespeare's tomb.[4]

Knowles's masque is consciously synoptic of the status and meaning of Scott and his works in 1832. It depicts, first of all, a writer who had achieved the status of a national bard – both in the sense that he was the inheritor of the minstrelsy of the north, and in the sense that his brilliant array of 'dramatic characters' and historical subject matter qualified him as the modern Shakespeare.[5] This London-based celebration describes Scott as both a Scottish and British bard, selecting a careful balance of Scottish and English tableaux. Second, it describes Scott in terms of a collected oeuvre that spans both poetry and fiction and that is organised chronologically in order of composition and publication, producing Scott very much in the terms that he had himself constructed through the 'Magnum Opus' edition that he authorised, introduced, and re-edited shortly before his death. Third, in keeping with the new introductions to individual volumes of the 'Magnum Opus' and the eventual status of the 'Magnum' as valedictory, the masque sets Scott's works within a biographical frame.

If Knowles depicts Scott as bard-like, he also describes him as a romantic author whose fully visualised homes and haunts can serve as an explanatory frame to the works, and which are therefore appropriate destinations for literary pilgrims, whether ancient bards, Scott's own dramatic characters, or, by extension and implication, modern-day literary tourists, armchair or actual. This, too, may be said to be very much in keeping with the ways in which Scott himself had chosen to promote the relation between himself and locality. He had certainly chosen Dryburgh Abbey as his final resting-place not merely out of social ambition but out of a sense of romantic fitness, and Abbotsford had functioned from its earliest conception not merely as a gen-tleman's country-seat but as a suitable place to entertain a celebrated writer's admirers, designed from the outset as a place that displayed and interrogated the relation between the man and his works. So powerful was this conceit that the Abbotsford edition of 1844 would simply translate it into print, por-traying the artefacts displayed at the house within the text so as to give the fictions 'whatever additional interest may be derived from the representation of what was actually in the contemplation or memory of the Author when he composed them'.[6] Similarly, J. M. W. Turner's commissioned illustrations to the *Poetical Works* and to the 'Magnum Opus' had worked to tie the author to works by depicting Scott in the foreground of the locations and landscapes which he had used as settings, showing the author, his publisher Cadell, and Turner himself picnicking overlooking Melrose Abbey, or the three of them making their way across the Tweed towards Abbotsford in an open carriage.[7]

Knowles's masque thus celebrates a Scott who is at once poet and novel-ist, Scottish and British, a man and a collected works, a bard and a romantic author. The final scene, however, moves beyond echoing Scott's own self-projections. Here Scott's characters may be cast as dutiful sons and daughters returning to attend a family funeral at the ancestral home, but they have clearly already left home. Their ability to survive their creator allegorises the future profitability of the works.

In fact, the masque projects some of the commercial directions in which the Scott industry would develop beyond the collected edition – in particular, adaptation and extraction. Knowles's production bears witness to an already established habit of adapting Scott's poetry and fiction to the stage; its staging of individual scenes as epitomes of whole works not only assumed audience familiarity with Scott's oeuvre but a shared understanding that individual scenes could stand for the whole work. Over the rest of the century, extensive stage adaptation (from straight dramatisation through melodrama, opera, and burlesque) enjoyed a symbiotic coexistence with visual representation of scenes from Scott in fine art;[8] it has been estimated that between 1805 and 1870 the Royal Academy and the British Institution between them exhibited more than a thousand 'Scott' works.

This habit of consuming Scott in reduced or epitomised form as public entertainment extended to private spaces. At the top of society Scott's works furnished inspiration for fancy-dress balls and the latest aristocratic amusement, *tableaux vivants*, both of which pleasures would at length filter down to the middle classes. In the middle-class Victorian parlour, the piles of music on the piano were very likely to include one or other of Scott's songs in one of the many settings for harp or pianoforte provided by composers ranging from Dr Kemp of Cambridge to the celebrated Franz Schubert. Other parlour amusements derived from Scott included specially shortened juvenile dramas for toy theatres and magic lantern slide-shows. From mid-century, less expert or committed readers, including women and children, could be familiarised with Scott's narratives through compilations of 'beauties', 'scenes', and 'readings', and through abridgements and re-tellings. One early such production, directed at women, was *The Female Characters of Scott, with Introduction and Memoir*, another was *Readings for the Young from the Works of Sir Walter Scott*, both published in 1848. This industry really got going with the multi-volume *Abbotsford Miscellany* series which A & C Black produced in 1855, which chopped up the novels and verse into 'Scottish scenes and characters', 'Characters of eminent persons', 'Humorous and poetical pieces', 'Narratives and descriptive pieces', 'Romantic narratives', and 'Tales of chivalry and romance'.

If the Victorians conceived of Scott in this way as a mine of enchanting moments, they were also interested in him as a man. The masque's sense of the pertinence of Scott's life as a frame to his works was vastly amplified by the publication of Lockhart's biography, which determined the Victorian view of Scott: to the sense of him as a national genius was added an apprehension of him as diligent (otherwise how could he have been so prolific?), honourable and courageous (otherwise he would not have undertaken to work off the debts contracted as a result of the 1825–6 crash), the model of a moral man, and a gentleman. Lockhart's narrative linked Scott's life to his works and both to landscapes and locations. His influence is clear in the *Abbotsford Miscellany*, which mixed extracts from the fiction and poetry with material from the letters and journal rendered canonical by Lockhart, under such headings as 'Scenes at Abbotsford – The Flitting, Rural Employment, Hogmanay, Death of Lady Scott', and 'Maxims, Observations and Anecdote'. On occasion, the pull towards collating the fictional and the biographical even entailed the extrapolation of the autobiographical from the works; thus 'Early feelings' are conveyed by a passage from *Marmion* on Smailholm Tower.[9]

The end-result of this conflation of man, works, and place was that Knowles's closing conceit of pilgrimage to Abbotsford proved prophetic. After Scott's death, Abbotsford developed into a full-blown tourist attraction, on the itinerary of almost anyone interested in contemporary European culture. Nor was Abbotsford the only place associated with Scott that attracted visitors. As in Scott's lifetime, tourists were also drawn to sites that he had used as settings. The most spectacular example of such tourist interest was the boom in visitor numbers to Loch Katrine, which lasted until the early twentieth century, and left by way of legacy the pleasure-steamer the SS *Walter Scott*, still in service there.[10] But by the end of the century, a much more extensive notion of 'Scott country' had developed, serviced by the convergence of illustrated collected editions of the Waverley Novels with expensive freestanding albums of topographical prints such as Leitch Ritchie's *Scott and Scotland; with twenty-one highly finished Engravings from Drawings by George Cattermole* (1835) and Finden's *Landscape-Historical Illustrations of Scotland, and the Waverley Novels* (1836–8) and the maps, topographical writing, travel writing and guidebooks which had begun to appear in relation to individual locales soon after the publication of *The Lady of the Lake*. Ritchie's rationale for his album – 'to delineate, with the utmost possible fidelity, existing scenes, and yet to superadd a moral interest, by peopling them with the creation of genius' – serves as a description of how the well-read were enabled to visit places and associate them with both Scott's biography and individual works.[11]

The tourist sense of Scott country as an amalgam of places he had lived and places he had written about was underscored by memorial practices, most spectacularly in the Scott monument in Edinburgh. A Gothic spire successively elaborated with a marble statue of a seated Scott and the subsequent encyclopaedic embellishment of the whole with statues of Scott's characters, it describes the way in which Scott and his fictions coalesced into a national icon. But although the practices of both tourism and memorialisation suggest a desire to localise Scott to Scotland, other memorials bear witness to the international reach of his appeal. He is commemorated in the imperial Pantheon of Poets' Corner in Westminster Abbey, but the rest of the world can provide its Scott memorials too, ranging from the simple plaque in Rome put up in 1882 to mark the place where Scott stayed in the last year of his life in an effort to retrieve his health, to the importantly-placed statue erected in 1897 in New York's Central Park, to the ivy that grows on the walls of a house in New York State descended from the cutting that Washington Irving took from a plant at Abbotsford in commemoration of his visit in 1817. One very quick way to calibrate the scale of Scott's hold upon the nineteenth-century anglophone global imagination is simply to Google the number of places – from buildings to towns to streets – that call themselves either

'Waverly' (mysteriously often dropping the original 'e') or 'Abbotsford' in the USA, in Canada, Australia, and elsewhere.

Tributes of this kind to the hold Scott's fiction had over international imaginations, and to the urge to translocate its power, also invoke the novel nineteenth-century readers rated as his most important – *Ivanhoe* (1820). They include the little town Ivanhoe in New South Wales, Australia, and, in the USA, Lake Ivanhoe in Orlando, Florida, Ivanhoe in California, a vast Ivanhoe frieze in the Los Angeles Public Library, an Ivanhoe temple in Kansas City Missouri, and an institution now long defunct, the Ivanhoe restaurant in Chicago. This last, executed in swashbuckling castle style, promised a themed and theatricalised dining experience in rooms such as 'Robin Hood's garden' and 'King Richard's prison', enhanced by the chance to eat off special themed Ivanhoe crockery. The afterlife of *Ivanhoe* can serve here as a useful case-study in the afterlives of the novels. Subject to all the forms of adaptation and dissemination surveyed above, it provides a way of describing these in more detail. In two respects its afterlife was atypical, however: firstly, *Ivanhoe* proved unusually resistant to being incorporated within 'Scott country'; secondly, its success outran that of any other Waverley Novel, travelling further around the globe, and lasting longer within twentieth-century culture.

2

Ivanhoe has long been regarded as a turning-point in Scott's writing career, the moment after the crisis of Peterloo when he turned away from Scottish subjects and settings and the relatively recent history of the previous century and a half, to explore more distant historical and geographical material in an urgent exercise in nation-building. It achieved extraordinary success: Lockhart was retailing a generally-felt sentiment when he noted: 'Ivanhoe is perhaps the first of all Scott's efforts whether in prose or verse.'[12] It was celebrated for its magnificence of pictorial representation, for its splendour of descriptive scenery, for its simultaneous vastness of scope and attention to elaborate detail, and for its air of high romance. Its relative vagueness of historical and geographical setting permitted the reapplication of Scott's story about a moment of English nation-making and empire-building to other nations and empires in the process of formation well beyond anglophone culture. By 1823 *Ivanhoe* had already been translated into Danish and Italian, by 1826 into Spanish, and by 1829 into Hungarian, and these qualities may well account in part for the mid-twentieth-century success of the novel in translation in Japan. The novel would exert substantial literary influence as a result; Hilaire Belloc identified it as the first of the great nineteenth-century historical novels, which 'founded in Europe what has now become at once a permanent form of fiction and a permanent historical method'.[13]

The history of *Ivanhoe* within popular global culture is a story of progressive multi-modal adaptation to a variety of uses, audiences, spaces, and agendas. It was adapted for a wide variety of stages, ranging from the theatres royal through to the illegitimate theatres in London, Edinburgh, the provinces, Paris, Copenhagen and elsewhere, inspiring at least thirty-seven adaptations as drama, melodrama, burlesque, opera, hippodrama (with real horses), and tournaments. Nor was this desire to realise the novel in other forms confined to the commercial theatre, penetrating deep into private life. High society indulged the *Ivanhoe* craze in the shape of costume balls such as that themed to the novel held in Brussels in 1823 and Victoria and Albert's Bal Costumé of 1842, which included an 'Ivanhoe Quadrille'. The Eglinton tournament given in August of 1839 was arguably equally indebted to *Ivanhoe*.[14] In 1837 six *tableaux vivants* inspired by *Ivanhoe* and the novel seen as its companion piece, *The Talisman*, were given in Prague. In 1882, the wealthy of Florida held a jousting tournament inspired by *Ivanhoe* in the Christmas holidays; and in 1889, the New York élite staged a winter costume ball with the same theme.[15] Indeed, the evidence suggests that no Victorian fancy-dress ball or party was complete without an Ivanhoe in attendance.[16] High society also provided a series of wealthy buyers for paintings on subjects drawn from the novel such as those by Eugène Delacroix, who produced no fewer than six treatments of subjects from *Ivanhoe*.[17]

The less well-heeled in Britain, Europe, America, and India contented themselves with cheaper versions of these pastimes. They provided their children with the juvenile drama of *Ivanhoe* that came out in 1822 in Hodgson's Juvenile Drama series to stage in toy theatres; they supplied them with board games (*Ivanhoe: A Social Game* was produced by G. Parker & Co. in the USA in 1886);[18] they entertained themselves with dramatic charades and tableaux derived from the novel;[19] they sang song-settings by Schubert;[20] they attended fancy-dress parties dressed up as Ivanhoe, Rebecca, and Rowena;[21] they lolled over drawing-room compilations such as Charles Swain's *Cabinet of Poetry and Romance; Female Portraits from the Writings of Byron and Scott, with Poetical Illustration* (1845); and they bought prints and lithographs illustrating the story.[22] The poor and the less literate were catered for as well, by cut-down chapbook versions such as *Ivanhoe, or, The Jew and his Daughter: an Interesting Old English Tale. Founded on Facts* (1820).

Ivanhoe, in short, saturated both public and private spheres in a wide variety of realisations and adaptations throughout the century. One result of this was that *Ivanhoe* slowly became one of those few books which, at any given period, it was possible to be familiar with almost without having read it, reduced to a number of instantly recognisable set-piece scenes which virtually all forms of adaptations or reiterations included, and which virtually all illustrators chose to depict. One early twentieth-century reader recalled it in just such a sequence of scenes:

> The great tournament at Ashby, the Robin Hood scenes, the interchange of buffets between Friar Tuck and the Black Knight; and above all the siege of Torquilstone – both the scene in which Rebecca describes the siege to the wounded Ivanhoe, as she sees it from the window, and the ravings of the dying Front de Boeuf when Ulrica tells him that the castle is on fire and he knows the flames will reach him before his mortal wounds have had time to do their work; again, the arrival of Ivanhoe as Rebecca's champion at Templestowe, his combat with Brian de Bois-Guilbert, the death of the unwounded warrior from his own evil passions [. . .] all these pictures were first known to a boy of ten; they are vivid still.[23]

This cultural familiarity meant that the story and characters of *Ivanhoe* could be, and were, used as moral touchstones within nineteenth-century fiction. This was especially true within fiction directed at women, because *Ivanhoe* was felt to have supplied a script not just for an idea of chivalric manhood, but for pure womanhood and proper relations between the sexes. Rebecca seems generally to have been felt to be a more interesting, glamorous, and possibly admirable character than her rival Rowena. This was the view of many early critics and commentators, and Rebecca's fate was regularly re-scripted, as in George Soane's *The Hebrew* (1820), in Thackeray's spoof sequel *Rebecca and Rowena* (1850), in which he kills off Rowena (that 'frigid piece of propriety', that 'icy, faultless, prim, niminy-piminy' and 'intoler-able' woman), and Thomas F. Plowman's (real name Thomas Forder) *Isaac Abroad; or, Ivanhoe Settled and Rebecca Righted: a Dramatic Version of a Final and Unpublished Volume of Scott's Novel* (1878), all pieces which married Rebecca to Ivanhoe.[24] The many representations of *tableaux vivants* derived from *Ivanhoe* in fiction are invariably included to serve as touchstones for character and courtships. Rebecca certainly had by far the better costume, allowing for the wearing of exotically coloured silks and a great many jewels. Rowena, by contrast, was thought of as 'that pompous, cold, disagreeable, insipid Rowena', to quote the heroine Ellen's mother in Samuel Griswold Goodrich's story 'The Consul's Daughter' when it is suggested that Ellen should be costumed as Rowena to accompany her friend Matilda as Rebecca, making up a trio with the man they are both in love with, who is going as Ivanhoe.[25] (In conformity with Scott, the modest Ellen eventually gets her man, while the showy Matilda retires baffled.)

In parallel, the history of adaptations aimed at children speaks of how important *Ivanhoe* was felt to be by as early as the 1860s to the promotion of proper values for both boys and girls. Charles Hunt's painting of middle-class children playing at Ivanhoe (1871) describes the hold that the book had, or that it was felt that it should have, over children's imaginations of the time. Two boys joust on tables and chairs in a borrowed helmet and toy breastplates for the entertainment of two rather self-consciously pretty girls sitting in a makeshift pavilion fashioned of a broken umbrella held by a couple of other boys, while a volume of Ivanhoe lies open on the floor in the foreground. Broadly speaking, as the painting suggests, boys were to find in Ivanhoe models of knightly and gentlemanly chivalry: in 1908, Baden-Powell's best-selling Scouting for Boys was in fact recommending it as appropriate reading for boys.[26] Girls were expected to find a model for pure, attractive, and admiring maidenhood in Rowena. Perhaps unsurprisingly, such evidence as there is to hand suggests that Ivanhoe was less equivocal as a reading experience for boys than girls. One male reader remembered that, 'It was reading the siege of Torquilstone which led me to make pasteboard armour for myself as a boy and procure a wooden sword and battle-ax and have many a hand-to-hand fight with my brother similarly accoutred, in which the occasional real wounds were a pride and joy.'[27]

In 1924, rather belatedly, W. P. Borland described what he himself had found as a boy in Ivanhoe and its companion tales, namely strongly inflected gender role-models: 'fearless, generous heroes, whose fortunes led them into strange and terrible places, into perilous adventures [. . .] heroines, beautiful and constant, whose misfortunes gave opportunities to the heroes of showing how brave and chivalrous they were'.[28] If boys concentrated on the scenes depicting fighting and perilous adventures and rescuing unfortunate heroines, girls had their attention again and again directed to the contrast drawn between Rebecca and Rowena. Louisa Caroline Tuthill's I will be a Lady: a Book for Girls (1845), for example, included a story entitled 'Tableaux Vivants' which focused on the staging of the interview between Rowena and Rebecca, and this time not to the advantage of the girl cast as Rowena:

> The scene was in the one in which Rebecca presents the casket, and asks to see the face that had won Ivanhoe. No one could have been more completely Saxon than the Rowena, and the dress, and the lights, and the contrast with the dark Jewess, made her look very prettily; – but the moment the curtain was lifted, Harriet Ann burst into a silly, girlish giggle, and entirely spoiled the picture. The passionate Rebecca was so angry that she would not attempt the scene again.[29]

Some girls may simply have rebelled; as a child, Ada Ellen Bayly seems to have bypassed the problem by taking the part of Ivanhoe herself.[30] The performance of such tableaux was regularly promoted as suitable child edutainment within the home and, later on, at school.[31]

By the last quarter of the century *Ivanhoe* was being regularly edited, abridged and retold for children. It had already featured in one selection designed for children, *Readings for the Young from the Works of Sir Walter Scott*, 1848, but it was really in the 1870s, according to Beiderwell and McCormick, that *Ivanhoe* began to be marketed in its entirety explicitly for children, by being included in publishers' lists for children and sold as a school text.[32] Lavish illustrated editions (Riau 1882, 1883; Brock 1900; and Soper 1910) were produced for the gift market. The Bodleian Library holds around twenty-four abridgments or retellings of *Ivanhoe* for children and young people published in Britain between 1875 and 1952; in America, Beiderwell and McCormick note that the first time it was published as a children's book was in Ginn's 'Classics for Children' (1886), and that thereafter the first abridgment appeared in the 1890s, the first school edition in 1892 and eight schoolroom editions between 1897 and 1899.[33] This is almost certainly only the tip of the iceberg of the re-versioning of the novel for children, which was also carried out in compilations from Scott, such as *Readings from Sir Walter Scott* (1887) and *The Peerless Reciter, or, Popular Program: containing the choicest recitations and readings from the best authors, for schools, public entertainment, social gatherings, Sunday schools etc.* (1894).

The high point of *Ivanhoe*'s cultural importance can conjecturally be dated to just before the First World War. In June and July 1913, a lavish adaptation was filmed on site at Chepstow Castle by the American-based Imperial Film Company. Chepstow had a history of hosting large-scale pageants, including one based on *The Talisman*; the film drew on this local infrastructure and dominant aesthetic, hiring 200 locals as part of a total cast of 500 actors and fifty horses; by all accounts the town existed in a state of permanent fancy-dress and excitement throughout the summer.[34] The next year, *Ivanhoe*'s ideals of gentlemanly chivalry were to be tested to breaking point by the realities of trench warfare – and would eventually break. The elaborate edition of 1919 produced by G. K. Chesterton, Holbrook Johnson, and R. Brimley Johnson is tellingly valedictory in its collecting up of 'critical appreciations old and new', which usefully describe how *Ivanhoe* appeared on the cusp of its catastrophic fall from favour. Each of the critical appreciations reiterate *Ivanhoe*'s overriding appeal to boys, its brilliant pageantry and pictorial qualities, its strong sense of the wider European political theatre, its impact upon the writing of history and historical fiction, its theatricality, and the importance of Rebecca as a model for the strong heroine. But the compilation also includes Leslie Stephen's regretful comment, made originally in his *Hours in a Library* (1892 version): '*Ivanhoe* cannot be given up [. . .] *Ivanhoe*, let it be granted, is no longer a work for men; but it still is, or still ought to be, delightful reading for boys.'[35] The 'boyishness' of *Ivanhoe* had begun by the 1890s to identify it as attractively residual or obsolete; by the 1920s it marked a vanished time in which manly chivalry and the national and imperial rationale with which it was associated were still viable.

To the twenty-first century eye, *Ivanhoe* might well seem to be radically dubious about the chivalric. Ivanhoe himself is conspicuously ineffective if gallant. Given to swooning at critical points, confined to a sick-bed and in danger of altogether missing the siege of Torquilstone, which is conveyed to him only by the running commentary of a girl, he is at the culminating moment unable through exhaustion brought on by a previous wound to finish off the formidable Bois-Guilbert, who in fact is only dispatched by a stroke brought on by his 'contending passions'. But the practice of adaptation to which the novel was subjected progressively throughout the century had had a tendency to write out these problems. As Philip Cox notes, the adaptations of *Ivanhoe* were sites of political and cultural contestation, re-describing the original sometimes to revalue the passionate heroine, sometimes to make Ivanhoe more clearly manly, often to address anxiety about the treatment of Jewishness. *The Hebrew*, for example, re-describes the original to render Isaac of York altogether nobler and Ivanhoe altogether manlier (in this version Ivanhoe really does kill Bois-Guilbert). With the writing out of Scott's scepticism, the habit of adaptation, which had, as Cox has argued, increased the popularity of the original while in many ways re-scripting it, ensured that the catastrophe of the First World War would deliver a mortal blow to the popularity of the novel itself, as it did to the ideology and social languages with which it was synonymous in Britain.[36]

Ivanhoe would survive longer in the United States, where, as Jonathan Stubbs has argued with regard to the multiple scripts for the 1952 film, 'images of Britain's Middle Ages functioned as a cultural space used to articulate ideas about democracy and race relations at home, and interventionism abroad'.[37] The novel retained its place on American school syllabuses until the mid-twentieth century (the protagonist of Harper Lee's *To Kill a Mockingbird*, 1960, remarks on being forced to read *Ivanhoe*) and it has also retained a place in children's popular culture in Anglo-American television adaptations, the most recent of which was made in 2000. However, when in a couple of episodes into the popular 1958 television series Roger Moore threw off the constricting silver armour and the absurdly vast white-plumed helmet of Ivanhoe ('I feel like a medieval fireman', he quipped), and re-costumed himself as a hero owing less to medieval chivalry than to Errol Flynn's Robin Hood (himself distantly derived from the plot of *Ivanhoe*), he and his successors exited anything much resembling Scott's story. By the end of the century, even in American culture, *Ivanhoe* becomes a marker of the past; it is mentioned as part of the nineteenth-century heroine's reading in Karen Cushman's children's fiction *The Ballad of Lucy Whipple* (1996), and specified as a part of the East Coast aesthetic she necessarily outgrows when she moves to California and into modernity.[38]

3

What is true of the afterlife of *Ivanhoe* is also, to a lesser extent and with occasional differences of emphasis, true in broad outline of the ways in which Scott's other works operated within the Victorian popular consciousness. Even this chapter's necessarily brief and imperfect effort to reanimate the shadow of Scott's meanings for the century or so after his death reveals the astonishing extent of his cultural reach at the time; in this respect the inscription on the plaque buried beneath the Scott monument's foundations was in part justified. Imagining a moment aeons ahead when the plaque might be unearthed by archaeologists of another civilisation because 'all the surrounding structures are crumbled to dust / By the decay of Time, or by Human or Elemental violence', this artefact is designed to testify to a distant posterity:

> that/His Countrymen began on that day [15 August 1840] / To raise an Effigy and Architectural Monument / TO THE MEMORY OF SIR WALTER SCOTT, BART. / Whose admirable Writings were then allowed to have given more delight and suggested better feeling / To a larger class of readers, in every rank of society, / Than those of any other Author, / With the exception of Shakespeare alone; / And which were therefore thought likely to be remembered / Long after this act of Gratitude / On the part of this first generation of his Admirers / Should be forgotten

Yet almost as astonishing as the extent of Scott's cultural reach for the Victorians and Edwardians was its erasure over the next century. The Victorian feeling of living on the edge of cultural collapse, which informed the burial of this plaque, Knowles's stage-fantasy of the ruins of Abbotsford, and Captain Basil Hall's equally apocalyptic 1841 vision of Abbotsford in decay, would prove within a hundred years eerily prophetic as regarded Scott's acknowledged power over the popular imagination.[39]

That said, Scott is currently showing renewed signs of (after)life under the animating influence of the Scots nationalism of the last three decades. Within the academy this has manifested itself most notably in an upsurge of criticism, in the Edinburgh Edition of the Waverley Novels, and in the new projected edition of the poetry. Beyond the academy this resurgence may be read miscellaneously but unmistakeably in the re-marking of Scott within Scotland: in the development of a walking trail called the 'Walter Scott Way'; in a recent proliferation of plaques in Kelso, including one marking 'The Garden Cottage; home of Scott's Aunt Janet where he stayed while at school in Kelso'; and, most strikingly and expensively, in the re-display of

Abbotsford as a twenty-first-century tourist attraction. The Victorians, with all their enthusiasm for the Scottishness of Scott, in particular as exhibited in *Waverley*, *The Heart of Mid-Lothian*, and *Rob Roy*, had an even stronger preference for the more unambiguously English *Ivanhoe* and other Waverley Novels with exclusively English settings which ran it close for popularity, novels that have all but fallen out of today's canon, most especially *Kenilworth* and *Woodstock*. By contrast, the twenty-first-century Scott looks set to be an emphatically Scottish localist rather than a British or anglophone imperialist. For the foreseeable future, that is to say, Ivanhoe and Robin Hood are probably doomed to live on only in the wooden swords and toy bows and arrows sold for the pleasure of visiting children in the gift-shops of every ruined castle that still covertly polices the border.

Endnotes

Introduction – Robertson

1. Muriel Spark, *The Prime of Miss Jean Brodie* ([[1961] Harmondsworth: Penguin, 1965), p. 57.
2. See Martin Stannard, *Muriel Spark: The Biography* (London: Weidenfeld & Nicolson, 2009): prize, p. 38 and illustrations section 1, number 10; 1994 lecture, p. 509.
3. Muriel Spark, 'What Images Return', in Karl Miller (ed.), *Memoirs of a Modern Scotland* (London: Faber, 1970), p. 153. Although the poet involved was, biographically, Louis MacNeice, see also 'The House of the Famous Poet' (begun 1952), *The Stories of Muriel Spark* (New York: E. P. Dutton, 1985), pp. 192–9 and Stannard, *Spark*, pp. 135, 349–50.
4. On some of the less frequently-discussed elements of this oeuvre see Julian D'Arcy and Kirsten Wolf, 'Sir Walter Scott and Eyrbyggja Saga', *Studies in Scottish Literature* 22 (1987), pp. 30–43; David Matthews, '"Quaint Inglis": Walter Scott and the Rise of Middle English Studies', *Studies in Medievalism* 7 (1995), pp. 33–48; Arthur Johnston, *Enchanted Ground: The Study of Medieval Romance in the Eighteenth Century* (London: Athlone Press, 1964); Alan Lupack, '*Sir Tristrem*: Reception and Perception', *Studies in Medievalism* 7 (1995), pp. 49–62; George Falle, 'Sir Walter Scott as Editor of Dryden and Swift', *University of Toronto Quarterly* 36 (1967), pp. 161–80; Daniel P. Watkins, 'Scott the Dramatist', in Terence Allan Hoagwood and Daniel P. Watkins (eds), *British Romantic Drama: Historical and Critical Essays* (Madison, NJ: Fairleigh Dickinson University Press, 1998), pp. 182–207; Fiona Robertson, 'Castle Spectres: Scott, Gothic Drama, and the Search for the Narrator', and Barbara Bell, 'Sir Walter Scott and the National Drama', in Alexander and Hewitt, *Scott in Carnival*, pp. 444–58 and 459–77 respectively.
5. In addition to the edition of the *Letters* cited in this volume, see the Millgate Union Catalogue, www.nls.uk/scott; J. H. Alexander, 'The Gurnal', in Alexander and Hewitt, *Scott in Carnival*, pp. 434–43.
6. See Bolton, *Scott Dramatized*; Richard M. Ford, *British Productions of the Waverley Dramatisations: A Catalogue* (Oxford: Oxford Bibliographical

156

Society, 1978) and 'The Waverley Burlesques', *Nineteenth-Century Theatre Research* 6:2 (1978), pp. 63–70; Jerome Mitchell, *Scott Operas* and *More Scott Operas* (Lanham, MD: University Press of America, 1996), and Jeremy Tambling, 'Scott's "Heyday" in Opera', in Pittock, *Reception in Europe*, pp. 285–92; Douglas Percy Bliss, *Sir Walter Scott and the Visual Arts* (Glasgow: Foulis Archive Press, 1971); Catherine Gordon, *Lamp of Memory*. The lines of enquiry suggested by Hugh Trevor-Roper in 'The Invention of Tradition: The Highland Tradition of Scotland', in Eric Hobsbawm and Terence Ranger (eds), *The Invention of Tradition* (Cambridge: Cambridge University Press, 1983), pp. 15–43, have been explored most authoritatively by Murray G. H. Pittock in *The Invention of Scotland: The Stuart Myth and the Scottish Identity, 1638 to the Present* (London: Routledge, 1991), and in essays by Pittock and Ian Brown in Ian Brown (ed.), *From Tartan to Tartanry: Scottish Culture, History and Myth* (Edinburgh: Edinburgh University Press, 2010).

7. Muir, *Scott and Scotland*, p. 11.
8. Hewitt, *Scott on Himself*, pp. 26, 39–40. Scott's youthful reading is generally taken to inform his account of Edward Waverley, *WN* vol. 1, pp. 14–15.
9. The Abbotsford Library Research Project Trust was established in 1996, under the directorship of Douglas Gifford. The preparation of a new catalogue of the collection is led by Lindsay Levy of the Library of the Faculty of Advocates, Edinburgh. To date, new discoveries in the collection include a medieval folio manuscript, the Bokenham mass, and a manuscript copy of *The Western Remonstrance*, from Covenanting history of the 1680s; representative of ongoing work is Lindsay Levy, 'Scott's Early Love Poems to Williamina Belsches', *Scottish Literary Journal* 3:2 (2011), pp. 45–53.
10. Hazlitt, 'Sir Walter Scott', in *Lectures on the English Poets* and *The Spirit of the Age: or Contemporary Portraits*, intro. Catherine Macdonald Maclean (London: Dent, 1967), p. 230.
11. Ibid., p. 231.
12. Ibid., p. 229.
13. See Pittock, *Reception in Europe*; Alexander and Hewitt, *Scott and his Influence*, for essays on individual writers from Britain, Europe, Canada, and the United States.
14. *Jane Eyre*, ed. Margaret Smith (Oxford: Oxford University Press, 1975), p. 381.
15. *The Tenant of Wildfell Hall*, ed. G. D. Hargreaves, intro. Winifred Gérin (Harmondsworth: Penguin, 1979), p. 91.
16. *The Tenant of Wildfell Hall*, television drama, directed by Mike Barker. London: BBC, 1996.
17. Although *Count Robert* has an unexpected literary afterlife: see Edward Larrissy, 'Yeats's "Sailing to Byzantium" and Scott's *Count Robert of Paris*', *Notes & Queries* 42:2 (1995), pp. 210–11.

1 – Ferris

1. 'Scott's Minstrelsy of the Scottish Border', *Monthly Review* 42 (1803), p. 21.
2. Ibid., p. 33.
3. [William Maginn], 'The Death of Sir Walter Scott', *Fraser's Magazine* 6 (1832), p. 380.
4. See Duncan, *Scott's Shadow*, ch. 1.
5. See Andrew Piper, *Dreaming in Books: The Making of the Bibliographic Imagination in the Romantic Age* (Chicago: University of Chicago Press, 2009), pp. 97–9.
6. Pierre Bourdieu, *The Rules of Art: Genesis and Structure of the Literary Field*, trans. Susan Emmanuel (Stanford: Stanford University Press, 1996).
7. See, for example, Joep Leerssen, 'Introduction', *Free Access to the Past: Romanticism, Cultural Heritage and the Nation*, ed. Lotte Jensen, Joep Leerssen, and Marita Marthijsen (Leiden and Boston: Brill, 2010).
8. Rosemary Sweet emphasises these developments in *Antiquaries: The Discovery of the Past in Eighteenth-Century Britain* (London and New York: Hambledon & London, 2004), ch. 9.
9. See Mark Salber Phillips, *Society and Sentiment: Genres of Historical Writing in Britain, 1740–1820* (Princeton: Princeton University Press, 2000) and Rigney, *Imperfect Histories*.
10. For Scott's sales figures, see William St Clair, *The Reading Nation in the Romantic Period* (Cambridge: Cambridge University Press, 2004), appendix 9.
11. Review of *Marmion*, *Scots Magazine* 70 (1808), p. 195.
12. *Reliquiae Trotcosienses*, ed. Gerard Carruthers and Alison Lumsden (Edinburgh: Edinburgh University Press, 2004).
13. Heather Jackson surveys the publishing/reading context of the period in *Romantic Readers: The Evidence of Marginalia* (New Haven and London: Yale University Press, 2005), pp. 1–59.
14. Garside, 'The Baron's Books', p. 248.
15. Yoon Sun Lee elaborates this argument in *Nationalism and Irony*, pp. 74–104.
16. See Fielding, *Scotland and the Fictions of Geography*, pp. 114–22.
17. 'Ancient History of Scotland', *Quarterly Review* 41 (1829), p. 154.
18. Ibid., p. 155.
19. Homer Obed Brown stresses the formative role of Scott's own periodical essays in *Institutions of the English Novel: From Defoe to Scott* (Philadelphia: University of Pennsylvania Press, 1997), pp. 8–22.
20. On the importance of the national tale as precursor of Scott's historical novel, see Trumpener, *Bardic Nationalism*, pp. 137–42.
21. Review of *Waverley*, *Antijacobin Review* 47 (1814), p. 217.
22. Review of *Ivanhoe*, *Edinburgh Review* 33 (1820), p. 1.

23. Review of *Alicia de Lacy; an historical Romance*, *British Critic* 2 (1814), p. 549.

24. Richard Maxwell, *The Historical Novel in Europe, 1650–1950* (Cambridge: Cambridge University Press, 2009), p. 3.

25. David Duff, *Romanticism and the Uses of Genre* (Oxford: Oxford University Press, 2009), p. 178.

26. Robertson, *Legitimate Histories*, p. 117.

27. *Waverley*, ed. Claire Lamont (Oxford: Oxford University Press, 1986), p. 344.

28. Robert Mayer, 'The Internal Machinery Displayed: *The Heart of Midlothian* and Scott's Apparatus for the Waverley Novels', *Clio* 17:1 (1987), p. 13.

29. Wordsworth, *Poetical Works*, ed. Ernest de Selincourt (Oxford: Oxford University Press, 1969), p. 735.

2 – McNeil

1. For the *Minstrelsy*'s evolution and publication see Millgate, *Making of the Novelist* and 'The Early Publication History of Scott's *Minstrelsy of the Scottish Border*', *PBSA* 94:4 (2000), pp. 551–64.

2. Ian Duncan has recently labelled the *Minstrelsy* 'one of the great neglected works of British Romanticism': *Modern Language Quarterly* 70:4 (2009), p. 409. For recent studies see Fielding, *Writing and Orality*; Maureen N. McLane, *Balladeering, Minstrelsy, and the Making of British Romantic Poetry* (Cambridge: Cambridge University Press, 2008); Steve Newman, *Ballad Collection, Lyric, and the Canon: The Call of the Popular from the Restoration to the New Criticism* (Philadelphia: University of Pennsylvania Press, 2007); Susan Stewart, *Crimes of Writing: Problems in the Containment of Representation* (New York: Oxford University Press, 1991). For discussion of Scott's influence on ballad collecting in Europe, see Tom Hubbard, 'European Reception of Scott's Poetry: Translation as the Front Line', in Pittock, *Reception in Europe*, pp. 268–84.

3. Jackson-Houlston established Scott's authorship in *Ballads, Songs, and Snatches: The Appropriation of Folk Song and Popular Culture in British Nineteenth-Century Realist Prose* (Aldershot: Ashgate, 1999). The *Antiquary* passage is doubly ironic in that there were two extant versions of 'The Battle of Red Harlaw' in Scott's day. Jackson-Houlston surmises that Scott must have assumed the original traditional version was lost and so rewrote the later version: *Ballads, Songs, and Snatches*, pp. 28–30.

4. Davis et al., *Scotland and the Borders of Romanticism*, p. 13.

5. See Nicholas Hudson, '"Oral Tradition": The Evolution of an Eighteenth-Century Concept', in Alvaro Ribeiro and James G. Basker (eds), *Tradition in Transition: Women Writers, Marginal Texts, and the Eighteenth-Century Canon* (Oxford: Clarendon Press, 1996), pp. 161–76; and Nick Groom, 'Celts, Goths, and the Nature of the Literary Source', in ibid., pp. 274–96.

6. Fielding, *Writing and Orality*, p. 4.

7. Ibid., pp. 1–11.
8. For a recuperation of the spinster figure as ballad source, see Adriana Craciun, 'Romantic Spinstrelsy: Anne Bannerman and the Sexual Politics of the Ballad', in Davis et al., *Scotland and the Borders of Romanticism*, pp. 204–24.
9. Janet Sorensen, 'Alternative Antiquarianisms of Scotland and the North', *Modern Language Quarterly* 70:4 (2009), pp. 415–41.
10. *Edinburgh Review* 6 (1805), p. 462.
11. McLane, *Balladeering*, p. 128.
12. Literally so, since the minstrel is a Scott. See McLane, *Balladeering*, pp. 130–2.
13. See for example Franco Moretti, *Atlas of the European Novel, 1800–1900* (London: Verso, 1998), pp. 34–41; Saree Makdisi, *Romantic Imperialism: Universal Empire and the Culture of Modernity* (Cambridge: Cambridge University Press, 1998), pp. 70–99.
14. See Trumpener, *Bardic Nationalism*, pp. 246–7.
15. See McLane, *Balladeering*, pp. 84–90, 117–22; and Eric Lott, *Love and Theft: Blackface Minstrelsy and the American Working Class* (Oxford: Oxford University Press, 1995).
16. The definition is Mary Louise Pratt's: *Imperial Eyes: Travel Writing and Transculturation* (London: Routledge, 1992), p. 7. See also James Buzard, *Disorienting Fiction: the Autoethnographic Work of Nineteenth-Century British Novels* (Princeton: Princeton University Press, 2005).
17. Pratt, *Imperial Eyes* pp. 7–8.
18. Susan Oliver sees Scott's attraction to borders life as reflecting more immediate and topical anxieties in the first half of the nineteenth century: *Poetics of Cultural Encounter*, ch. 2.
19. Homi K. Bhabha, *The Location of Culture* (London: Routledge, 1994), pp. 206, 219.
20. See Scott Michaelsen and David E. Johnson, *Border Theory: The Limits of Cultural Politics* (Minneapolis: University of Minnesota Press, 1997).
21. Ramón Saldívar argues that Paredes's comparison between Chicano and Scottish ballad traditions links 'the struggles of the "Border people" of south Texas with other peoples at the peripheries of power globally and historically': *The Borderlands of Culture: Américo Paredes and the Transnational Imaginary* (Durham, NC: Duke University Press, 2006), p. 36.

3 – Lumsden and McIntosh

1. For example, *The Cambridge Companion to Romantic Poetry*, ed. James Chandler and Maureen N. McLane (Cambridge: Cambridge University Press, 2008) contains many passing references to his poetry but no sustained discussion.
2. *Letters* vol. 1, p. 349 (to Archibald Constable & Co., 31 January 1807).

3. For full details of the publishing history see Todd and Bowden, *Bibliographical History*, pp. 175–89.

4. Davis et al., *Scotland and the Borders of Romanticism*, p. 5.

5. Murray Pittock also proposes that constructions of Romanticism have not always thought of it in a fully archipelagic sense, so that Scotland's contribution has been too often neglected: *Scottish and Irish Romanticism* (Oxford: Oxford University Press, 2008), p. 6.

6. These include Marilyn Butler, Nigel Leask, Tim Fulford, Lynda Pratt and Mark Storey. For an overview of the rehabilitation of Southey in recent years see Lynda Pratt, 'Introduction' in *Robert Southey and the Contexts of English Romanticism*, ed. Lynda Pratt (Aldershot: Ashgate, 2006), pp. xvii–xxix.

7. In, respectively, Marilyn Butler, 'Repossessing the Past', in Marjorie Levinson, Marilyn Butler, Jerome McGann, Paul Hamilton (eds), *Rethinking Historicism: Critical Readings in Romantic History* (Oxford: Blackwell, 1989), p. 79; and 'Plotting the Revolutions: The Political Narratives of Romantic Poetry and Criticism', in *Romantic Revolutions: Criticism and Theory*, ed. Kenneth R. Johnston, Gilbert Chaitin, Karen Hanson and Herbert Marks (Indianapolis: Indiana University Press, 1990), pp. 141–2.

8. David Hewitt, 'Scott, Sir Walter (1771–1832)', *Oxford Dictionary of National Biography* (Oxford: Oxford University Press, 2004), vol. 49, pp. 490–510 (p. 495).

9. Scott's excitement: 'Essay on Imitations of the Ancient Ballad', in *PW* vol. 4, p. 39; and liberation, Hewitt, 'Scott, Sir Walter', p. 496.

10. See Trumpener, *Bardic Nationalism*, p. 6.

11. Those who have drawn attention to this aspect of Scott's poetry include Goslee, *Scott the Rhymer* and Fielding, *Writing and Orality*. McLane, *Balladeering*, argues that, via their notes and apparatuses, ballad collections offered a taxonomy of thinking for the Humanities as we now know them.

12. Francis Jeffrey in J. H. Alexander, *Two Studies in Romantic Reviewing: Edinburgh Reviewers and the English Tradition; The Reviewing of Walter Scott's Poetry: 1805–1817* (Salzburg: Institut für Englische Sprache und Literatur Universität Salzburg, 1976), p. 48.

13. Marshall Brown notes that in the Romantic ballad 'Time moves fast and jerkily if it moves at all, avoiding the smooth unfolding of cause and consequence': 'Poetry and the Novel', in *The Cambridge Companion to Fiction in the Romantic Period*, ed. Richard Maxwell and Katie Trumpener (Cambridge: Cambridge University Press, 2008), p. 117.

14. Lincoln, *Scott and Modernity*, p. 36.

15. Ibid., p. 31; Pittock, *Scottish and Irish Romanticism*, p. 187; and Oliver, *Poetics of Cultural Encounter*, p. 11.

16. Elaborated in Alison Lumsden, *Walter Scott and the Limits of Language* (Edinburgh: Edinburgh University Press, 2010), ch. 1.

17. Pittock, *Scottish and Irish Romanticism*, p. 189.

18. Lincoln, *Scott and Modernity*, p. 31.
19. This can also be seen in the poem's treatment of the 'magic book' of Michael Scott. See Lumsden, *Limits of Language*, pp. 62–3.
20. Tara Ghoshal Wallace, 'Competing Discourses in *Ivanhoe*', in Alexander and Hewitt, *Scott in Carnival*, p. 294.
21. Pittock, *Scottish and Irish Romanticism*, p. 191.
22. Millgate, *The Making of the Novelist*, p. 25.
23. MS 3877, fo. 2v. [2 April 1808].
24. See Jill Rubenstein, 'Scott's Historical Poetry', Johns Hopkins University, unpublished PhD, 1969, p. 132.
25. J. H. Alexander, *'Marmion': Studies in Interpretation and Composition* (Salzburg: Institut für Anglistik und Amerikanistik Universität Salzburg, 1981) p. 3.
26. J. D. McClatchy, 'The Ravages of Time: The Function of the *Marmion* Epistles', *Studies in Scottish Literature* 9 (1972), p. 262.
27. Lincoln, *Scott and Modernity*, p. 37.
28. Goslee also notes this connection between fiction and forgery, positing Marmion's crime as 'a metaphor not only for the self-indulgence but for the opportunism involved in the writing of romance fictions', *Scott the Rhymer*, p. 43.
29. Andrew Hook, 'Scotland and Romanticism: the international scene', in *The History of Scottish Literature*, 4 vols (1987–98), vol. 2, p. 319.
30. Hogg, 'Highland Adventures', in *Winter Evening Tales*, ed. Ian Duncan (Edinburgh: Edinburgh University Press, 2004), p. 109.
31. Marshall Brown, 'Poetry and Novel', p. 117.

4 – McCracken-Flesher

1. See Cairns Craig, *The Modern Scottish Novel: Narrative and the National Imagination* (Edinburgh: Edinburgh University Press, 1999), p. 117.
2. For example N. T. Phillipson, 'Nationalism and Ideology', in J. N. Wolfe (ed.), *Government and Nationalism in Scotland* (Edinburgh: Edinburgh University Press, 1969), p. 186. Also David McCrone, *The Sociology of Nationalism: Tomorrow's Ancestors* (London: Routledge, 1998), p. 60.
3. Francis Jeffrey, review of *Waverley*, *Edinburgh Review* 24 (1814), pp. 208–43. See Hayden, *Critical Heritage*, p. 79.
4. James Hogg declared: 'The Whig ascendancy in the British cabinet killed Sir Walter', Hogg, *Memoirs*, p. 132; Thomas Carlyle imagines Scott writing himself to death for bourgeois ends in his review of vols 1–6 of Lockhart's biography, *London and Westminster Review* (1837–8), pp. 293–345, rpt. in Hayden, *Critical Heritage*, pp. 345–73.
5. 'Sawney in the Bog-house', c. 1745, attributed to George Bickham the Younger, imitated 1779 by James Gillray. *Catalogue of Political and Personal*

Satires, British Museum, print 2678, 3988, 5539. See Michael Duffy, *The Englishman and the Foreigner* (Cambridge: Chadwyck-Healey, 1986), plate 36.

6. See McCracken-Flesher, *Possible Scotlands*, pp. 73–113.
7. Hugh Miller, 'The Centenary of the "Forty-Five"', in *Essays Historical and Biographical, Political and Social, Literary and Scientific* (Edinburgh: Adam and Charles Black, 1862), pp. 82–95. See p. 85.
8. Lukács, *Historical Novel*, pp. 19–88. Edwin Muir remarks: 'Scott [. . .] lived in a community which was not a community and set himself to carry on a tradition that was not a tradition': *Scott and Scotland*, pp. 11–12. Phillipson, 'Nationalism and Ideology', p. 186.
9. Pittock, *The Invention of Scotland*, pp. 86–7; D'Arcy, *Subversive Scott*, p. 52.
10. Cairns Craig, *Out of History: Narrative Paradigms in Scottish and English Culture* (Edinburgh: Polygon, 1996), pp. 13, 40, 45–6.
11. Judith Williamson, *Decoding Advertisements* (London: Marion Boyars, 1978).
12. *Monthly Review* 104 (1824), pp. 198–209; see esp. pp. 199–200.
13. Andrew Bisset, Review of *Tales of a Grandfather*, Second Series, *Westminster Review* 10 (1829), pp. 257–83.
14. Review of *The Black Dwarf* and *Old Mortality*, *Critical Review* 5:4 (1816), pp. 614–25. Rpt. in Hayden, *Critical Heritage*, pp. 106–12: see p. 107.
15. Review of *Redgauntlet*, *Examiner* (11 July 1824), p. 441.
16. Lukács, *Historical Novel*, p. 38.
17. See Welsh, *Hero of the Waverley Novels*, esp. ch. 2.
18. Review of *Redgauntlet*, *London Magazine* 10 (1824), pp. 69–78; see p. 71.
19. See Millgate, *The Making of the Novelist*, pp. 35–6; Wilt, *Secret Leaves*, pp. 28–37.
20. Wilt, *Secret Leaves*, p. 5.
21. Ibid., p. 17.
22. See Cairns Craig, *Associationism and the Literary Imagination: From the Phantasmal Chaos* (Edinburgh: Edinburgh University Press, 2007), p. 17.
23. McCracken-Flesher, *Possible Scotlands*, pp. 73–113.
24. Bisset, Review, pp. 260–1.
25. Welsh, *Hero of the Waverley Novels*, p. 58; Millgate, *The Making of the Novelist*, p. 56.
26. Robertson, *Legitimate Histories*, p. 62.
27. For example, review of *Redgauntlet*, *Edinburgh Magazine* Second Series 14 (1824), pp. 641–7, and *Monthly Review* 104 (1824): 198–209.

5 – Jones

1. Thomas Carlyle, *Two Note Books of Thomas Carlyle, from 23d March 1822 to 16th May 1832*, ed. Charles Eliot Norton (New York: The Grolier Club, 1898), pp. 214–15.

2. Thomas Thomson to Francis Horner, 25 May 1816, in Cosmo Innes, *Memoir of Thomas Thomson* (Edinburgh: Constable, 1854), pp. 155–6.

3. Marinell Ash, *The Strange Death of Scottish History* (Edinburgh: Ramsay Head Press, 1980), p. 47.

4. [J. G. Lockhart], *Memoirs of the Life of Sir Walter Scott, Bart.*, 7 vols (Edinburgh, 1837–8), vol. 1, p. 202. See also Arthur Melville Clark, *Sir Walter Scott: The Formative Years* (Edinburgh and London: Blackwood, 1969), p. 249. Scott mentions Thomson in his report on the 'Mountain Boys' in a letter to William Erskine of 24 April 1796 (*Letters*, vol. 1, p. 47).

5. Tristram Clarke, 'Thomson, Thomas (1768–1852)', in *Oxford Dictionary of National Biography*, vol. 54, p. 555.

6. Anderson, *Scott and History*, pp. 2–3.

7. Horner to Thomson, 30 May 1816, in Innes, *Memoir of Thomas Thomson*, pp. 156–7.

8. Lockhart, *Memoirs*, vol. 4, pp. 26–7. See also Thomas Constable, *Archibald Constable and His Literary Correspondents*, 3 vols (Edinburgh: Edmonston and Douglas, 1873), vol. 3, p. 92.

9. Hugh Blair, *Lectures on Rhetoric and Belles Lettres*, 3 vols (Dublin: Whitestone, Colles, Burnett et al., 1783), vol. 3, p. 43.

10. Scott to Archibald Constable, 10 October 1816, *Letters* vol. 4, pp. 277–8. 'Pauls Letters from the Continent' is a reference to a series of imaginary letters by Scott entitled *Paul's Letters to His Kinsfolk* (1816), which document his personal reactions to the scenes he passed through on his tour of the Netherlands and France the previous year, including the post-battle field of Waterloo, and provides a detailed history of Napoleon's last campaign based on interviews with participants and eyewitnesses. Scott's model for his 'History' was Oliver Goldsmith's *An History of England in a Series of Letters from a Nobleman to his Son* (1784). See Scott's letter to John Murray of 20 October 1814 (*Letters* vol. 3, p. 509).

11. Constable to Scott, 25 October 1816, NLS MS 789, fos 669–70.

12. Lockhart, *Memoirs*, vol. 4, p. 27.

13. Hewitt, *Scott on Himself*, p. 31. Alexander Fraser Tytler was appointed, jointly with John Pringle, professor of universal history at Edinburgh University on 16 February 1780. In 1786 he became full professor of civil history (see *Oxford Dictionary of National Biography*, vol. 55, pp. 822–4).

14. John W. Burgon, *The Portrait of a Christian Gentleman: A Memoir of Patrick Fraser Tytler* (London: Murray, 1859), p. 174.

15. Scott to Lord Montagu, 17 July 1823, *Letters* vol. 8, p. 48. Scott refers to David Dalrymple, Lord Hailes's *Annals of Scotland* (1776–9); John Pinkerton's *The History of Scotland from the Accession of the House of Stuart to that of Mary* (1797); William Robertson's *History of Scotland, During the Reigns of Queen Mary and of King James VI. till his Accession to the Crown of England* (1759); and Malcolm Laing's *History of Scotland, from the Union of the Crowns on the*

Accession of James VI. [. . .] to the Union of the Kingdoms in the Reign of Queen Anne (1800).

16. Burgon, *The Portrait of a Christian Gentleman*, pp. 175, 176.

17. Patrick Fraser Tytler, *History of Scotland*, 9 vols (Edinburgh: Tait, 1828–43), vol. 1, p. vi.

18. See ibid., vol. 1, pp. 425–57.

19. Jane Millgate, *Macaulay* (London and Boston: Routledge & Kegan Paul, 1973), p. 120.

20. Thomas Babington Macaulay, 'History', in *The Complete Works of Lord Macaulay*, 12 vols (London: Longmans, Green, 1898), vol. 7, p. 217.

21. Macaulay, 'Hallam', *Complete Works*, vol. 7, pp. 221–326; see also Mark Phillips, 'Macaulay, Scott, and the Literary Challenge to Historiography', *Journal of the History of Ideas*, 50:1 (1989), pp. 117–33.

22. Hewitt, *Scott on Himself*, pp. 22, 27.

23. See Garside, '"Philosophical" Historians', p. 504.

24. Scott notes in his 'Memoirs' that he was 'selected by [John Bruce] as one of the students whose progress he approved to read an essay before Principal Robertson' (Hewitt, *Scott on Himself*, p. 31).

25. Sylvia Sebastiani, 'Conjectural History vs. the Bible: Eighteenth-Century Scottish Historians and the Idea of History in the *Encyclopaedia Britannica*', *Lumen* 21 (2002), pp. 213–31; Sylvia Sebastiani, '"Race", Women and Progress in the Scottish Enlightenment', in *Women, Gender and Enlightenment*, ed. Sarah Knott and Barbara Taylor (Basingstoke: Palgrave Macmillan, 2005), pp. 75–96.

26. Colin Kidd, '*The Strange Death of Scottish History* revisited: Constructions of the Past in Scotland, c.1790–1914', *Scottish Historical Review*, 76, part 1, no. 201 (April 1997), pp. 86–102 (p. 87); see also his *Subverting Scotland's Past: Scottish Whig Historians and the Creation of an Anglo-British Identity, 1689–c.1830* (Cambridge: Cambridge University Press, 1993).

27. Letter to William Straham, August 1770, in *The Letters of David Hume*, ed. J. Y. T. Grieg, 2 vols (Oxford: Clarendon Press, 1932), vol. 2, p. 230; Murray Pittock, 'History and the Teleology of Civility', in *Enlightenment and Emancipation*, ed. Susan Manning and Peter France (Lewisburg: Bucknell University Press, 2006), p. 83.

28. Kidd, '*The Strange Death of Scottish History* revisited', p. 87.

29. Moritz Baumstark, 'David Hume: The Making of a Philosophical Historian: A Reconsideration', unpublished PhD thesis (University of Edinburgh, 2007), p. 137.

30. Kidd, '*The Strange Death of Scottish History* revisited', p. 87.

31. Ibid., p. 87; Karen O'Brien, 'Robertson's Place in the Development of Eighteenth-Century Narrative History', in *William Robertson and the Expansion of Empire*, ed. Stewart J. Brown (Cambridge: Cambridge University Press, 1997), pp. 74–91.

32. See, for example, Duncan Forbes, 'The Rationalism of Sir Walter Scott', *Cambridge Journal* 7 (1953), pp. 20–35; McMaster, *Scott and Society*; Sutherland, 'Fictional Economies'; David Kaufmann, *The Business of Common Life: Classical Economics and the Novel from Revolution to Reform* (Baltimore and London: Johns Hopkins University Press, 1995).

33. Ferris, *Achievement of Literary Authority*, p. 205.

34. *WN* vol. 1, p. 98. Castruccio Castrucani was Duke of Lucca and leader of the Ghibelline party in the political wars in early fourteenth-century Italy.

35. Claire Lamont, 'The Poetry of the Early Waverley Novels', *Proceedings of the British Academy* 61 (1975), p. 322.

36. P. D. Garside, 'Historical Note', *WN* vol. 1, p. 505.

37. John Home, *The History of the Rebellion in the Year 1745* (London: T. Cadell, Jun., and W. Davies, 1802), p. 150; *WN* vol. 1, pp. 296–7; Garside, 'Historical Note', *WN* vol. 1, p. 505.

38. Robert Louis Stevenson, 'Victor Hugo's Romances', *Cornhill Magazine* 30 (August 1874), p. 182.

39. Ibid., p. 180. On the links between historical fiction in Scotland and France, see Richard Maxwell, *The Historical Novel in Europe, 1650–1960* (Cambridge: Cambridge University Press, 2009).

40. David Hume, *The History of Great Britain: Vol. 1: Containing the Reigns of James I. and Charles I.* (Edinburgh: Hamilton, Balfour, and Neill [1754]), pp. 245–6.

41. David Hume, *Baron David Hume's Lectures 1786–1822*, ed. G. Campbell H. Paton (Edinburgh: Printed for the Stair Society by Skinner, then Cunningham, 1939–58), vol. 1, p. 8.

42. David Hume, *Commentaries on the Law of Scotland, Respecting Crimes*, 2 vols (Edinburgh: Bell and Bradfute, and Balfour, 1797), vol. 2, pp. 231–2.

43. Ibid., vol. 2, p. 428.

44. David Hewitt and Alison Lumsden, 'Historical Note', in *WN* vol. 6, p. 587.

45. Mark Salber Phillips, *Society and Sentiment: Genres of Historical Writing in Britain, 1740–1820* (Princeton: Princeton University Press, 2000), p. 65.

46. Susan Manning, *The Puritan-Provincial Vision: Scottish and American Fiction in the Nineteenth Century* (Cambridge: Cambridge University Press, 1990), p. 180.

47. Scott to James Ballantyne, 10 September 1818, *Letters* vol. 5, p. 186.

48. John Ruthven's father, William, first Earl of Gowrie, had kidnapped the boy-king James VI in the 'Raid' of Ruthven. He had at first been pardoned, then banished, then beheaded in 1584, after entering into a conspiracy to capture Stirling Castle.

49. *WN* vol. 7a, p. 66; see also Anderson, *Scott and History*, pp. 69–70.

50. William Robertson, *The History of Scotland*, 2 vols (Dublin: Ewing, 1759), vol. 2, p. 222.

51. D. J. Womersley, 'The Historical Writings of William Robertson', *Journal of the History of Ideas*, 47:3 (1986), p. 502.

52. Tytler, *History of Scotland*, vol. 9, p. 343.

53. Ibid. vol. 9, pp. 358–9.

54. [Patrick Fraser], *Tytler's History of Scotland Examined: A Review* (Edinburgh: Constable, 1848), p. 245.

55. *Oxford Dictionary of National Biography*, vol. 55, p. 828.

6 – Baker

1. In his 1975–6 Collège de France lectures published as *Society Must Be Defended* (2003), Michel Foucault argues that conquest, as a basic mode of power relations, persisted as an underlying social framework well after its supposed supplanting by emergent techniques of political government, and that Carl von Clausewitz's famous formulation that 'war is politics by other means', by inverting what had been a general if increasingly tacit understanding of this persistence, induced, at a crucial historical juncture, a certain amnesia about conquest. Scott too keeps conquest ever in sight as an order of historical event, its immanence to what might seem political or even intimate personal affairs.

2. Chris Hedges, *War is a Force That Gives Us Meaning* (New York: Public Affairs, 2002).

3. Curry, *Edinburgh Annual Register*, p. 100.

4. On Scott and the early modern transition from absolutism to more distributed modalites of power relations, see Amy Witherbee, 'Habeas Corpus: British Imaginations of Power in Walter Scott's *Old Mortality*', *New Literary History* 39 (2008), pp. 355–67.

5. In so doing, this chapter will draw, for the most part tacitly, on a group of excellent recent studies of Romanticism and war. See Mary Favret, *War at a Distance* (Princeton: Princeton University Press, 2010); Gillian Russell, *The Theatres of War* (Oxford: Clarendon Press, 1995); J. R. Watson, *Romanticism and War* (Basingstoke: Palgrave, 2003); Simon Bainbridge, *Napoleon and English Romanticism* (Cambridge: Cambridge University Press, 1995) and *British Poetry and the Revolutionary and Napoleonic Wars* (Oxford: Oxford University Press, 2003); Philip Shaw (ed.), *Romantic Wars: Studies in Culture and Conflict* (Aldershot: Ashgate, 2000), and Shaw, *Waterloo and the Romantic Imagination* (Basingstoke: Palgrave, 2002).

6. This anecdote, reported by Scott himself, appears in Lockhart, *Memoirs*, vol. 1, p. 13.

7. Twain, *Life on the Mississippi* (New York: Penguin, 2009), p. 249. On Twain and Scott, see Wilt, 'Steamboat Surfacing: Scott and the English Novelists', *Nineteenth-Century Fiction* 35:4 (1981), pp. 459–86, and Manning, 'Did Mark Twain Pull Down the Temple on Scott's Shoulders?', in Janet Beer and Bridget Bennett (eds), *Special Relationships* (Manchester: Manchester University Press, 2002), pp. 9–27.

8. Whereas critics like Daniel Cottom, in *The Civilized Imagination*, were as late as 1985 still presenting Scott as nostalgic for absolutism, the more dialectical view of Scott's achievement, elaborated by Lukács and Daiches from hints already available in contemporaneous authors like William Hazlitt and George Sand, now holds general sway: see Duncan, *Modern Romance* and *Scott's Shadow*, which convincingly attributes the high Tory reading of Scott to his appropriation by reactionaries in the 1820s and 1830s.

9. See David Daiches, 'Scott's Achievement as a Novelist' [1951], in Daiches, *Literary Essays* (Chicago: University of Chicago Press, 1956), pp. 88–121, esp. pp. 91–6.

10. On Stoicism, war, and narrative in Scott's early fiction, see Baker, 'Scott's Stoic Characters', pp. 443–71.

11. On this see Witherbee, 'Habeas Corpus', p. 365.

12. See Lincoln, *Scott and Modernity*, pp. 137–47.

13. Evan Gottlieb usefully unpacks the significance of Knockdunder's tolerance of the bandit gang in *Feeling British* (Lewisburg: Bucknell University Press, 2007), pp. 199–200.

7 – Marshall

1. Nicholas Tyacke (ed.), *England's Long Reformation, 1500–1800* (London: University College London Press, 1998).

2. John Bossy, *Christianity in the West 1400–1700* (Oxford: Oxford University Press, 1985), p. 171.

3. Carlos M. N. Eire, *War Against the Idols: The Reform of Worship from Erasmus to Calvin* (Cambridge: Cambridge University Press, 1986), p. 2.

4. See Peter Marshall, 'Saints and Cinemas: A Man for All Seasons', in S. Doran and T. S. Freeman (eds), *Tudors and Stuarts on Film* (London: Palgrave Macmillan, 2009), pp. 46–74.

5. Thomas McCrie, *A Vindication of the Scottish Covenanters: consisting of a review of the first series of the 'Tales of my Landlord'* (Glasgow: Maurice Ogle, 1824).

6. Alec Ryrie, *The Origins of the Scottish Reformation* (Manchester: Manchester University Press, 2006), pp. 5, 139 and 203; Michael Lynch, 'In Search of the Scottish Reformation', in E. J. Cowan and R. J. Finlay (eds), *Scottish History, The Power of the Past* (Edinburgh: Edinburgh University Press, 2002), pp. 73–94, especially p. 76. See also Christopher Hague (ed.), *The English Reformation Revised* (Cambridge: Cambridge University Press, 1987); and Peter Marshall and Alec Ryrie (eds), *The Beginnings of English Protestantism* (Cambridge: Cambridge University Press, 2002).

7. Anderson, *Scott and History*, p. 6.

8. Edward Chaney, *The Evolution of the Grand Tour: Anglo-Italian Cultural Relations since the Renaissance* (London: Cass, 1998), pp. 278–313.

9. Alison Shell, *Oral Culture and Catholicism in Early Modern England* (Cambridge: Cambridge University Press, 2007), p. 33; and *WN* vol. 9, p. 123.

10. A. Ross, 'Some Notes on the Religious Orders in Pre-Reformation Scotland', in D. McRoberts (ed.), *Essays on the Scottish Reformation* (Glasgow: Burns, 1962), pp. 185–244, especially p. 188. Mark Dilworth, *Scottish Monasteries in the Late Middle Ages* (Edinburgh: Edinburgh University Press, 1995), p. 29.

11. Penny Fielding, 'Historical Note', *WN* vol. 9, p. 436; Mark Dilworth, *Scottish Monasteries in the Late Middle Ages*, p. 44; and J. Kirk, *Patterns of Reform: Continuity and Change in the Reformation Kirk* (Edinburgh: T. & T. Clark, 1989), pp. xvii–xviii.

12. Mark Dilworth, 'The Commendator System in Scotland', *The Innes Review* 37 (1986), pp. 51–72.

13. Dilworth, *Scottish Monasteries*, pp. 27–8.

14. A. Ross, 'Reformation and Repression', in McRoberts, *Essays on the Scottish Reformation*, pp. 371–414, esp. p. 409.

15. W. C. Dickinson and G. Donaldson (eds), *A Source Book of Scottish History*, vol. 3, pp. 93–104 and 122–5; and Cowan, 'The Covenanting Tradition in Scottish History', pp. 121–3.

16. Galt, *Ringan Gilhaize*, ed. P. J. Wilson (Edinburgh: Canongate, 1995), p. 3. See also E. J. Cowan, 'The Covenanting Tradition', pp. 121–2; Lynch, 'In Search of the Scottish Reformation', p. 75.

17. Kirk, *Patterns of Reform*, pp. xiv–xv.

18. Eire, *War Against the Idols*, pp. 2, 5, 17, 28, and 314.

19. Anderson, *Scott and History*, p. 23; Brown, *Scott and the Historical Imagination*, pp. 82–3. For another view see Luc Racaut and Alec Ryrie, 'Between Coercion and Persuasion', in Luc Racaut and Alec Ryrie (eds), *Moderate Voices in the European Reformation* (Aldershot: Ashgate, 2005), pp. 1–12.

20. Brown, *Scott and the Historical Imagination*, p. 88.

21. *TLS*, 6 March 2009.

22. *Commonweal*, 29 March 2009.

8 – Robertson

1. Wordsworth, *Poetical Works*, pp. 741, 734–5.

2. Frye, 'The Drunken Boat: The Revolutionary Element in Romanticism', in *Romanticism Reconsidered: Selected Papers from the English Institute* (New York: Columbia University Press, 1963), pp. 1–25 (p. 16).

3. Hayden, *Critical Heritage*, p. 347.

4. *Shelley's Poetry and Prose*, ed. Donald H. Reiman and Sharon B. Powers (New York: Norton, 1977), p. 483.

5. Ibid., p. 487.

6. Ibid., p. 378.

7. Hewitt, *Scott on Himself*, p. 80.

8. Sutherland, *Scott: A Critical Biography*, p. 64.

9. E. M. Forster, *Aspects of the Novel* (1927), ed. Oliver Stallybrass (Harmondsworth: Penguin, 1974), p. 44.

10. Ibid., pp. 47, 73. See, in response, J. H. Alexander, '"Only Connect": The Passionate Style of Walter Scott', *Scottish Literary Journal* 5:2 (1979), pp. 37–54.

11. Woolf, 'The Antiquary', from *The Moment*, repr. in *Collected Essays*, vol. 1 (London: Hogarth Press, 1966), pp. 134–43.

12. Lukács, *Historical Novel*, p. 34.

13. Ibid., p. 33.

14. Hazlitt, *Spirit of the Age*, p. 252.

15. Hawthorne, *The House of the Seven Gables*, ed. Milton R. Sterne (Harmondsworth: Penguin, 1981), p. 1.

16. Stewart, 'Romantic Meter and Form', in Chandler and McLane, *Cambridge Companion to British Romantic Poetry*, pp. 53–75.

17. Blake, *The Complete Poems*, ed. W. H. Stevenson and David V. Erdman (London: Longman, 1971), p. 629.

18. *Shelley's Poetry and Prose*, pp. 503–4. For the history of the idea see Timothy J. Clark, *The Theory of Inspiration: Composition as a Crisis of Subjectivity in Romantic and Post-Romantic Writing* (Manchester: Manchester University Press, 1997).

19. See Fiona Robertson, 'Romance and the Romantic Novel: Sir Walter Scott', in Corinne Saunders (ed.), *A Companion to Romance: From Classical to Contemporary* (Oxford: Blackwell, 2004), pp. 287–304.

20. To John Taylor, in *Letters of John Keats*, ed. Robert Gittings (Oxford: Oxford University Press, 1987), p. 341.

21. *The Female Portrait Gallery*, in Laman Blanchard, *The Life and Literary Remains of L.E.L.*, 2 vols (London: Henry Colburn, 1841), vol. 2, pp. 101–2, 134.

22. Ibid., vol. 2, p. 142.

23. Ibid., vol. 2, p. 150.

24. St Clair, *Reading Public*, pp. 638–9; on the 'quickening' international issue in these years, Todd and Bowden, *Bibliographical History*, p. 452.

25. See George Dekker, *The American Historical Romance* (Cambridge: Cambridge University Press, 1987); Fiona Robertson, 'Walter Scott and the American Historical Novel', in J. Gerald Kennedy and Leland Person (eds), *American Novels to 1870*, vol. 5 of *The Oxford History of the Novel in English* (Oxford: Oxford University Press, 2013).

26. *Shelley's Poetry and Prose*, pp. 227, 486.

27. Hazlitt, *Spirit of the Age*, p. 233.

28. Lockhart, *Memoirs*, vol. 5, pp. 315–16.

29. See for example three works of 1792: Blake, *Visions of the Daughters of Albion*, Thomas Holcroft, *Anna St Ives*, Mary Wollstonecraft, *A Vindication of the Rights of Woman*.

30. See Mark A. Weinstein, 'Essay on the Text', *WN* vol. 16, p. 390; Richard D. Jackson, 'George Crabbe and Scott's *Saint Ronan's Well*', *Scott Newsletter* 36 (2000), pp. 7–23.

31. Wordsworth, *Poetical Works*, p. 735. On general links, see Frank Jordan, 'Scott and Wordsworth; or, Reading Scott Well', *Wordsworth Circle* 4 (1973), pp. 112–23. For other reflections on this particular textual relationship, see David Chandler, 'Scott's *Saint Ronan's Well* and Wordsworth's "Hart-Leap Well"', *Notes & Queries* 51:2 (2004), pp. 152–7.

32. See W. J. B. Owen, '*The White Doe of Rylstone* in Its Time', *Wordsworth Circle* 29:1 (1998), pp. 20–5; E. C. Pettet, 'Echoes of *The Lay of the Last Minstrel* in *The Eve of St. Agnes*', *Review of English Studies* 3:9 (1952), pp. 39–48; Claire Lamont, 'Meg the Gipsy in Scott and Keats', *English* 36 (1987), pp. 137–45.

9 – Ghoshal Wallace

1. Charles S. Olcott, *The Country of Sir Walter Scott* (Boston: Houghton Mifflin, 1913), p. 376; Arthur Melville Clark, 'Preface' to *The Abbot* (London: Dent, 1969), p. vii; Stephanie Chidester, 'Scott as Jacobite: Reason and Romance in *Kenilworth* and *The Abbot*', *Encycla* 68 (1991), p. 315; Pittock, *The Invention of Scotland*, p. 84.

2. Cottom, in *The Civilized Imagination* (p. 186), notes that Scott 'dwells upon weak or irresponsible rulers'; see also McMaster, *Scott and Society*, p. 226.

3. Elizabeth I, *Collected Works*, ed. Leah S. Marcus, Janel Mueller, and Mary Beth Rose (Chicago: University of Chicago Press, 2000), pp. 52, 326. For a genealogy of the concept see Ernst H. Kantorowicz, *The King's Two Bodies: A Study in Mediaeval Political Theology* (Princeton: Princeton University Press, 1997).

4. Kantorowicz, *The King's Two Bodies*, p. 438.

5. Quoted in ibid., p. 223. Elizabeth used the same figure to deflect pressures to marry in 1559 and in 1561: *Collected Works*, pp. 59, 65.

6. *The Constitutional Documents of the Puritan Revolution, 1625–1660*, ed. Samuel Rawson Gardiner, 3rd edn (Oxford: Clarendon Press, 1906), p. 375.

7. Thomas P. Slaughter, *Ideology and Politics on the Eve of Restoration: Newcastle's Advice to Charles II* (Philadelphia: The American Philosophical Society, 1984), p. 12.

8. See Cockshut, *The Achievement of Walter Scott*, p. 76.

9. *Letters of King James VI & I*, ed. G. P. V. Akrigg (Berkeley: University of California Press, 1984), p. 226.

10. See Shaw, *The Forms of Historical Fiction*, pp. 173–6 and Robertson, *Legitimate Histories*, p. 229. For the damaging consequences of Scott's representation see Michael B. Young, *King James and the History of Homosexuality* (New York: New York University Press, 2000), p. 7; Leanda De Lisle, *After Elizabeth: The*

Rise of James of Scotland and the Struggle for the Throne of England (New York: Ballantine Books, 2005), p. 284. However, James's courtier Sir Anthony Weldon describes the quilted stiletto-proof doublets and the ungainly gait that Scott portrays in *Nigel*, and is the source of the famous quip that James was 'the wisest fool in Christendom' (*The Court and Character of King James, Written and Taken by Sir A. W., Being an Eye, and Rare Witnesse* [London: R. J., 1817, Kessinger Legacy Reprint, 2010], p. 58).

11. See John Buchan, in *Sir Walter Scott* (Port Washington, NY: Kennikat Press, 1967), p. 249; Hart, *The Plotting of Historical Survival*, p. 198; Stephen Bann, *Romanticism and the Rise of History* (New York: Twayne Publishers, 1995), p. 24.

12. Stephen Greenblatt, *Renaissance Self-Fashioning: From More to Shakespeare* (Chicago: University of Chicago Press, 1980), pp. 140–1, 167.

13. See Gordon, *Under Which King*, p. 135.

14. Wilt, *Secret Leaves*, p. 106. Jayne Elizabeth Lewis, in *Mary Queen of Scots: Romance and Nation* (London: Routledge, 1998), pp. 147–9, describes how Caroline of Brunswick appeared at her trial in 1821 costumed as Mary.

15. Chidester, 'Scott as Jacobite', p. 315, Buchan, *Sir Walter Scott*, p. 229.

16. Greenblatt, *Renaissance Self-Fashioning*, p. 141.

17. James Melville, *The Memoirs of Sir James Melville of Halhill. Containing an impartial Account of the most remarkable AFFAIRS of STATE during the Sixteenth Century, not mentioned by other Historians: more particularly relating the Kingdoms of ENGLAND and SCOTLAND, under the Reigns of Queen ELIZABETH, MARY, Queen of Scots, and King JAMES. In most of which TRANSACTIONS the AUTHOR was Personally and Publicly Concerned*, ed. Gordon Donaldson (London: The Folio Society, 1969), p. 58.

18. See Jane Millgate, '"In Thy Rightful Garb": Roles and Responsibilities in Scott's *The Abbot*,' *English Studies in Canada* 3:2 (1977), p. 200.

19. For contrasting views, see Sutherland, *The Life of Walter Scott*, p. 239; Chidester, 'Scott as Jacobite', p. 317; Lukács, *The Historical Novel*, pp. 47–8; Shaw, *Forms of Historical Fiction*, p. 157; McMaster, *Scott and Society*, pp. 180–1.

20. James I, *Basilikon Doron*, in *A Miscellany, containing Richard of Bury's Philobiblon, The Basilikon Dōron of King James I, Monks and Giants by John Hookham Frere, The Cypress Crown by De La Motte Fouqué, and The Library, A Poem by George Crabbe*, intro. Henry Morley (London: George Routledge and Sons, 1888; Nabu Public Domain Reprint, 2010), p. 147.

21. Quoted in Slaughter, *Ideology and Politics*, p. xxvi.

22. Hart, *Plotting of Historical Survival*, p. 98; and on the 'uchronian' Charles at the end of *Woodstock* see Regina Hewitt, *Symbolic Interactions: Social Problems and Literary Interventions in the Works of Baillie, Scott, and Landor* (Lewisburg: Bucknell University Press, 2006), p. 182.

23. Elizabeth I, *Collected Works*, p. 326.

24. On this climactic moment see Hart, *Plotting of Historical Survival*, p. 99; Wilt, *Secret Leaves*, p. 173.
25. Watson, *Revolution and the Form of the British Novel*, p. 110.

10 – Dick

1. Carlyle, 'Sir Walter Scott', in *Essays: Scottish and Other Miscellanies* (London: Dent, 1967), p. 66; Bagehot, 'Thomas Babington Macaulay', in Forrest Morgan (ed.), *The Works of Walter Bagehot*, vol. 2 (Hartford: Traveller's Inn Company, 1889), pp. 85–6.
2. See Ferris, *Achievement of Literary Authority*; Duncan, *Modern Romance*; Michael Gamer, *Romanticism and the Gothic* (Cambridge: Cambridge University Press, 2000), pp. 163–99; McCracken-Flesher, *Possible Scotlands*; Gottlieb, *Feeling British*.
3. The phrase is from Gary F. Langer, *The Coming of Age of Political Economy 1815–1835* (New York: Greenwood Press, 1987).
4. See especially Duncan Forbes, 'The Rationalism of Walter Scott', *Cambridge Journal* 7 (1953), pp. 20–35; Garside, 'Philosophical Historians'; Sutherland, 'Fictional Economies'.
5. Garside, 'Philosophical Historians', p. 500. See also Richard B. Sher, *Church and University in the Scottish Enlightenment: The Moderate Literati of Edinburgh* (Princeton: Princeton University Press, 1985).
6. On the curriculum and structure of Scottish universities see George Elder Davie, *The Democratic Intellect: Scotland and Her Universities in the Nineteenth Century* (Edinburgh: Edinburgh University Press, 1961); S. Leslie Hunter, *The Scottish Educational System* (Oxford: Pergamon, 1968); G. S. Osborne, *Change in Scottish Education* (London: Longmans, 1968); Clifford Siskin, *The Work of Writing; Literature and Social Change in Britain 1700–1830* (Baltimore: Johns Hopkins University Press, 1998), pp. 90–3.
7. Philip Connell, *Romanticism, Economics, and the Question of Culture* (Oxford: Oxford University Press, 2000), pp. 72–3.
8. Donald Winch, *Riches and Poverty: An Intellectual History of Political Economy in Britain 1750–1834* (Cambridge: Cambridge University Press, 1996), pp. 127–36.
9. Biancamaria Fontana, *Rethinking the Politics of Commercial Society: the Edinburgh Review 1802–1832* (Cambridge: Cambridge University Press, 1985) and Joanne Shattock, *Politics and Reviewers: the Edinburgh and the Quarterly in the Early Victorian Age* (Leicester: Leicester University Press, 1989), pp. 5–22.
10. See Keith Tribe, *Land, Labour, and Economic Discourse* (London: Routledge, 1978), pp. 116–20; Boyd Hilton, *Corn, Cash, and Commerce: The Economic Policies of Tory Governments 1815–1830* (Oxford: Oxford University Press, 1977).
11. *Principles of Political Economy*, in Piero Sraffa and M. H. Dobb (eds), *The*

Works and Correspondence of David Ricardo, vol. 1 (Cambridge: Cambridge University Press, 1951), pp. 67–84.

12. See G. S. Checkland, 'The Propagation of Ricardian Economics in England', *Economica* 16 (1949), pp. 40–52; Mark Blaug, *Ricardian Economics: A Historical Study* (New Haven: Yale University Press, 1957); Connell, *Romanticism, Economics*, pp. 76–92.

13. See Hilton, *Corn, Cash, Commerce*, pp. 26–8.

14. See Connell, *Romanticism, Economics*, pp. 147–59 and Kevin Gilmartin, *Writing Against Revolution: Literary Conservatism in Britain 1790–1832* (Cambridge: Cambridge University Press, 2007), pp. 207–52.

15. Sutherland, 'Fictional Economies', p. 108.

16. Thomas Robert Malthus, *An Essay on the Principle of Population as it Affects the Further Improvements of Society, with Remarks on the Speculations of Mr. Godwin, M. Condorcet, and Other Writers* (London: Johnson, 1798).

17. A. M. C. Waterman, *Revolution, Economics, and Religion: Christian Political Economy, 1798–1833* (Cambridge: Cambridge University Press, 1991).

18. Malthus expanded and republished the essay in 1803, 1806, 1807, 1817, and 1826 with the title *An Essay on the Principle of Population or, A View of its Past and Present Effects on Human Happiness, with an Inquiry into our Prospects Regarding the Future Removal or Mitigation of the Evils it Occasions.*

19. On Malthus and the Romantics, see Winch, *Riches and Poverty*, pp. 288–348 and Connell, *Romanticism, Economics*, pp. 13–62.

20. Shelley's critique of Malthus is taken up in Maureen McLane, *Romanticism and the Human Sciences: Poetry, Population, and the Discourse of the Species* (Cambridge: Cambridge University Press, 2000), pp. 113–18.

21. Malthus declined (if he was even asked) and continued to write for the *Edinburgh* until 1815 when he fell out with the editors over his support for the Corn Laws.

22. Eric Richards, *A History of the Highland Clearances Volume 2: Emigration, Protests, Reasons* (London: Croom Helm, 1985), p. 61.

23. Susan Oliver, 'Planting the Nation's "Waste Lands": Walter Scott, Forestry, and the Cultivation of Scotland's Wilderness', *Literature Compass* 6/7 (2009), pp. 589–91.

24. Makdisi, *Romantic Imperialism*, p. 89.

25. Charlotte Sussman, 'The Emptiness at *The Heart of Midlothian*: Nation, Narration, and Population', *Eighteenth-Century Fiction* 15 (2002), p. 122.

26. Ibid., p. 108. See also Duncan, *Modern Romance*, p. 168.

27. The standard accounts of these changes are Albert O. Hirschman, *The Passions and the Interests: Political Arguments for Capitalism Before Its Triumph* (Princeton: Princeton University Press, 1977); Neil McKendrick, John Brewer, and J. H. Plumb, *The Birth of a Consumer Society: The Commercialization of Eighteenth-Century England* (Bloomington: Indiana University Press, 1982); and J. G. A. Pocock, *Virtue, Commerce, and History:*

Essays on Historical and Political Thought, Chiefly in the Eighteenth Century (Cambridge: Cambridge University Press, 1985).

28. Carl Wennerlind, 'The Death Penalty as Monetary Policy: The Practice and Punishment of Monetary Crime, 1690–1830', *History of Political Economy* 36 (2004), pp. 129–59.

29. On the persistence of feudal notions of credit see Craig Muldrew, *The Economy of Obligation: The Culture of Credit and Social Relations in Early Modern England* (Basingstoke: Palgrave, 1998); Margot Finn, *The Character of Credit: Personal Debt in English Culture 1740–1914* (Cambridge: Cambridge University Press, 2003); Deborah Valenze, *The Social Life of Money in the English Past* (Cambridge: Cambridge University Press, 2006).

30. For Scott's and his publishers' experiments with marketing and the resulting controversies over 'cultural authority' see Duncan, *Scott's Shadow*, ch. 1.

31. See Frank W. Fetter, *The Development of British Monetary Orthodoxy 1797–1875* (Cambridge, MA: Harvard University Press, 1965) and John Houghton, *Culture and Commerce: Cultural Bias in Monetary Theory and Policy* (Boulder: Westview, 1991).

32. See Ricardo, *Principles*, pp. 45–7. Ricardo had already responded to the Bullion Report in *The High Price of Bullion* (1810): Piero Sraffa (ed.), *The Works and Correspondence of David Ricardo* (Cambridge: Cambridge University Press, 1951), vol. 3, pp. 47–98. For Ricardo's part in the bullion controversy and his ties to 'philosophical radicalism', see Murray Milgate and Shannon C. Stimson, *Ricardian Politics* (Princeton: Princeton University Press, 1991), pp. 66–71.

33. See Alexander Dick, 'The Ghost of Gold: Forgery Trials and the Standard of Value in Shelley's *The Mask of Anarchy*', *European Romantic Review* 18 (2007), pp. 381–400.

34. Silvana Colella, 'Monetary Patriotism: *The Letters of Malachi Malagrowther*, *The Antiquary*, and the Currency Question', *Nineteenth-Century Studies* 17 (2003), pp. 53–71; Yoon Sun Lee, 'A Divided Inheritance: Scott's Antiquarian Novel and the British Nation', *ELH* 64 (1997), pp. 537–67.

35. Lawrence H. White, 'Free Banking in Scotland before 1944', in *Free Banking in Britain: Theory, Experience, and Debate 1800–1845* (Cambridge: Cambridge University Press, 1984), pp. 23–49; Matthew Rowlinson, '"The Scotch Hate Gold"; British Identity and Paper Money', in Emily Gilbert and Eric Helleiner (eds), *Nation-States and Money: The Past, Present, and Future of National Currencies* (London: Routledge, 1999), pp. 47–67.

36. Larry Neal, 'The Financial Crisis of 1825 and the Restructuring of the British Financial System', *Federal Reserve Bank of St. Louis Review* 80 (May–June 1998), pp. 53–76.

37. The first letter was published as a pamphlet, *Thoughts on the Proposed Change of Currency* (1826). Towards the end of the year, the three letters were

collected and reissued as *The Letters of Malachi Malagrowther*. See P. H. Scott (ed.), *The Letters of Malachi Malagrowther* (Edinburgh: Blackwood, 1981), pp. xi–xxxiv.

38. Scott, *Malagrowther*, p. 38.

39. Ibid., p. 39.

40. On the 'nationalism' of the *Letters*, see N. T. Phillipson, 'Nationalism and Ideology', in J. N. Wolfe (ed.), *Government and Nationalism in Scotland* (Edinburgh: Edinburgh University Press, 1969), p. 186, and McCracken-Flesher, *Possible Scotlands*, pp. 142–8.

41. Louis J. Jennings, *The Croker Papers: The Correspondence and Diaries of the Late Right Honourable John Wilson Croker* (London: Murray, 1889), p. 318.

11 – Duncan

1. See Theodor W. Adorno, 'Late Style in Beethoven', in *Essays on Music*, ed. Richard Leppert (Berkeley: University of California Press, 2002), pp. 564–7; also Edward W. Said, *On Late Style: Music and Literature Against the Grain* (New York: Vintage, 2007).

2. See Baker, 'Scott's Stoic Characters'.

3. See Wilt, *Secret Leaves*, pp. 170–6; Robertson, *Legitimate Histories*, pp. 265–73; and McCracken-Flesher, *Possible Scotlands*, pp. 127–38.

4. On these effects see Robertson, *Legitimate Histories*, pp. 242–4.

5. See Kenneth McNeil, 'The Limits of Diversity: Using Scott's "The Two Drovers" to Teach Multiculturalism in a Survey or Nonmajors Course', in *Approaches to Teaching Scott's Waverley Novels*, ed. Evan Gottlieb and Ian Duncan (New York: MLA, 2009), pp. 123–8. For the larger issues at stake see James Buzard, *Disorienting Fiction: The Autoethnographic Work of Nineteenth-Century British Novels* (Princeton: Princeton University Press, 2005); and Fielding, *Scotland and the Fictions of Geography*.

6. Slavoj Žižek, *Tarrying with the Negative: Kant, Hegel and the Critique of Ideology* (Durham, NC: Duke University Press, 1993), pp. 203–4.

7. *WN* vol. 1, p. 6; compare *Ivanhoe*, *WN* vol. 8, p. 10.

8. Lukács, *Historical Novel*, pp. 23–5, 53.

9. See James A. Secord, 'Edinburgh Lamarckians: Robert Jameson and Robert E. Grant', *Journal of the History of Biology* 24:1 (1991), pp. 1–18.

10. See McMaster, *Scott and Society*, pp. 214–15; Clare Simmons, 'A Man of Few Words: The Romantic Orang-Outang and Scott's *Count Robert of Paris*', *Scottish Literary Journal* 17:1 (1990), pp. 21–34.

11. Giorgio Agamben, *The Open: Man and Animal*, trans. Kevin Attell (Stanford: Stanford University Press, 2004), p. 16.

12. Alexander, 'Essay on the Text', *WN* vol. 23b, p. 209.

13. On Scott as Thomas the Rhymer see McCracken-Flesher, *Possible Scotlands*,

pp. 180–1; on Scott's 'minstrel autobiography' see McLane, *Balladeering*, pp. 196–9.

12 – Watson

1. Playbill in the John Johnson Collection, Bodleian Library, Oxford. London Playbills folder 3 (15) – Covent Garden.
2. Playbill inserted in the *Theatrical Observer*, quoted Diana E. Henderson, in *Collaborations with the Past: Reshaping Shakespeare Across Time and Media* (Ithaca, NY: Cornell University Press, 2006), p. 99.
3. *The London Literary Gazette and Journal of Belles Lettres, Arts, Sciences etc. for the year 1832* (London, 1832), pp. 683–4.
4. Henderson, *Collaborations with the Past*, p. 99.
5. For the identification of Scott with Shakespeare see Nicola J. Watson, 'Walter Scott', in Adrian Poole (ed.), *Great Shakespeareans* vol. 5 (London: Continuum, 2011), pp. 14–22.
6. Prospectus (March 1842) for the Abbotsford edition. Quoted Richard Maxwell, 'Walter Scott, Historical Fiction, and the Genesis of the Victorian Illustrated Book', in Richard Maxwell (ed.), *The Victorian Illustrated Book* (Charlottesville and London: University Press of Virginia, 2002), p. 28.
7. Frontispieces, *PW* vol. 6 and vol. 12 respectively.
8. For detailed discussion of Scott and the 'National Drama', see Barbara Bell, 'The National Drama, Joanna Baillie and the National Theatre', in Ian Brown et al. (eds), *Edinburgh History of Scottish Literature* (Edinburgh: Edinburgh University Press, 2007), vol. 2, pp. 228–35, and 'The National Drama and the Nineteenth Century', in Ian Brown (ed.), *Edinburgh Companion to Scottish Drama* (Edinburgh: Edinburgh University Press, 2011), pp. 47–59.
9. *The Abbotsford Miscellany: Scottish Scenes and Characters* (Edinburgh: A. & C. Black, 1855), contents; fly-leaf; pp. 172, 197.
10. For detailed discussion of this phenomenon see Ian Brown, *Literary Tourism*.
11. Leitch Ritchie, *Scott and Scotland; with twenty-one highly finished Engravings from Drawings by George Cattermole* (London: Longman, Rees, Orme, Brown, Green, and Longman, 1835), p. iv.
12. G. K. Chesterton, Holbrook Jackson, and R. Brimley Johnson, *Ivanhoe by Sir Walter Scott with Critical Appreciations Old and New* (Bath: Cedric Chivers, 1919), p. 18, which quotes Lockhart from *Memoirs* vol. 6, p. 176.
13. Ibid., p. 15.
14. See Sarah Stevenson and Helen Bennett, *Van Dyck in Check Trousers: Fancy Dress in Art and Life 1700–1900* (Edinburgh: Scottish National Portrait Gallery, 1978), p. 83; *Dresses worn at her Majesty's Bal Costumé, May 12th* (London: Charles and Leopold Morton, 1842); Coke Smyth and J. R.

Planché, *Souvenir of the Bal Costumé* (London, 1843); Mark Girouard, *The Return to Camelot: Chivalry and the English Gentleman* (New Haven and London: Yale University Press, 1981), p. 90.

15. Kevin M. McCarthy, *Christmas in Florida* (Florida: Pineapple Press, 2000), p. 38; Jerry E. Patterson, *The First Four Hundred: Mrs Astor's New York in the Gilded Age* (New York: Rizzoli, 2000), p. 26.

16. See *Memorials of the Preston Guilds* (Preston: G. Toulmin, 1882), p. 130; *Dancing: A Journal devoted to the Terpsichorean Art* 1:10 (1892), p. 119.

17. See Richard D. Altick, *Paintings from Books: Art and Literature in Britain 1760–1900* (Columbus, OH: Ohio State University Press, 1985), p. 123.

18. See http://indiana.edu/-liblilly/games/ivanhoe.

19. For parlour amusements derived from *Ivanhoe* see *Round Games for all Parties* (London: David Bogue, 1854), p. 120ff; *Dick's Standard Charades and Comedies for Home Representation* (London: J. Dicks, c.1883); Leger d. Mayne [William Brisbane Dick], *What shall we do tonight? Or, Social Amusements for Evening Parties* (New York: Dick and Fitzgerald, 1873), p. 188. For *tableaux vivants* based on *Ivanhoe* held in Britain, see Henrietta Horatia Gaisford's letter to W. H. Fox-Talbot (2 December 1830), www.foxtalbot.arts.gla.ac.uk/letters; *The Court Journal: Court Circular and Fashionable Gazette* 5 (1833), p. 84; *The Spectator* 6 (19 January 1833), pp. 61–2. For *tableaux vivants* in the USA, see *The Journal of Southern History* 3:343; 'Long Branch', *The Knickerbocker* 14 (1839), p. 234; *Journals of Charlotte Forten Grimké*, ed. Brenda Stevenson (New York, Oxford: Oxford University Press, 1988), p. 335; Frank Boott Goodrich, *The Tribute Book: A Record of the Munificence, Self-sacrifice and Patriotism of the American People during the War for the Union* (New York: Derby and Miller, 1865), p. 352; *Report of the Boston Young Men's Christian Union 1879* (Boston: The Union, 1879), p. 39; Francis Garvin Davenport, *Cultural Life in Nashville on the Eve of the Civil War* (North Carolina: University of North Carolina Press, 1941), p. 164; *The Daily Ledger* (3 December 1886, Tacoma-Pierce County Genealogical Society). In India, see Emily Eden, *Up the Country; Letters Written to her Sister from the Upper Provinces of India* (London: R. Bentley, 1867), p. 288; William Tayler, *Thirty-Eight Years in India: from Juganath to the Himalayan Mountains* (London: W. H. Allen, 1881), vol. 2, p. 467; Edward Spencer Mott, *A Mingled Yarn: The Autobiography of Edward Spencer Mott* (London: E. Arnold, 1898), p. 153; Francis Cornwallis Maude and John Walter Sherer, *Memories of the Mutiny* (London: Remington & Co., 1894), vol. 1, p. 261. For fictional tableaux see 'The Winter Night's Club', *The Southern Literary Messenger* 9 (1843), p. 52; William Pitt Lennox, *The Tuft-hunter* (London: H. Colburn, 1843), vol. 1, p. 248; Louisa May Alcott, 'The Inheritance' (1849), ed. Joel Myerson and Daniel Shealy (Harmondsworth: Penguin, 1998), p. 84; Elizabeth Missing Sewell, *Ivors: or, the Two Cousins* (London: Longmans, Brown, Green, Longmans and Roberts, 1858), p. 137; William Mathews, *The Two Homes* (London: Smith, Elder,

1859), p. 129; Ann Sophia Stephens, 'The Soldier's Orphans', *Peterson's Magazine* 49–50 (1866), p. 213ff; Charlotte Mellen Packard, 'The Key to a Life', in *Arthur's Home Magazine* 35–6 (1867), p. 96; William Pitt Lennox, *Lord of Himself* (London, 1880), p. 31; Bithia Mary Croker, *Diana Barrington: A Romance of Central India* (London: George Munro and Sons, 1887), p. 161; and Henry James, 'Paste' (1899), in Leon Edel (ed.), *The Complete Tales of Henry James* vol. 10 (New York: Lippincott, 1962), p. 451ff.

20. *Romanze des Richard Lowenherz aus Walter Scott's Ivanhoe; für eine Singstimme mit Begleiitung des Pianoforte* (Vienna: Diabelli, 1828).

21. For a fictional account of such a fancy-dress party, see William Gilmore Simms, *Flirtation at the Moultrie House* (Charleston: Edward C. Connell, 1850), p. 37; for an actual party see Elizabeth Lindsay Lennox, *Leaves from an old Washington Diary 1854–63*, ed. Lindsay Lennox Wood (New York: Books Inc., 1943), p. 85.

22. Lithograph series by Hayez (1828–9) and Maurin (1836).

23. Chesterton et al., *Ivanhoe*, pp. 20–1.

24. William Makepeace Thackeray, 'Proposals for a continuation of *Ivanhoe* in a letter to Mr Alexandre Dumas', *Fraser's Magazine* (1846), in Chesterton et al., *Ivanhoe*, p. 52.

25. Samuel Griswold Goodrich, *The Consul's Daughter: And Other Interesting Stories* (New York: Nafis & Cornish, 1841), p. 72.

26. Girouard, *Return to Camelot*, p. 255.

27. Chesterton et al., *Ivanhoe*, p. 21.

28. W. P. Borland (ed.), *The Scott Book: Scenes from the Novels of Sir Walter Scott* (London: G. Bell & Sons, 1924), p. x.

29. Louisa Caroline Tuthill, *I will be a Lady: A Book for Girls* (Boston: Crosby and Nichols, 1845), p. 104.

30. Jesse Maria Escreet, *The Life of Edna Lyall (Ada Ellen Bayly)*, (London: Longmans, Green & Co., 1904), p. 19.

31. See *Our Young Folks* vol. 8 (1872), p. 116; *Suggested Programs for Special Day Exercises* (Nebraska: Department of Public Instruction, 1913), p. 182; Winifred Ward, *Playmaking with Children from Kindergarten to High School* (New York, London: D. Appleton-Century Company, 1947), p. 70.

32. Cited Bruce Beiderwell and Anita Hemphill McCormick, 'The Making and Unmaking of a Children's Classic: The Case of Scott's *Ivanhoe*', in Donelle Ruwe (ed.), *Culturing the Child 1690–1914: Essays in Memory of Mitzi Myers* (Lanham, MD: Scarecrow Press, 2005), pp. 166, 167–8, 170.

33. Ibid., pp. 171–2.

34. See Anne Rainsbury (ed.), *Chepstow and the River Wye: From the Collections of Chepstow Museum* (Stroud: The History Press, rev. edn, 2009), pp. 18–20.

35. Chesterton et al., *Ivanhoe*, p. 54.

36. Philip Cox, *Reading Adaptations: Novels and Verse Narratives on the Stage, 1790–1840* (Manchester: Manchester University Press, 2000), p. 166.

37. Jonathan Stubbs, 'Hollywood's Middle Ages: The Development of *Knights of the Round Table* and *Ivanhoe* 1935–53', *Exemplaria* 21:4 (Winter 2009), p. 398.
38. Beiderwell and McCormick, 'Making and Unmaking of a Children's Classic', p. 173.
39. Captain Basil Hall, *Patchwork* (London: E. Moxon, 1841), vol. 2, p. 288.

Further Reading

Alexander, J. H., and David Hewitt (eds), *Scott and his Influence* (Aberdeen: ASLS, 1983).

Alexander, J. H., and David Hewitt (eds), *Scott in Carnival* (Aberdeen: ASLS, 1993).

Anderson, James, *Sir Walter Scott and History* (Edinburgh: Edina Press, 1981).

Arata, Stephen, 'Scott's Pageants: The Example of *Kenilworth*', *Studies in Romanticism* 40:1 (2001), pp. 99–107.

Baker, Samuel, 'Scott's Stoic Characters: Ethics, Sentiment, and Irony in *The Antiquary*, *Guy Mannering*, and "The Author of *Waverley*"', *Modern Language Quarterly* 70:4 (2009), pp. 443–70.

Bautz, Annika, *The Reception of Jane Austen and Walter Scott: A Comparative Longitudinal Study* (London: Continuum, 2007).

Beiderwell, Bruce, *Power and Punishment in Scott's Novels* (Athens, GA: University of Georgia Press, 1992).

Bolton, H. Philip, *Scott Dramatized* (London: Mansell, 1992).

Brown, David, *Scott and the Historical Imagination* (London: Routledge, 1979).

Brown, Ian (ed.), *Literary Tourism, The Trossachs and Walter Scott* (Glasgow: Scottish Literature International, 2012).

Buchan, John, *Sir Walter Scott* (London: Cassell, 1932).

Cockshut, A. O. J., *The Achievement of Walter Scott* (London: Collins, 1969).

Corson, James C., *Notes and Index to Sir Herbert Grierson's Edition of the Letters of Sir Walter Scott* (Oxford: Clarendon Press, 1979).

Cottom, Daniel, *The Civilized Imagination: A Study of Ann Radcliffe, Jane Austen, and Walter Scott* (Cambridge: Cambridge University Press, 1985).

Curry, Kenneth (ed.), *Sir Walter Scott's Edinburgh Annual Register* (Lexington: University of Kentucky Press, 1977).

Daiches, David, 'Scott's Achievement as a Novelist', two parts, *Nineteenth-Century Fiction* 6 (1951), pp. 81–95, 153–73.

D'Arcy, Julian, *Subversive Scott: The Waverley Novels and Scottish Nationalism* (Reykjavik: University of Iceland Press, 2005).

Davis, Leith, *Acts of Union: Scotland and the Literary Negotiation of the British Nation, 1707–1830* (Stanford: Stanford University Press, 1998).

Davis, Leith, Ian Duncan, and Janet Sorensen (eds), *Scotland and the Borders of Romanticism* (Cambridge: Cambridge University Press, 2004).

Duncan, Ian, *Modern Romance and Transformations of the Novel: The Gothic, Scott, Dickens* (Cambridge: Cambridge University Press, 1992).

Duncan, Ian, *Scott's Shadow: The Novel in Romantic Edinburgh* (Princeton: Princeton University Press, 2007).

Duncan, Ian, Ann Wierda Rowland, and Charles Snodgrass (eds), *Scott, Scotland, and Romantic Nationalism*, special issue of *Studies in Romanticism* 40:1 (2001).

Ferris, Ina, *The Achievement of Literary Authority: Gender, History, and the Waverley Novels* (Ithaca: Cornell University Press, 1991).

Fielding, Penny, *Writing and Orality: Nationality, Culture, and Nineteenth-Century Scottish Fiction* (Oxford: Clarendon Press, 1996).

Fielding, Penny, *Scotland and the Fictions of Geography: North Britain, 1760–1830* (Cambridge: Cambridge University Press, 2009).

Garside, Peter, 'Scott and the "Philosophical" Historians', *Journal of the History of Ideas* 36 (1975), pp. 497–512.

Garside, Peter, 'The Baron's Books: Scott's *Waverley* as a Bibliomaniacal Romance', *Romanticism* 14:3 (2008), pp. 245–58.

Gordon, Catherine, *The Lamp of Memory: Scott and the Artist* (Derby: Derbyshire Museum Service, 1979).

Gordon, Robert C., *Under Which King? A Study of the Scottish Waverley Novels* (Edinburgh: Oliver & Boyd, 1969).

Goslee, Nancy Moore, *Scott the Rhymer* (Lexington: University Press of Kentucky, 1988).

Gottlieb, Evan, and Ian Duncan (eds), *Approaches to Teaching Scott's Waverley Novels* (New York: MLA, 2009).

Hart, Francis Russell, *Scott's Novels: The Plotting of Historical Survival* (Charlottesville: University Press of Virginia, 1966).

Hayden, John O. (ed.), *Scott: The Critical Heritage* (London: Routledge, 1970).

Hennelly, Mark, '*Waverley* and Romanticism', *Nineteenth-Century Fiction* 28 (1973), pp. 194–209.

Hewitt, David (ed.), *Scott on Himself: A Selection of the Autobiographical Writings of Sir Walter Scott* (Edinburgh: Scottish Academic Press, 1981).

Hill, Richard J., *Picturing Scotland through the Waverley Novels: Walter Scott and the Origins of the Victorian Illustrated Novel* (London: Ashgate, 2010).

Johnson, Edgar, *Sir Walter Scott: The Great Unknown*, 2 vols (London: Hamish Hamilton, 1970).

Jones, Catherine, *Literary Memory: Scott's Waverley Novels and the Psychology of Narrative* (Lewisburg: Bucknell University Press, 2003).

Lee, Yoon Sun, *Nationalism and Irony: Burke, Scott, Carlyle* (Oxford: Oxford University Press, 2004).

Lincoln, Andrew, *Walter Scott and Modernity* (Edinburgh: Edinburgh University Press, 2007).

Lukács, Georg, *The Historical Novel* (1937), trans. Hannah and Stanley Mitchell (London: Merlin Press, 1962).

Lumsden, Alison, *Walter Scott and the Limits of Language* (Edinburgh: Edinburgh University Press, 2010).

Manning, Susan, *The Puritan-Provincial Vision: Scottish and American Literature in the Nineteenth Century* (Cambridge: Cambridge University Press, 1989).

Manning, Susan, *Fragments of Union: Making Connections in Scottish and American Writing* (Basingstoke: Palgrave, 2002).

McCracken-Flesher, Caroline, *Possible Scotlands: Walter Scott and the Story of Tomorrow* (Oxford: Oxford University Press, 2005).

McMaster, Graham, *Scott and Society* (Cambridge: Cambridge University Press, 1981).

McNeil, Kenneth, *Scotland, Britain, Empire: Writing the Highlands, 1760–1860* (Columbus: Ohio State University Press, 2007).

Millgate, Jane, *Walter Scott: The Making of the Novelist* (Toronto: University of Toronto Press, 1984).

Mitchell, Jerome, *The Walter Scott Operas* (Alabama: University of Alabama Press, 1977).

Muir, Edwin, *Scott and Scotland: The Predicament of the Scottish Writer* (London: Routledge, 1936).

Oliver, Susan, *Scott, Byron, and the Poetics of Cultural Encounter* (Basingstoke: Palgrave Macmillan, 2005).

Pittock, Murray (ed.), *The Reception of Sir Walter Scott in Europe* (London: Continuum, 2006).

Rigney, Ann, *Imperfect Histories: The Elusive Past and the Legacy of Romantic Historicism* (Ithaca: Cornell University Press, 2001).

Rigney, Ann, *The Afterlives of Walter Scott: Memory on the Move* (Oxford: Oxford University Press, 2012).

Robertson, Fiona, *Legitimate Histories: Scott, Gothic, and the Authorities of Fiction* (Oxford: Clarendon Press, 1994).

Robertson, Fiona (ed.), *Scott*, vol. 3 in *The Lives of the Great Romantics by Their Contemporaries*, 2nd series (London: Pickering and Chatto, 1997).

Shaw, Harry E., *The Forms of Historical Fiction: Sir Walter Scott and His Successors* (Ithaca: Cornell University Press, 1983).

Shaw, Harry E., *Narrating Reality: Austen, Scott, Eliot* (Ithaca: Cornell University Press, 1999).

Sutherland, John, *The Life of Walter Scott: A Critical Biography* (Oxford: Blackwell, 1995).

Sutherland, Kathryn, 'Fictional Economies: Adam Smith, Walter Scott and the Nineteenth-Century Novel', *English Literary History* 54 (1987), pp. 97–127.

Todd, William B., and Ann Bowden, *Sir Walter Scott: A Bibliographical History, 1796–1832* (New Castle, DE: Oak Knoll Press, 1998).

Trumpener, Katie, *Bardic Nationalism: The Romantic Novel and the British Empire* (Princeton: Princeton University Press, 1997).

Tulloch, Graham, *The Language of Sir Walter Scott* (London: Deutsch, 1980).

Wallace, Tara Ghoshal, 'The Elephant's Foot and the British Mouth: Walter Scott on Imperial Rhetoric', *European Romantic Review* 13:3 (2002), pp. 311–24.

The Walter Scott Digital Archive, Department of Special Collections, Edinburgh University Library, www.walterscott.lib.ed.ac.uk.

Walter Scott Research Centre, University of Aberdeen, www.abdn.ac.uk/english/centres/walterscott.

Watson, Nicola J., *Revolution and the Form of the British Novel, 1790–1825: Intercepted Letters, Interrupted Seductions* (Oxford: Clarendon Press, 1994).

Watson, Nicola J., *The Literary Tourist: Readers and Places in Romantic and Victorian Britain* (Basingstoke: Palgrave Macmillan, 2006).

Welsh, Alexander, *The Hero of the Waverley Novels* (New Haven: Yale University Press, 1963).

Welsh, Alexander, *The Hero of the Waverley Novels: With New Essays on Scott* (New Haven: Yale University Press, 1992).

Wickman, Matthew, *The Ruins of Experience: Scotland's 'Romantick' Highlands and the Birth of the Modern Witness* (Philadelphia: University of Pennsylvania Press, 2007).

Wilt, Judith, *Secret Leaves: The Novels of Walter Scott* (Chicago: University of Chicago Press, 1985).

Notes on Contributors

Samuel Baker is Associate Professor of English at the University of Texas, Austin. He is the author of *Written on the Water: British Romanticism and the Maritime Empire of Culture* (2010), and of essays on Scott, Romantic-period poetry and prose, and intertextual and interdisciplinary studies.

Alexander Dick is Tenured Assistant Professor of English at the University of British Columbia. He is the author of essays on Romantic poetry, prose, and drama, the co-editor of four collections of essays, and the author of *Romanticism and the Gold Standard: Money, Literature, and Economic Debate in Britain 1790–1830* (2013).

Ian Duncan is Florence Green Bixby Professor of English at the University of California, Berkeley. His books include *Scott's Shadow: The Novel in Romantic Edinburgh* (2007), *Modern Romance and Transformations of the Novel: The Gothic, Scott, Dickens* (1992), *Scotland and the Borders of Romanticism* (co-editor, 2004), *Approaches to Teaching Scott's Waverley Novels* (co-editor, 2009), and *The Edinburgh Companion to James Hogg* (co-editor, 2012). He has edited novels by Scott and Hogg and is a General Editor of *The Collected Works of James Hogg*.

Ina Ferris is Professor of English at the University of Ottawa. Her books include *The Romantic National Tale and the Question of Ireland* (2002) and *The Achievement of Literary Authority: Gender, History, and the Waverley Novels* (1991). She is co-editor of *Bookish Histories: Books, Literature, and Commercial Modernity, 1700–1900* (2009) and *Romantic Libraries* (2004), and has published numerous articles on Scott and other nineteenth-century British authors.

Catherine Jones is Lecturer in English at the University of Aberdeen. She is the author of *Literary Memory: Scott's Waverley Novels and the Psychology of Narrative* (2003) and the co-editor of *Scotland, Ireland, and the Romantic*

Aesthetic (2007), and has published essays on Romantic opera, de Staël, travel writing, and James Beattie. Her forthcoming book is *Literature and Music in the Atlantic World, 1767–1867*.

Alison Lumsden is Professor of English Literature at the University of Aberdeen, co-director of the Walter Scott Research Centre and a General Editor of the *Edinburgh Edition of the Waverley Novels*, for which she has co-edited *The Pirate*, *The Heart of Mid-Lothian*, and *Reliquiae Trotcosienses* and edited *Peveril of the Peak*. Author of *Walter Scott and the Limits of Language* (2010) and co-editor of *Contemporary Scottish Women Writers* (2000), she has published on many Scottish writers and is lead editor of a new edition of Scott's poetry.

George Marshall retired as Principal of Trevelyan College, University of Durham, in 1996. His main scholarly interests are in literature – especially, in recent years, Scott and Wordsworth – and in religious history. He is the author of *In a Distant Isle: the Orkney Background of Edwin Muir* (1987) and of essays on the autobiographies of Edwin Muir, Ronald Knox, and Robert Hugh Benson.

Caroline McCracken-Flesher is Professor of English at the University of Wyoming. Her publications range over Scottish culture, the novel, and the nineteenth century. Books include *Possible Scotlands: Walter Scott and the Story of Tomorrow* (Oxford, 2005), *The Doctor Dissected: A Cultural Autopsy of the Burke and Hare Murders* (2011), and, as editor, *Scotland as Science Fiction* (2011), *Culture, Nation, and the New Scottish Parliament* (2007), and *Approaches to Teaching the Works of Robert Louis Stevenson* (2012).

Ainsley McIntosh is affiliated to the Walter Scott Research Centre at the University of Aberdeen. Her research interests lie in the poetry and fiction of the British Romantic period, especially Walter Scott. She has also written on the domestic fiction of Mary Brunton and Susan Ferrier for the *Edinburgh Companion to Scottish Women's Writing*.

Kenneth McNeil is Professor of English at Eastern Connecticut State University. He is the author of *Scotland, Britain, Empire: Writing the Highlands 1760–1860* (2007) and of essays on Scott, John Galt, Anne Grant, and eighteenth- and nineteenth-century Scottish literature and history. His current project is a study of Scottish literature and the transatlantic world.

Fiona Robertson is Horace Walpole Professor of English Literature at St Mary's University College. Her books include *Legitimate Histories: Scott,*

Gothic, and the Authorities of Fiction (1994), *Scott* in *Lives of the Great Romantics by Their Contemporaries* (1997), *Women's Writing 1778–1838* (2001), *The United States in British Romanticism* (2013), and the Oxford World's Classics edition of *The Bride of Lammermoor* (1991). She is the author of essays on Romantic-Period poetry and prose, nineteenth-century American writing, and co-editor of the fiction of Stephen Crane (1998).

Tara Ghoshal Wallace is Professor of English at George Washington University. Her books include *Jane Austen and Narrative Authority* (1995) and *Imperial Characters: Home and Periphery in Eighteenth-Century Literature* (2010). She is the editor of Frances Burney's *A Busy Day* and co-editor of *Women Critics, 1660–1820* and the author of essays on Scott, Austen, Frances Burney, Samuel Johnson and Elizabeth Hamilton.

Nicola J. Watson is Professor of English Literature at the Open University, and has published widely on eighteenth- and nineteenth-century literature and culture. Books include *Revolution and the Form of the British Novel, 1790–1825* (1994), *England's Elizabeth: An Afterlife in Fame and Fantasy* (co-authored, 2002), and *The Literary Tourist: Readers and Places in Romantic and Victorian Britain* (2006). She has edited Scott's *The Antiquary* for Oxford World's Classics (1999), has co-edited *At the Limits of Romanticism* (1994), *Literary Tourism and Nineteenth-Century Culture* (2009), and is completing a study of US writers' houses as tourist sites.

Index

Note: Works by Sir Walter Scott are listed in the index under their titles; other works are listed under the names of their authors, where known.